Vulnerability and Glory

Vulnerability and Glory

A Theological Account

KRISTINE A. CULP

WESTMINSTER
JOHN KNOX PRESS
LOUISVILLE · KENTUCKY

© 2010 Kristine A. Culp
First edition
Published by Westminster John Knox Press
Louisville, Kentucky

10 11 12 13 14 15 16 17 18 19—10 9 8 7 6 5 4 3 2 1

Unless otherwise indicated, Scripture quotations are from the New Revised Standard Version of the Bible, copyright © 1989 by the Division of Christian Education of the National Council of the Churches of Christ in the U.S.A., and are used by permission.

Excerpts from John Calvin, *Calvin: Institutes of the Christian Religion*, ed. John T. McNeill, trans. Ford Lewis Battles, LCC (Philadelphia: Westminster Press, 1960). Used by permission. Excerpts from *Praisesong for the Widow* by Paule Marshall, copyright © 1983 by Paule Marshall. Used by permission of G. P. Putnam's Sons, a division of Penguin Group (USA), Inc. and Joan Daves Literary Agency. Some material in chapter 5 was previously published in the introduction to H. Richard Niebuhr, *"The Responsibility of the Church for Society" and Other Essays by H. Richard Niebuhr*, ed. Kristine A. Culp (Louisville, KY: Westminster John Knox Press, 2008). Used by permission. Chapter 7, "Always Reforming, Always Resisting" is a revised and expanded version of a chapter by the same name originally published in pp. 152–68 of *Feminist and Womanist Essays in Reformed Dogmatics*, ed. Amy Plantinga Pauw and Serene Jones (Louisville, KY: Westminster John Knox Press, 2006). Some material in chapter 3 was previously published in that chapter. Used by permission.

Book design by Drew Stevens
Cover design by Night & Day Design
Cover illustration: © iStockphoto.com

Library of Congress Cataloging-in-Publication Data

Culp, Kristine A. (Kristine Ann)
    Vulnerability and glory : a theological account / Kristine A. Culp.
        p. cm.
    Includes bibliographical references and index.
    ISBN 978-0-664-23522-2 (alk. paper)
    1. Suffering—Religious aspects—Christianity.   I. Title.
    BT732.7.C83 2010
    248.8'6—dc22

                                                                        2010017885

Contents

Acknowledgments

This book offers an account of the vulnerability and glory of personal and shared life. Numerous conversations and contexts have made it possible to reflect on those realities and to shape that account. I especially thank Larry Bouchard, David Hall, Claudia Highbaugh, Verity Jones, Cynthia Lindner, Holly McKissick, Amy Northcutt, Kay Northcutt, Stephanie Paulsell, Richard Rosengarten, William Schweiker, and Clark Williamson. They encouraged this book's "itinerary" with shared meals, conversation, and friendship over many years. William Schweiker was particularly generous as a reader of early and late versions of chapters. I am grateful for the support of the Disciples Divinity House of the University of Chicago and the University of Chicago Divinity School, and for the colleagues and students with whom I have been privileged to work. The Association of Disciples for Theological Discussion and the Forrest-Moss Institute of Disciples Women Scholars have continued to provide lively discussion and hearty collegiality. Chapter 7, "Always Reforming, Always Resisting," is a revised and expanded version of a chapter first written at the invitation of Amy Plantinga Pauw and Serene Jones for *Feminist and Womanist Essays in Reformed Dogmatics*; I thank them for that invitation and for what it meant to participate in that conversation. Chapter 4 discusses material that first oriented my theological reflections on sociality and community; it conveys some of my indebtedness to three teachers, James M. Gustafson, Lois Gehr Livezey, and the late Anne E. Carr. I am grateful for them and for Betty Culp, Karen and Tim Moklestad, and Gary and Lisa Culp, who have extended care throughout my life as well as for this book.

Introduction:
Vulnerable to Devastation and Transformation

An alert crossed the top of *The New York Times* online: a 7.0 magnitude earthquake had been registered in Haiti, with its epicenter near Port-au-Prince. Ominous news. Within the hour, images and information began to reveal devastation far beyond my own and probably most anyone's worst imagining. As I write this, only a few days later, survivors are still being pulled from the ruins, and the numbers of lives lost have hardly begun to be counted. The January 12 earthquake shook the city horrifically, crumbling dwellings from the humblest to the presidential palace, collapsing parliament and the national cathedral, and ruining hospitals, schools, shops, and offices; it crushed lives, symbolic life, and means of livelihood. The enormity of the catastrophe will likely grow for weeks, months, perhaps years.

Outside the decimated Cathédrale Notre-Dame in Port-au-Prince, a woman cried, "This is what God did!" And a man, whose brother and nephew died, said, "God is angry at the world." To the same reporter, Sister Berta Lopez Chavez commented, "Haiti lives two realities: this catastrophe, and their catastrophe of every day, of poverty and ignorance and daily hunger. . . . What else can happen to them? The little they had is gone." A parishioner, Francois Voleile, kept vigil for a priest who had been buried alive under a collapsed building and worked with rescue teams. " 'We are not discouraged,' parishioner Voleile said, 'We are still alive and can go on.' "[1] Tens of thousands of people spent the first nights in the streets, where they took refuge from possible aftershocks and solace in each other. Into the immense darkness of a night without electricity, they sang hymns and prayers.[2]

Haiti's earthquake, together with other disasters and threats, reminds us how vulnerable persons, other living things, and this planet are. When survivors of disasters suffer the loss of persons with whom their lives have been bound and places from which their lives seem inseparable, they may also be reminded, painfully so, of how profound these relations are. We humans are vulnerable not only to being harmed, but also to the love and care of others. That suffering can be both heightened and ameliorated by such connections points to the complexity of vulnerability.

The Hebrew prophets, Jesus, and the apostle Paul, among others, viewed persons as vulnerable to transformation as well as to devastation, to love and joy as well as to harm and suffering. How to attend to vulnerability is a perennial religious question. In a world where horrible things happen, where harm sometimes seems to multiply cruelly, and where people are sometimes capable of incomprehensible brutality, it remains an urgent matter. Direct aid, prayer, comfort, and lamentation are among responses that are often sorely needed. Matters of theology and theodicy also arise. While theodicy—to justify God's goodness in the face of evil and suffering—is one way of thinking theologically about vulnerability, it is not the only way. Moreover, when theodicy becomes part of an attempt to "fix things"—including God—it may have the effect of diverting attention from the depths of creaturely plights and possibilities, and from a living God. In this book, I focus on how devastation and transformation are related in creaturely existence and before God. I attend to vulnerability—here defined as susceptibility to being changed, for good and for ill—as basic to this existence. Vulnerability is the situation in which persons and communities may receive and bear the glory of God; it is also the situation in which earthly existence may be harmed and degraded.

VULNERABILITY

In the last two decades a significant literature has emerged in response to disasters, terrorism, global climate change, and other risks. Initiatives by the United Nations, World Health Organization, governments, universities, and corporations assess "vulnerability and risk." This literature, and the specific threats and risks that it tracks, suggests something of the globalized concerns that are shaping our time and place. In this literature, definitions of vulnerability point to the risk of harm from hazards, epidemics, and disasters; the contrasting term is resilience. In other words, damage has a force of inevitability, and the main questions are how to prevent it and, if and when hazards are met, whether persons, communities, and environments will be able to resist and rebound from it. There is "menace in the air" of contemporary existence.[3] The implied narrative of damage, loss, and, at best, resilience contrasts with early twentieth-century confidence in seemingly sure progress.

If in our day vulnerability garners global attention and generates analysis, it is neither a new idea nor a recent sensibility. The Latin root of *vulnerability* points to "wounds" and "wounding." Over the centuries, Christian theologies have attended to a moral and spiritual vulnerability at the heart of personal and social existence. Through the notion of original sin, theologians have been teaching for centuries about an inescapable wounding. For example, medieval thinkers pondered the wounds of sin: the devastating effects of original sin and how actual sins exacerbated these wounds of ignorance, malice, weakness, and concupiscence.[4]

The biblical notion that humans are creatures made of earth and breath likewise suggests vulnerability—but to transformation as well as to devastation. In this perspective, which I will take up, human creatures are susceptible to ill and to good. Vulnerability encompasses not only the capacity to suffer harm and to be damaged, but also capacities implied by contrast: to be kept safe and whole, to have integrity and dignity, and to be healed and lifted. This robust notion of vulnerability can be read from the beginning to the end of the Bible in the stories of creatures who rise and fall, who make and break covenants, who are astounding in their perversity and cruelty and also in their capacities to love and do justice. It is suggested by Gospel narratives in which Jesus and his disciples are vulnerable to rejection and to welcome. The complexity of vulnerability is indicated in the story of Jacob wrestling through the night at the ford of the river Jabbock with a mysterious stranger, who leaves Jacob both limping and transformed. It is found at the very heart of the Christian gospel in Jesus' life, death, and resurrection.

As the prophet Jeremiah and the apostle Paul taught, humans are earthen vessels, susceptible to being shattered and also capable of bearing great treasure, the grace and glory of God. Vulnerability is an enduring feature of creaturely existence; it is not a temporary condition that can be or ought to be overcome. Persons and communities remain vulnerable: they are always susceptible to harm and therefore almost inevitably marked by suffering and wrong—sometimes by unfathomable tragedy or brutality—and yet they are always also susceptible to transformation. Note, then, that vulnerability does not equate with or necessarily entail powerlessness or weakness. Vulnerability is intrinsic to being creatures who are interdependent with other persons, living things, and the earth. Creaturely life is also tinged with glory—so the heavens and the lilies of the field attest, according to the Psalms and the Gospels. Vulnerability and glory are part of being creatures who are situated in particular times and places with particular bodies, desires, capacities, needs, and life spans, and who come to know something of their situatedness and interdependence in relation to vaster contexts and purposes. Rather than assigning vulnerability to creatures exclusively or glory only to God, this account affirms the glory of God as known in the glory of creation and through creaturely life, and likewise it affirms the vulnerability of creaturely life and of a living God.

I pair vulnerability with "glory" rather than with "risk" or "resilience" to indicate the possibilities of transformation as well as the realities of devastation. In changing the central contrast from "risk/resilience" to "glory," I am not disputing the real hazards that contemporary analyses address. The characterization of seemingly inevitable damage fits scores of threatened communities and cultures—and the whole planet in the face of global climate change. Furthermore, risks ought to be minimized, damage prevented, and capacities for resilience fostered. Nor am I advocating a renewed confidence in progress. The threats are real and the damage is significant. Indeed, with many theologians through the centuries, I argue that an awareness of devastation and tragedy is heightened by a correlative awareness of the grace and glory of God manifest in creation and transformation. The point, then, is not to encourage greater optimism or pessimism—neither progress nor regress is inevitable—but rather to provide ways of thinking critically about and living transformatively within these global realities.[5]

LIFE BEFORE GOD

This account of vulnerability to devastation and transformation is, more exactly, an account of life given by and lived before God as vulnerable and as capable of bearing glory. I want to say something here about the phrase "life before God" and how I use it to designate two related spaces of reflection and existence.

First, "life before God" indicates a locus of theological reflection, a field of systematic inquiry. I use the phrase as an analogue to what theologians conventionally have discussed within the systematic loci of theological anthropology (the nature and condition of human life) and ecclesiology (the nature and purpose of the church). However, these conventional topics designate more specific objects and narrower fields of inquiry than I want to signal with life before God. This account attends to the individuality, sociality, responsibility, and interdependence of earthly existence—of human creatures especially—before God. Neither individual piety nor churches exhaust the reality of life before God.

In fact, theological strategies for depicting Christian life and community have been more varied historically than is typically understood. Diverse approaches did not only address the authority of institutions, rituals, and dogma and their purity. Rather, as theologians depicted the church descriptively and normatively, they also grappled with vulnerability and suffering, with the ambiguity of persons and institutions, with the devastations of poverty, hunger, and persecution, with tyranny and freedom, with how organizations, texts, practices, and traditions mediate "salvation," and with the presence and sometimes seeming absence of God in history. Once the vitality and breadth of these questions are regained, then historical theological perspectives can offer vital resources for an account of life before God as vulnerable and capable of bearing glory.

Rather than constructing a new ecclesiology or theological anthropology, the aim of this book is to attend to possibilities of devastation and transformation in life that is shared with and for others before God. My method, about which I will say more below, is to focus on figurations of individual and communal existence and the transforming reality of God as they respond, or fail to be responsive, to creaturely vulnerability and ambiguity. Note that I construe persons and communities as not only vulnerable—that is, susceptible to deleterious and positive change—but also ambiguous. They have already been harmed and transformed and therefore always already live within vectors of devastation and transformation. I retrieve and "condense" theological metaphors, tropes, and logics in order to depict conversion, salvation, and sanctification in relation to such threats and possibilities. Thus this book offers a fairly comprehensive theology of the vulnerability and glory of creaturely existence, especially in personal and shared Christian life, and of transformation and devastation, interpreted in relation to the grace and glory of God.[6]

Second, "life before God" designates the space of existence as encompassed and indwelt by the transforming reality of God. "Before God" or *coram Deo*, "in the sight or presence of God," is a phrase often associated with Martin Luther. The scene that typically illustrates Luther's *coram Deo* is of the man at the Imperial Diet of Worms, bearing his conscience's solitary witness to God against a hostile gathering: "Here I stand, I can do no other." In fact, although Luther and other sixteenth-century theologians, perhaps John Calvin especially, prized the testimony of conscience, they also insisted that the whole world was before God. There was no secular exclusion, no place that was farther from the presence of God; neither was there any place, any church structure, authority, or ritual, that could be said to possess or control the presence of God. God's grace and glory ought to be proclaimed and made manifest particularly in Christian life and ministry, but all life, from the depths of individual conscience to the breadth of public life, from the misery of betrayal to the marvel of love, exists before God. Luther may have crystallized the formulation *coram Deo*, but the insight was already there in Augustine's vision of the city of God, in Paul's vision of a world aching with the pains of new birth, in Jesus' welcoming of strangers and outcasts, in the prophets who announced the presence of the Lord in the midst of the poor and oppressed, and in stories of a creator who sculpted a world and pronounced it good.

In this account, the basic meaning of "before God" is an affirmation of the reality of God as the horizon that delineates and orients creatures and cosmos. The focus of this account is on *life before God*, that is, not on the horizon, God, but on the moving space of creaturely and cosmic existence that is encompassed and transformed by this horizon. This is a space constituted by the relation between God and cosmos and among God and creatures in their individuality, sociality, and interdependence. Moreover, it is a space shaped by the relations of creatures with each other in the earth and in response to God. These are moving, changing relations that defy simple definitions, grammars, or logics. Life before God is a field of ongoing tensions and conversions—among God and creatures, among creatures and cosmos, between past and future, between glory that is known and glory that is yet emerging. A theological account of vulnerability and glory must be adequate to this moving field of life and to a living God.

In the face of threats, perceived and actual, persons and communities often attempt to reduce tensions and control change; they turn to what I call strategies of invulnerability. Metaphorically and literally, they reinforce barriers and restrict movement of goods and people. At times such measures may be crucial, but relying on defense as the exclusive or primary strategy represents a failure to recognize already existing interdependencies.[7] Similarly, Christian theologies and communities sometimes have attempted to safeguard salvation by elevating "the church" above "the world," or to secure sanctity and doctrine by removing "the Christian life" from "the world." Such approaches fail to recognize the presence of God in the whole world and that persons cannot dwell with God apart from others and the places and history that they share. Moreover, no shield of invulnerability—be it a dogmatic, ecclesial, or moral strategy for defending the true faith, the true church, or the true identity—can secure earthly existence from possibilities of harm and devastation . . . or from the movement of God's grace and glory.

Although the triumphalist approach of elevation and the sectarian approach of separation differ from each other theologically and sociologically, both can function as strategies of invulnerability. They attempt to elevate or segregate the church from the world and to raise the barriers between them. By contrast, central figures in the history of Christian thought—Paul, Augustine, Luther, and Calvin among others—sought to avoid both triumphalism and sectarianism. They affirmed the presence of a living God in creaturely life and possibilities of transformation in vulnerable, ambiguous existence. In this account I engage their work along with the Prophets and the Gospels, more recent theologies, and varied experiences and situations.

As the Prophets and Gospels attest, possibilities for transformation and devastation are always appearing in the midst of life. To live open to the grace and glory of God requires ongoing conversion in which attention, affections, and action are attuned to God and others. It involves not only ongoing tensions and conversion, but also multiple transformations. I portray a way of moving through suffering that resists the valorization of suffering and also the denigration of God and creatures. This movement of resistance is held in ever-converting tension with a movement of affirmation that receives and shares life as a gift of God. I depict the former as the testimony and call of resistance and the latter as an itinerary of delight and gratitude.

OVERVIEW

This account of vulnerability and glory is given in three parts. The first part identifies and evaluates historical figurations (e.g., metaphors, tropes, logics) that contribute to a picture of life before God as vulnerable, ambiguous, and yet capable of bearing glory.

Chapter 1 begins with Paul's figure of treasure in earthen vessels and follows it through changing construals of vulnerability, ambiguity, and transformation. I explore its use in relation to other figurations and to the felt sensibilities and meanings that shape and are shaped by these figurations. The chapter ends with Augustine, who offered a dynamic depiction of divine transformation of the whole world and yet whose ideas, including the distinction between visible and invisible church, set in motion a history of effects that tended toward triumphalism. Chapters 2 and 3 follow these figurations and their significance through the work of Luther and Calvin. They each turned to these and other tropes to diagnose the threats and corruption of their day, and also to teach confidence in the saving grace of God. Of special note for the constructive work of this book are Luther's attention to suffering as an epistemological key to reality, his notion of Christendom as a gathered people rather than an institution, Calvin's insistence on transformation in history, and both of their uses of the marks of the church.

It is as much tropes and strategies that these chapters follow as thinkers. Nonetheless, Paul, Augustine, Luther, and Calvin have central roles in this book because their formulations offered powerful and complex perspectives on God, personal and social existence, and salvation. Undeniably, their work—individually and in interconnection—has given enduring shape to Christianity, especially Protestant Christianity. Moreover, their ideas and language reverberate not only in churches and Christian theology, but also, often implicitly and indirectly, in history and cultures. In my admittedly, although not exclusively, Protestant account of life before God, I engage their ideas and sensibilities critically. When their ideas are recalibrated and combined with other resources, they can inform responses to present-day quandaries. Note that there are other perspectives that might also be engaged and to which I offer some gestures; moreover, I do not take Paul, Augustine, Luther, and Calvin as arbiters of which other perspectives can be engaged fruitfully.

Chapter 4 bridges the historical engagement of part 1 with the constructive work of parts 2 and 3. Titled "Modern Treasure?" it examines twentieth-century approaches to church and salvation. It rejects strategies of invulnerability and calls for an account oriented to the ongoing conversion of creaturely existence and the transforming reality of God.

In the rest of the book, resources from Part I are layered, condensed, and built upon in relation to contemporary situations and to additional biblical, historical, and contemporary material. Figurations of contemporary situations and situatedness articulate with historical sensibilities, patterns, and strategies—variously critiquing them, resonating with them, extending and altering them. This interrelation and condensation of resources allows a complex and dynamic depiction of the vulnerability and glory of creaturely existence with others before God.

Part 2 returns to contemporary questions about devastation and transformation, taking them up in relation to theological themes of discipleship and conversion and of bearing suffering. Drawing on a pattern of witness and welcome from the Gospels and from the work of theologian H. Richard Niebuhr, chapter 5 depicts life before God as "A Field of Tensions and Conversions." As Jesus' calling and sending of disciples indicates, the transforming reality of God is made manifest in the midst of daily places and interactions. Chapter 6, "Vulnerability in a World Marked by Suffering," reengages Luther's sign of the cross and Calvin's problematic excursus on bearing the cross. Distinguishing the acknowledgment of vulnerability from the valorization of suffering, it asks whether the mark of suffering can offer a key for interpreting the presence of God in creaturely life.

Part 3 explores tensively related ways of living before God. The disciplined movements and training of sensibilities that they portray are compared with, but not equated to, the ancient *vias negativa* and *affirmativa*. The seventh chapter, "Always Reforming, Always Resisting," explores the call to resist idolatry and tyranny in relation to the Reformed slogan *ecclesia reformata sed semper reformanda* (the church reformed but always being reformed). Recognition of vulnerability as a basic aspect of creaturely existence entails the need for vigilance in the face of idolatry and inhumanity; moreover, to resist the degradation of creatures, cosmos, and God is in part what love of God and of neighbor require in our day. Chapter 8, "An Itinerary of Delight and Gratitude," depicts a way of ongoing conversion that is tutored by the taste of God's goodness and fashioned in grateful interdependence with and for others. It develops this itinerary by drawing together historical resources in relation to a conversion story told by novelist Paule Marshall. Despite real devastation and loss, vulnerable life can come to receive and bear the glory of God.

This book offers a theological account of vulnerability and glory, offering within that account ways of attending to harm and delight, and ways of interpreting possibilities of participation and transformation in the life that we are given to share with others before God. In her 2003 book, *Regarding the Pain of Others*, cultural critic Susan Sontag suggested that, to the extent that understanding of others' pain is ever possible, it involves refusing to be only a spectator and requires responding to the reality of pain, whether distant or close at hand.[8] That is, possibly, what the images and cries of Haiti ask, and it is where this book begins.

January 17, 2010

PART 1

Vulnerability and Community

CHAPTER 1

From Paul's Earthen Vessel to Augustine's Mixed Body

> We have this treasure in clay jars, so that it may be made clear that this extraordinary power belongs to God and does not belong to us. We are afflicted in every way, but not crushed; perplexed, but not driven to despair; persecuted, but not forsaken; struck down, but not destroyed; always carrying in the body the death of Jesus, so that the life of Jesus may also be made visible in our bodies.
>
> —2 Corinthians 4:7–10

The apostle Paul explained to the Corinthian Christians that their "clay"—their vulnerable, earthen existence—receives and bears God's glory. We come from the earth, are given breath and life, and will perish; and yet, Paul wrote, the glory and power of God are made manifest in vulnerability, especially in the life and the death of Jesus. Three hundred some years later, when Christianity gained an established place in the Roman Empire, the problem was no longer how to bear the glory of God under persecution. Instead, Augustine, bishop of Hippo, saw moral and religious ambiguity in the church; he viewed it as a decidedly "mixed body." In order to reject what we might today call a sectarian view of Christianity, he formulated the distinction between the visible and invisible church. The boundaries of the church were overrun by a dubious crowd of humanity, yet he viewed the church's pure order as being preserved in God. Augustine portrayed the rule of God as stretching beyond the church to the entire society and beyond time to the eternal city of God. The whole of history became the field of divine transformation. However, his concern to safeguard order also opened the way to a triumphalist view of the church.

This chapter moves from Paul to Augustine as they and other theologians sought to interpret the transforming reality of God in relation to the vulnerability of creaturely life and the ambiguity of Christian communities. This treatment is by no means exhaustive. It focuses on the trajectories of the metaphor of treasure in earthen vessels and of the logic of the relation of visible and invisible church, while also attending

13

to other biblical and theological tropes. Through such tropes, these early theologians indicated and depicted the theological realities that they believed and experienced. Later theologians—I focus on Martin Luther and John Calvin—reinterpreted and resituated many of the same tropes. In this chapter and the following ones, I explore the dynamic complexity of shifting theological depictions and felt sensibilities associated with them. If contemporary theological thinking is to be adequate to the complexities of the past and the present, it must be able to evoke and critically engage these dense interactions of language, meaning, felt import, situation, and situatedness.

PAUL: VULNERABLE VESSELS, GLORIOUS TREASURE

"We have this treasure in clay jars" (2 Cor. 4:7). Paul's words to the Corinthian church echoed the creation story in which God forms the human from the dust of the earth and breathes life into it (Gen. 2:7). As the first human being, Adam, was "from the earth, a man of dust" (1 Cor. 15:47), so is the Corinthian church. The divine *pneuma*—breath, spirit—inhabits and enlivens these perishable vessels. The animating spirit of God is known in its luminous power through the life, death, and resurrection of Jesus the Christ. Paul referred to this treasure as the "light of the gospel" (2 Cor. 4:4), that is, "the knowledge of the glory of God in the face of Jesus Christ" (4:6). He explained to the Corinthians that the "extraordinary power" that infuses their earthenness "belongs to God and does not come from us" (4:7). They are created from the earth, given breath and life, and are perishing, "wasting away." At the same time, they are being transformed: the inmost stuff of their existence is "being renewed day by day" (4:16).[1]

These clay vessels suggest earthenware used in the temple as well as in mundane places. Paul's earthen pot, *skeuos ostrakinon*, also alludes to Jeremiah's allegory of the irreparable shattering of the potter's vessel (Jer. 18:1–12). Paul and other agents of the gospel may have felt as "breakable" as everyday pottery. In his letter to the Corinthians, however, Paul fashioned clay pots as a testimony of power rather than as a portent of judgment. The apostle's catalog of affliction contrasts with the incomparable reality of God.[2] "We are afflicted in every way, but not crushed; perplexed, but not driven to despair; persecuted, but not forsaken; struck down, but not destroyed; always carrying in the body the death of Jesus, so that the life of Jesus may also be made visible in our bodies" (2 Cor. 4:8–10). As Paul and others endure persecution without being crushed, God's glory is made manifest in their vulnerability. "For while we live, we are always being given up to death for Jesus' sake, so that the life of Jesus may be made visible in our mortal flesh" (4:11).

These treasure-bearing vessels stand in not only for Paul, but also for the whole Corinthian body. Like the first human, Adam, the Corinthians are subject to strife, hardship, and death. Yet they already also exist "in Christ": through baptism they have been incorporated into the very body of Christ. Paul's trope of treasure in clay jars and the synecdoche of the body interpreted threats of affliction as existing in interrelation with manifestations of glory. In 2 Corinthians 4, the same earthenness that makes them susceptible to suffering, corruption, and death contrasts with and, in some sense, is also a condition for empowerment, renewal, and transformation.

In other places, Paul construed the earthen stuff of human life and particularly the "flesh" (*sarx*) more negatively, as more threatened and threatening. First Corinthians portrayed the Corinthians as particularly susceptible to discord and contamination: they are an assembly that is sometimes divided by status and also a body whose boundaries are threatened by hostile agents. According to Dale Martin, underlying Paul's depictions of threat were two competing explanations of disruption and disease. Martin contrasts the logic of an "invasion etiology of disease," evident in Paul's anxieties about pollution and firm boundaries, to an "imbalance etiology" found in Greco-Roman medicine and indicated by concerns for equilibrium and moderation. Each of these etiologies involves a physiology and corresponding therapy and can be correlated with a political theory. Martin elaborates: "The etiology of balance reflects a sense of control over one's body and the environment. Fears of invasion and loss of power over one's self are not paramount." In it, disease occurs when the body becomes imbalanced or, analogically, when the stability of the political order is disturbed by strife between the classes. Therapeutic interventions involve restoring proper balance and reestablishing the body's "natural" hierarchy. By contrast, in Paul and in the invasion etiology in general, "the body is not a secure microcosm of the balanced universe but a site of cosmic battles between good and evil." This view, Martin notes, "evinces a social position of helplessness in the face of outside powers. The world is a much more precarious place, with threats on every side."[3] Note how the etiology of invasion and the threat of persecution coalesce: in 2 Corinthians 4:8–10 Paul's catalog of afflictions conveys the sense of being threatened on every side.

Martin concludes that Paul "struggles to disrupt the hierarchy of 'this world' and restructure both it and the body to reflect the topsy-turvy status system of apocalyptic eschatology and faith in a crucified Messiah."[4] Paul's revolutionary vision was sometimes constrained by a physiology that remains hierarchical, as indicated by his treatment of the women prophets in 1 Corinthians 11.[5] Other passages and images, including that of clay jars bearing glorious treasure, convey a less mixed message.

Paul's depiction of the animating power of God made manifest in clay jars and his disruption of the status of "this world" will reverberate through the ages. The logics of imbalance and invasion will have analogues in later interpretations of personal and communal existence. As we shall see, the trope of treasure in earthen vessels will come to bear different meanings, partly as the effective etiologies of Augustine and other theologians shift from concern about external risks, especially persecution, to concern about the unity of the church and moderation in Christian life. These changing emphases correlated with changing views of transformation and also related to whether and how hierarchical status, ideology, and polity were disrupted or maintained.

In the ancient world, change and flux themselves were viewed as threatening; the etiologies of invasion and of imbalance both suggest this. The word *vulnerability* is also caught up with the view of change as threat; it typically connotes a risk to harmful change being effected by prevailing powers. While *vulnerability* as such is not found in Paul's Letters to Corinth, there are analogues. Paul offered his reader varied depictions of demise: destruction, putrefaction, affliction, rejection, pollution, and bondage to sin. However, he also outlined a horizon of hope that involves positive change: "We will all be changed, in a moment, in the twinkling of an eye, at the last trumpet" (1 Cor. 15:51b–52a). Paul's appeal to creation and renewal, as well as to resurrection and redemption, underscored possibilities of positive transformation.[6] Persons are also vulnerable to healing and strengthening by the extraordinary power of God.

In this book I develop this broader construal of vulnerability. I consider how susceptibility to devastation and transformation are entwined and how capacities for healing and harm are linked. Vulnerability is always experienced in particular bodies and situations, and is often signaled by threats of trauma and torture; yet in this interpretation, vulnerability is not embodiment or emplacement as such. Vulnerability is susceptibility to being changed, for good and for ill.

Paul's deceptively simple metaphor of clay jars brings us close to the heart of matter. It conveys a range of threats by associating malleable and breakable vessels with the dust of creation and of death. It signals, too, a range of possibilities: of creation pronounced "good," of everyday vessels suited for holy use, and of divine *pneuma* moving through and manifest in human life. The interrelations of threats and possibilities with those of bodies, creation, mortality, transformation, and glory, are difficult to convey other than through the layers of allusions and associations that rich metaphors offer. By contrast, note the pervasive, nearly rote, use of the dialectic of flesh and spirit (or body and spirit) in much of Western Christian thought. To be sure, careful exegesis can complicate a dualistic rendering of this pair. Nonetheless, use of the body/spirit dialectic, especially as interpreted in relation to dialectics of visible and invisible and of historical existence and spiritual essence, has often served to flatten and reduce complex relationships. With renewed attention to the layers of meanings condensed in metaphors and this construal of vulnerability, I attempt to broaden the bandwidth, as it were, adding dimension and dynamism to our understanding of creaturely plights and possibilities and their interrelation in the glory of God.

IRENAEUS: RELIABILITY AND RENEWAL

Paul exhorted the Corinthians to be mindful that their earthenness bore the glory of God. A century or so later, a subtle but decisive shift had occurred. Irenaeus placed confidence in the Christian assembly because it was a reliable vessel that is ever being renewed by the Spirit of God. He explained how the trustworthiness of the vessel and the treasure are interdependent:

> We receive our faith from the Church and keep it safe; and it is as it were a precious deposit stored in a fine vessel, ever renewing its vitality through the Spirit of God, and causing the renewal of the vessel in which it is stored. . . . For where the Church is, there is the Spirit of God; and where the Spirit of God is, there is the Church and every kind of grace.[7]

On the one hand, the treasure renews the vessel: the Spirit of God is ever at work renewing the vitality of faith in the church. On the other hand, the reliability of the vessel ensures the treasure: the church has passed on and preserved the true teaching of the faith from the apostles. There were reasons for Irenaeus to seek confidence in the vitality of the treasure and the reliability of the vessel. Authorities threatened Christians with torture and horrible deaths while Gnostic views challenged Pauline teaching about divine transformation of mortal life. For Irenaeus, the reality of the church stood as testimony that God's power prevails over such threats.

Since the apostle Paul's own martyrdom, the threat of persecution had remained over the church in the Mediterranean world. Irenaeus became bishop of Lyon in the Roman province of Gaul after his predecessor, Pothinus, was martyred. Altogether, 47 Christians, 24 males and 23 females, were martyred in Lyon in 177–178 CE.[8] In this context, a central concern for Irenaeus and his contemporaries was, in the phrasing of historian Peter Brown, "how the frail, mortal body might become a reliable container for the Spirit of God."[9] What would enable Christians to bear affliction and not be crushed? To be struck down but not destroyed? Irenaeus answered: the restoring power of God. Having already created the human race from dust, God has now made a recapitulation in the Word of God become flesh. God has repaired and restored humanity, gathering up the human race in Christ's humanity and, in Christ as the second Adam, repeating and annulling the first Adam. Christ has demonstrated and the Spirit of God has empowered a fullness of life that prevails over torture and the fear of death.[10]

Irenaeus insisted that Christians "gradually become accustomed to receive and to bear God."[11] The martyrs of Lyon, especially the young slave woman Blandina, received and bore the glory of God in an exemplary manner. Note that glory was associated with luminosity and vitality, with an evident life-giving power. For Paul, God's power was manifest particularly in creation and new creation; here Blandina's luminous endurance attested to God's transcendent power over against the empire's prosecution of death. According to the account preserved in the memory of the church, "Blandina was filled with such power that even those who were taking turns to torture her in every way from dawn to dusk were weary and exhausted." The crowd was "bloodthirsty" and the Roman governor eager "to please the mob."[12] Blandina survived ordeals of whipping, being mauled by wild animals, and being seared by fire, before dying in a ring with a bull, "while the pagans themselves admitted that no woman had ever suffered so much in their experience."[13] After being tortured to death, the martyrs' dead bodies were guarded and denied burial for several days, presumably also to deny them resurrection. In effect, imperial authorities claimed power to determine life and death and also to obliterate everlasting existence in God. In response, Christian testimony about the martyrs of Lyon circumscribed the limits of imperial power with the power of God and also with the powers of language and communal faith. Attestations to the martyrs' exemplary power rose in the memory of communities of believers.

If we turn for a moment to the work of contemporary theorist Elaine Scarry, we can develop another perspective on persecution and the inversion of power that will eventually return us to Irenaeus's concern with strengthening Christians "to receive and bear God." Scarry's book, *The Body in Pain*, begins with the observation that intense pain not only resists expression—how does one convey the pain that one has?—but that it "actively destroys" language. Pain is certain to the person suffering it, even if it cannot easily be shared with another. "For the other person," she explains, "it is so elusive that 'hearing about pain' may exist as the primary model of what it is 'to have doubt.'"[14] Scarry does not comment on early Christian martyrs, but she does examine Amnesty International's contemporary efforts against torture. She observes that their work, like a physician's diagnosis of pain, builds on "the assumption that the act of verbally expressing pain is a necessary prelude to the collective task of diminishing pain."[15] Amnesty International's efforts to end torture depend upon the ability to communicate the reality of pain to others who are removed not only from the pain, but also from the culture, language, and daily realities of the tortured person's life. When these realities become believable to those removed from them, such belief can become the ground for action against torture.

In the account of the martyrs of Lyon, there is no doubt that Blandina suffers intensely: "the pagans themselves" admitted the extremity of it. Her pain traverses the gap of unreality to find expression in Christian testimony. According to Scarry, torture involves an inversion whereby an increase in the prisoner's pain diminishes the prisoner's world and thus increases the torturer's power.[16] The torturer not only gains control over the prisoner's physical and mental state and survival, but also power to describe "reality" and circumscribe the prisoner's world. Interestingly, the early church recounts that "Blandina was filled with such power" that *her torturers* "were weary and exhausted." Their exhaustion foreshadows how God's transcendent power, attested in Blandina's endurance, and the power of her testimony and that of other martyrs will ultimately be increased, not diminished, in response to persecution. Through the martyrs' testimony, the glory and power of God will rise in the faith of the early church.

The account of the martyrs' ordeal and endurance is preserved against the language-destroying, world-destroying power of torture. Scarry observes that torturers deconstruct their prisoner's world by turning ordinary domestic acts and objects—a chair, water, "ovens"—into weapons of torture.[17] Early Christians, by contrast, transmuted torture's weapons into domestic utensils that produce testimony and community. For example, Ignatius, bishop of Antioch after the turn of the second century, wrote while he was on his way to Rome to face execution, "I am God's wheat, and I am ground by the teeth of wild beasts that I may be found the pure bread of Christ."[18] In this Christian "domestication" of torture's weapons, the horror of being mauled to death and the deconstructive power of torture are not minimized. Rather, their terrible reality makes all the more powerful the inversion that takes place in the domestication of weapons of torture. Acts of torture that unmake the world become acts that create symbols of bread and water and voice; these, in turn, build up the church. The church becomes the artifact made by articulating and confessing the unmaking that reigns in torture, by preserving the agency of victims of torture, and by preserving in them the agency of the church against the action of Roman authorities. The world-creating power of God is affirmed over against the claims of empire to determine life and death.[19] This affirmation is also at the heart of early Christians' confession that God has repaired the world in the resurrection of a tortured Savior.

When Blandina is executed, the narrator interprets, "She too was sacrificed."[20] She too is placed with Jesus and others as a victim of imperial power and as a witness to the sovereign power of God. Historian Elizabeth Castelli notes that "martyrdom and sacrifice are integrally linked" in these and other early Christian texts.[21] The experience of persecution was interpreted "within a framework of meaning that drew upon broader metanarratives about temporality, suffering and sacrifice, and identity."[22] Additionally, this framework "articulated a competing theory of power" that transformed "'persecution' into 'martyrdom' and powerlessness into power."[23] Castelli places this narrative and theory of power at the heart of "early Christian culture making."

Without a doubt, "culture making" is also central to Irenaeus's concerns: he conveys a palpable sense both of standing within the church's tradition of witness, which includes martyrdom, and of the church's reliability and renewal. However, for Irenaeus it is *restoration*, not sacrifice—the renewal and repair of the world over against destruction—that epitomizes divine power and glory. Such an insistence on restoration, not sacrifice, can orient a contemporary account of vulnerability and glory, while offering continuity with Paul's emphasis on creation and new creation.

For Irenaeus, however powerful the witness of martyrs was, it was the whole church, persisting over time and "scattered through the whole world,"[24] that was the primary vessel of the power and glory of God. More than the apostle Paul did or could have, Irenaeus relied on the church—its Scripture, tradition, and practice—as a sure mediator of divine restoration through the work of the Spirit.

According to Irenaeus, ordinary flesh-and-blood lives *are* transformed in the church. Baptism effects a new humanity, and the Eucharist nourishes it. This view contrasted with a view of corruption that he found in the Gnostics:[25]

> How can they say that flesh passes to corruption and does not share in life, seeing that flesh is nourished by the body and blood of the Lord? . . . We offer to him what his own [in the Eucharist], suitably proclaiming the communion and unity of flesh and spirit. For as the bread, which comes from the earth, receives the invocation [*epiklēsis*] of God, and then it is no common bread, but Eucharist, consists of two things, an earthly and a heavenly; so our bodies, after partaking of the Eucharist, are no longer corruptible, having the hope of the eternal resurrection.[26]

Through the sacraments and in teaching rendered as continuous with the apostles' own, Irenaeus's church offered tangible assurance and means of participating in the Spirit.

Irenaeus's church, then, was not an expendable vessel. Neither was its corporate existence as tenuous as that of Paul's Corinthian community seems to have been. Paul offered an image of the Corinthians as infants in Christ (1 Cor. 3:1–2), by contrast Irenaeus pictured the church as a nursing mother who assures sustenance. "She is the entrance to life," he wrote.[27] "Those who have no share in the Spirit are not nourished and given life at their mother's breast; nor do they enjoy the sparkling fountain that issues from the body of Christ."[28]

SECOND AND THIRD CENTURIES: "THE PIVOT OF SALVATION"

Through the second and third centuries and in urban centers around the Mediterranean, theologians such as Irenaeus at Lyon, Ignatius at Antioch, Clement of Rome, Melito of Sardis, Tertullian and later Cyprian at Carthage, Origen and, before him, Clement at Alexandria— all assumed that the church was essentially a tangible, empirical society, not an otherworldly or invisible one.[29] Although they affirmed that there was more to the church than meets the eye, they never imagined the church as anything less than an actual, tangible society. "Is it conceivable that God has consigned to some very cheap receptacle the reflection of his own soul, the breath of his own spirit, the workmanship of his own mouth, and has thus, by giving it an unworthy lodging, definitely brought about its damnation?" Tertullian asked, his rhetorical flourish revealing the day's prevailing assumptions.[30] To be sure, Tertullian stressed the corruptibility and corruption of the flesh. Indeed, he is often criticized by contemporary scholars for seemingly dualist castigations of the body and for misogyny. Nonetheless, even for him, "*caro salutis est cardo*: the flesh is the pivot of salvation."[31]

That summation, "the flesh is the pivot of salvation," could apply to many of Tertullian's contemporaries as well. They contemplated the mutilated bodies of martyrs; they also lived in warm Mediterranean cities where foodstuffs and cadavers were always already rotting. In such a figurative and literal climate, the dualistic teachings of the Valentinians and Marcionites might have been appealing. Against such dualistic views, Irenaeus, Tertullian, and others affirmed the goodness of the material world as God's creation.[32] Concurrently, they affirmed the church as a place filled with the glory of God and the possibility of full life. Yes, there were differences and shifts in tacit understandings and explicit articulations about the nature of the church. Nonetheless, according to historian J. N. D. Kelly, "they had little or no inkling of the distinction which was later to become important between a visible and an invisible church."[33] Indeed, they had little or no inkling of the ambiguities within churches—the mixtures of good and ill, of holy and profane, of morality and immorality—that this distinction would be formulated to address.

Even so, the status of Christians in the Roman Empire was already changing from the days when Irenaeus found himself among martyrs and potential martyrs. A generation later and at Alexandria on the other end of the Mediterranean, Origen wrote poignantly, wistfully, of how the community changed when threats of persecution were relieved:

> That was the time when Christians were really faithful, when the noble martyrdoms were taking place, when after conduct-

ing the martyrs' bodies to the cemeteries we returned thence
to meet together, and the entire church was present without
being afraid, and the catechumens were being catechized during the very time of the martyrdoms and while people were
dying who had confessed the truth unto death. . . . Then we
knew and saw wonderful and miraculous signs.[34]

Christian holiness was not otherworldly or invisible; rather, it was
evident in believers' lives and tangibly present in doctrine and sacraments.[35] For Origen, the faith of the few was evident in their persever-
ance through persecution and in the community's sanctity. "Now, when
we have become many," he observed, ". . . there are extremely few who
are attaining to the election of God and to blessedness."[36]

As it turns out, Origen was writing in the lull before the widespread
Decian persecution, the first persecution of Christians to be directed
by central imperial decree rather than by provincial authorities. Nonetheless, theological attention was beginning to shift from the matter of
how Christians might be strengthened to receive and bear God despite
threats of persecution and heresy, to the problem of the reliability and
holiness of the church, that is, from the vulnerability of Christians to the
ambiguity of the church as an institution.

THE PROBLEM OF AMBIGUITY WITHIN CHURCHES

The Pauline figure of treasure in earthen vessels came to bear different
meanings in changing social and rhetorical contexts. For example, it was
reconfigured in relation to interpretations of bodies as vessels, especially
suffering bodies and the bodies of women. These changed meanings
effected further changes in new contexts. This chapter can only suggest these associations through some references to interpretations of a
church of martyrs and the church as mother. These references gesture to
the surrounding political, economic, cultural, intellectual, and religious
atmospheres.[37] As the figure of treasure and vessels transmogrified over
the course of centuries, so also did interpretations of life before God.
Ironically, the figure that Paul used to sound threats to and possibilities for vulnerable existence sometimes came to bolster ideas about the
church's invulnerability.[38]

Recognition of what I refer to as the problem of ambiguity, that is,
the problem of ambiguity *within churches*, emerged in Christianity's
first few centuries. For the earliest Christians, ambiguity within their

communities was not a pressing practical matter; what pressed upon them were concerns with their status in the wider religious and political world and about their susceptibility to persecution, false teaching, and alien powers. Indeed, Paul and Irenaeus depicted these communities as reliable vessels that bore the grace and glory of God. When churches were increasingly perceived to contain mixtures of morality and laxity and of true and false teaching—that is, to be ambiguous—the reliability of the church as a means of God's grace and manifestation of God's glory came under question. In response to the problem of ambiguity, theologians often turned to strategies of institutional, dogmatic, or moral invulnerability.

By the turn of the fifth century, theologians and church leaders had shifted their attention from external threats to threats of falsehood and defilement within Christian churches. Augustine observed that the church was a "mixed body." Could churches bear God's grace when truth and falsehood were mixed within them? Introducing the distinction between the visible and invisible church, Augustine affirmed that actual churches exhaust neither the reality of Christian communion nor the glory of God. He broadened the horizon of transformation to the whole world and to all history. At the same time, his use of the visible/invisible antithesis accompanied and undergirded increasing theological and practical emphasis on the creation and maintenance of a properly ordered institution that minimized discord and bolstered unity.

The second half of this chapter traces the emergence of the problem of ambiguity and follows the introduction of the distinction between the visible and invisible church as a central theological response. In doing so, it follows a more-or-less Pauline-Augustinian strand of thought. It looks quickly at Cyprian's treatise on the church before focusing on Augustine's response to the problem of ambiguity. One concern of this and the next three chapters is to examine how responses to ambiguity, particularly the use of the distinction between visible and invisible church, articulate with approaches to vulnerability and transformation.

When *culture* and *world* are interpreted broadly, they reach to all spheres of human activity: political, economic, interpretive, social, moral, religious, intellectual, aesthetic, and so forth. Understood in these terms, Christians and their communities are always already in culture; threats may be external or internal to the community, but churches and cultures are never wholly "external" to each other. At issue is the nature of the relations among Christians and cultures.[39] The problem of strengthening persons and communities to bear God arises when

Christians perceive themselves to be threatened externally, for example, by the authorities of Roman provinces. Early Christian practices of strengthening persons and communities were in themselves cultural practices and processes. Christian life was tangible, material, the result of human activity. Yet neither did early Christians merely affirm the "world" in which they lived. They also met competing worldviews at every turn. Thus they engaged "culture" while resisting "culture," all the while attesting to the transforming power of God. The problem of securing churches against impurity and falsity, and thus to ensure confidence in salvation, becomes evident when the dominant culture tolerates Christianity (and therefore the relations among churches and cultural authorities and practices become more fluid); the problem of ensuring salvation against the ambiguities of culture becomes pervasive when Christianity gains a privileged status in culture.

As the problem of ambiguity in churches comes to the fore, theologians and church leaders will not always avoid a simplistic construal of the relation of church and world. Some will veer toward opposition, some toward accommodation. Others, notably Augustine, will advocate for complex and dynamic strategies for transforming the "world" while being located in its midst. Many will neglect the affirmations of the second and third centuries that embodied persons and encultured communities are the "pivot of salvation."

CYPRIAN'S SPIRITUAL-STRUCTURAL UNITY

When the Decian persecution ended in 251, church leaders were left with the question of what to do with the "lapsed," those who had compromised their faith in various ways during the persecution. This situation, and the clerical rebellion and ecclesial division that ensued, was the context in which Cyprian, bishop of Carthage from 248 until his martyrdom in 258, wrote his treatise *On the Unity of the Catholic Church*. Cyprian used the metaphor of vessels to argue that judgment of the lapsed belongs solely to God:

> Even though there seem to be "unclean vessels" in the church, there is no reason why we ourselves should withdraw from the church; rather, . . . we must strive as much as we can to be vessels of gold and silver. But the breaking of earthen vessels belongs solely to the Lord, to whom has been entrusted an iron rod.[40]

Here Cyprian summoned Paul's earthen vessel and Jeremiah's shattered vessels and, with the phrase "vessels of gold and silver," alluded to martyrs' bodies. (In the account of Polycarp's martyrdom, ca. 156–157, Polycarp's "burning flesh" is likened to "gold and silver refined in a furnace.")[41] Thus Cyprian upheld the martyrs as exemplars of faith while asserting that God is the ultimate judge of all persons. In this passage the earthen vessels referred to individuals, not the corporate body; Cyprian's church was sturdier and purer than the individual vessels that were found in it. His church, though susceptible to God's judgment, was invulnerable to damage caused by the laxity or fallibility of church members.

Against the threats of schisms and heresies, Cyprian took the unity of the church to be axiomatic.[42] Its unity is an organic reality that is divinely given. Just as a tree has many branches, the sun many rays, and a spring has many streams but one source, so also for Christians: "There is one head, one source, one mother boundlessly fruitful. Of her womb we are born, by her milk we are nourished, by her breath we are quickened."[43] With his recurring use of the image of church as mother, Cyprian held together in an organic whole, as it were, a sense of the church's life-giving inner vitality with an absolute insistence on its structural integrity. There is no spiritual vitality—no ministry, no sacraments, and hence no salvation—apart from the one church fastened together in the unity of the episcopacy.

Accordingly, Cyprian taught that, without episcopal succession and concord with the bishop, there is no church. His organic-structural images reinterpreted what were formerly charismatic "gifts" of ministry as "possessions" for which bishops alone have the power of the "keys." This structural interpretation of the church, albeit still a far cry from later views of the institution of papal monarchy, would not have been possible even a hundred years earlier. His teaching that there is no salvation outside the church assumed this structural and indeed legalistic view of the church as well as a view of its life pulsing with the vitality of the Spirit.[44] Both views were entailed when he wrote, "You cannot have God for your father unless you have the Church for your mother."[45]

Cyprian's teaching about the spiritual-structural unity of the church is summarized in a passage at the end of the treatise:

> There is one God and one Christ and one faith and one people, fastened together into a solid corporate unity by the glue of concord. The unity cannot be rent, nor can the one body be divided by breaking up its structure; it cannot be broken into

fragments by tearing and mangling the flesh. Whatever leaves the womb cannot live and breathe apart. It loses the substance of health.[46]

So certain was Cyprian of the church's holiness and vitality that he taught that "good men cannot leave the Church."[47] In effect, he asserted that resolving the question of whether the church is holy also resolved the question of moral ambiguity—whether the people of God are good. Cyprian's teaching may have offered "clarity and coherence," but as S. L. Greenslade commented, the pastoral consequences were dire for those who were judged to be outside the church and hence without salvation.[48]

CHANGING CIRCUMSTANCES

Imperial favor, granted to Christianity with Constantine's conversion in 312, changed both the status and the constituency of Christian churches. By the time Augustine became bishop of Hippo in North Africa in 395 (where he served until his death in 430), he judged the persons gathered in the church to be a decidedly "mixed body." He viewed the church like a threshing floor where the grain is nearly invisible among the chaff.[49]

North African Christians, like pious Christians elsewhere in the early fifth century, found churches filled with a full complement of humanity. Augustine described the dubious scene one might find in a church:

> The man who enters is bound to see drunkards, misers, tricksters, gamblers, adulterers, fornicators, people wearing amulets, assiduous clients of sorcerers, astrologers. . . . He must be warned that the same crowds that press into the church on Christian festivals, also fill the theatres on pagan holidays.[50]

Yet if moral markers between "church" and "world" seemed to disappear in such assemblies, North African Christians also thought of the church as a place that existed to protect and nourish the believer. Thus they were confronted with a "disconcerting double-image" of the church.[51]

In that context, the Donatists held to the idea of the moral and ritual purity of the church and set it in contrast to a hostile, impure world.[52] They appealed to the authority of Cyprian. Augustine viewed the situation differently and refuted what we can call, in retrospect, sectarianism. He believed that Christianity would continue to grow rapidly and encompass more of society. Rather than maintaining what he considered to be a defensive, static view of the church as an alternative to society, he interpreted the church in relation to the idea of the unity of the human race. Augustine held that all humanity came from the same mother, including those who descend from Abel, Abraham, and Moses to apostles, martyrs, "and all good Christians," and also those who descend from Cain and Ham to Judas, Simon Magus, and to "all the other false Christians."[53] According to Brown, "Augustine believed that the church might become coextensive with human society as a whole: that it might absorb, transform and perfect, the existing bonds of human relations."[54]

The differences between North African Christianity and society at the turn of the fifth century and North American Christianity and society at the turn of the twenty-first century are manifest. Nevertheless, fifth-century concerns about the evident ambiguity of religious communities have a certain resonance today. Like the Donatists of Augustine's day, some advocate for strict boundaries drawn according to absolute moral, ritual, or doctrinal purity, for example, fundamentalist Christianity, the Nation of Islam, and countercultural enclaves on the "right" and on the "left." Such strategies of invulnerability are no more adequate for our day than for Augustine's. They sacrifice a vision of a single humanity for group security. Augustine instead depicted salvation as a long process of transformation that addressed the ambiguous breadth of humanity.

THE VISIBLE AND INVISIBLE CHURCH IN AUGUSTINE

The distinction between the visible and the invisible church was central to Augustine's answer to Donatist concerns about the church's purity. To respond to the controversy, he introduced the notion of the *corpus permixtum*, the mixed body of the church. According to Augustine, actual churches include both true and false members. However, in the mystery of grace, the dividing line between true and false cannot be determined by external membership in the church or by baptism alone. Rather, the true church consists of "the fixed number of the saints predestined before the foundation of the world." Moreover, to ensure the sovereignty of God's grace, Augustine held that there is no sure correspondence of the elect with those who participate in the sacraments or evidence moral rectitude. Indeed, among the "fixed number" are some who continue presently in wickedness and heresy. Augustine was reluctant to judge anyone to be utterly beyond salvation, whether they were "misers, tricksters, gamblers" or Donatists. His own experience taught him that God's irresistible grace will confound human judgment. "In that unspeakable foreknowledge of God," Augustine wrote, "many who seem to be without are in reality within, and many who seem to be within yet really are without."[55]

The holiness of the church is derived from participation in Christ, established solely by God, and anchored in "the never failing fruitfulness of the root of the Catholic Church."[56] While the actual practice of the ministry and the observance of the sacraments are necessary means for a righteous life, they do not in themselves ensure the church's holiness.[57] The perfection of the church is seen only from the perspective of its future fulfillment. "The church, without spot or wrinkle, must not be understood as if it actually were so, but as destined to become so, when it is in glory."[58]

Augustine associated the glory of God with a still hidden but changeless perfection more than with a luminous, enlivening power of creation and renewal. To view the holiness of the church as a future destiny that is veiled in present actuality would have been inconceivable to Paul, Irenaeus, Origen, or Cyprian. Although they did not believe that the full glory of God was known in present life, they focused on the communities they knew and strove to explain how those communities offered both tangible means for entering into the power of the Spirit and the fullness of life and tangible assurances of salvation.

Faced with the challenges of a different day and a different church, Augustine turned to Neoplatonist metaphysics to help interpret the grace and power of God at work in the church and world. Peter Brown explains: "The whole world appeared to him as a world of 'becoming.' . . . This universe was in a state of constant, dynamic tension, in which the imperfect forms of matter strove to 'realize' their fixed, ideal structure, grasped by the mind alone."[59] Neoplatonism provided a way to conceptualize the circulation of life in God. Imperfect forms of matter can be moved (by God) toward their perfect or ideal reality in God, but they can also fall away and fall short of the glorious reality of the city of God. The city of God and the true church are ideal realities. By contrast, actual churches and their sacraments remain a "shadow of reality" that offer only emergent, partial indications of the full glory of God. They strive—imperfectly—to realize the glory of the heavenly Jerusalem and the mystical body of Christ. Augustine's church thus became "a field of innumerable, personal evolutions" and "long processes of spiritual growth."[60]

Augustine's effective etiology shifted from a concern with maintaining boundaries against invasion to a concern with the dynamic reality of the whole and how the whole is ordered toward God. Martin observes that in balance therapeutics, "health is restored by reestablishing the natural equilibrium of the body's elements and forces."[61] For Augustine, right order emerges as the forms of Christian life align with and take on the glorious perfection of divine reality. For example, in one of his sermons Augustine identifies Christ's ecclesial body with the eucharistic body. He portrays growth in the Christian life through a metaphysic of forms striving to realize their ideal, and exhorted his listeners:

> You hear the words "body of Christ," and you answer "Amen."
> Then *be* a member of the body of Christ, that your "Amen" may
> be true. . . . Remember that a loaf is not made of one grain,
> but of many. When you were exorcized you were, so to speak,
> ground. When you were baptized you were, so to speak, moist-
> ened. When you received the fire of the Holy Spirit you were, so
> to speak, baked. Be what you see [upon the table] and receive
> what you *are*.[62]

Participants in the Eucharist are instructed and empowered to make actual what they already are in Christ. Eucharist, baptism, and creed are mere forms—and therefore are inherently ambiguous—without the Spirit's enlivening power. The Spirit quickens and binds Christ's body together in love and effects the realization of full life through the forms of the Christian life. Ultimately, this "body" could expand to the whole civilized world.

DYNAMIC COMPLEXITY OR STABILITY AND MASTERY?

Jaroslav Pelikan argued that Augustine's definition of the church as the number of the saved "enabled him to accept a distinction between the members of the empirical catholic church and the company of those who would be saved, while at the same time he insisted that the empirical catholic church was the only one in which salvation was dispensed." J. N. D. Kelly thought otherwise. He contended that, with this distinction and definition, "the notion of the institutional Church ceases to have any validity." Eric Jay wrote that Augustine "ardently desired to open a way for Donatists to enter into communion with the Catholics, and so to enter into the sphere of the spirit of charity in which alone he believed they could find salvation." But in so doing, his "pastoral concern overcame logic." Peter Brown admired the complex and dynamic unity of life that Augustine sought, but also judged the resulting formulations to be inherently unstable. "While the Donatist view of the Church had a certain rock-like consistency," Brown noted, "Augustine's Church was like an atomic particle: it was made up of moving elements, a field of dynamic tensions, always threatening to explode."[63]

Kelly rightly judged that Augustine's concepts of mystical body and the invisible church ultimately diminish—or more precisely, the history of their effects ultimately diminishes—the importance of actual communities. Nevertheless, some critical dynamic such as Augustine's tension between visible and invisible church is needed to interpret the transforming reality of God present in creaturely existence. Sole reliance on the antithesis of visible and invisible—or its modern counterparts—is ultimately inadequate to the multiple transformations and regressions that Augustine at his best conveys. In chapter 5, we will return to the image of a field of dynamic tensions, albeit perhaps a different field than the one to which Brown referred.

Brown implies that Augustine's "atomic" church finally did explode, unleashing, as the tensions split apart, a potency intent on absorbing and perfecting society. In a fission of unstable elements—African Christians' sensibilities about the distinctiveness of the church, biblical themes of divine sovereignty and sin, Neoplatonism, Augustine's own experiences of the church in Rome and Milan—Augustine's church had become "a church set, no longer to defy society, but to master it."[64] Brown looked back to a passage written before Augustine came to Hippo in which Augustine attributes to "the Catholic Church, most true Mother of Christians," the power to align virtually the whole society in hierarchical relation:

> It is You [Mother Church] who make wives subject to their husbands . . . by chaste and faithful obedience; you set husbands over their wives; you join sons to their parents by a freely granted slavery, and set parents above their sons in pious domination. You link brothers to each other by bonds of religion firmer and tighter than those of blood. You teach slaves to be loyal to their masters, . . . masters . . . to be more inclined to persuade them than to punish. You link citizen to citizen, nation to nation, indeed, You bind all men together in the remembrance of their first parents, not just by social bonds, but by some feeling of their common kinship. You teach kings to rule for the

> benefit of their people; and You it is who warn the peoples to
> be subservient to their kings.[65]

The mother church of this passage is close kin to Cyprian's mother church. Perhaps her power resembles that of Augustine's own strong mother, Monica. In the centuries to come, she and her descendants, even more formidable churches, will unite with patriarchally ordered societies, administering a firm rule of the Christian life.

In our time we may notice stasis and mastery especially in this passage; yet other things are worth noting. First, Augustine depicts the church as constituted in its relationships, practices, and life—albeit hierarchically ordered ones—rather than by the enforcement of its boundaries against invasive powers in culture or "the world." Were we to summarize and paraphrase this passage in language that anticipates John Calvin's, we might say that "wherever human life is rightly ruled, properly ordered, and united toward God, do not doubt that there is the true church, the mother of all believers."[66] Calvin's ideas themselves have been charged with unleashing a bureaucratic potency, but this sense of intrinsic order (again, echoes of the balance etiology) also enabled moderation and relative openness. Second, accompanying this image of the church as a teaching, disciplining mother are images of a mother who gives birth to and nourishes Christians. She agonizes over her children, both wayward and exemplary ones.[67] These arguably more basic aspects of the image of church as mother pervade early Christian thought.

By the late medieval period, the image of mother church had taken on formidable reality. Martin Luther, unlike reformers Hildegard of Bingen before him and John Calvin after him, found nothing to recommend the image or reality of mother church. For Luther, as Pelikan observed, "the church was the daughter of the word, not the mother of the word."[68] Luther judged the notion of a powerful mother church to be another of the "ridiculous conceits" that accompanied papal pretensions to power and authority:

> The chief cause that I fell out with the pope was this: the pope
> boasted that he was the head of the church, and condemned all
> that would not be under his power and authority. . . . He made
> himself lord over the church, proclaiming her at the same time
> a powerful mother, and empress over the Scriptures, to which
> we must yield and be obedient; this was not to be endured.
> They who, against God's Word, boast of the church's authority
> are mere idiots. The pope attributes more power to the church,

which is begotten and born, than to the Word, which has begotten, conceived, and borne the church.[69]

Luther did not view papal claims and attributions of power as fore-
shadowing the glorious city of God, but rather as exemplifying a (false)
theology of glory. He charged that the pope and the empress-mother
church are so deceitful as to propagate the lie that they possess authority
over salvation. This church was anything but the mother of all believers;
in other places, he described her as "the whore-church of the devil."[70] In
Luther's earthy—and sexist—image, she is an impure "vessel," capable of
shameless falsehood and innovation, but incapable of bearing the truth.
He insisted, by contrast, that the Word of God alone—that is, not the
vessel but the treasure—gives birth to a holy Christian people.

Before turning to Luther and the next chapter, I want to save this
chapter's last word for Augustine. Augustine sketched a mother church
whose glorious power might unite not only all Christians but all humanity. Such unity remained a hope that was unrealized in his time, even as
the church spread throughout the Mediterranean world. In actuality, as
Peter Brown explains, "African society creaked with ills. The powerful
victimized the poor. Armed gangs of slave traders wandered with impu-
nity through a defenseless countryside. Members of Augustine's own
clergy set themselves up as petty tyrants in the villages."[71] Then, too,
death remained a "bitter sign of human frailty" and sexual desire a sign
of the "twisted human will." Only in the city of God would "the ache of
discord . . . give way to a *pax plena*, to a fullness of peace."[72] Until that
city at the end of time, the human race would suffer conflict and disorder, with humanity being unified in tragedy more than in glory.

CHAPTER 2

Assembled under the Cross: Martin Luther's Christendom

> Naked children, men, women, farmers, citizens, who possess no ton-
> sures, miters, or priestly vestments also belong to the church.
> —*Martin Luther*[1]

The gap between the faltering chaos of human society and the peace of the city of God caused Augustine to suffer "the ache of discord."[2] Even as he yearned for the glorious city of God, Augustine knew the disorder of human cities and souls. What Martin Luther underwent was something else. He, too, lived in a time of social trauma, some of it of his own making, much of it a response to the terror of the plague and to economic and intellectual upheaval.[3] Within this general climate of fear and anxiety, Luther suffered specific torments, his much-discussed episodes of *Anfechtungen*, spiritual trials. Like the apostle Paul, he felt assailed by the powers of sin and death. The remedies of his day offered no relief—not the best of monastic discipline, not arduous pilgrimages, penitence, or the cult of relics. None of these methods provided the deep inner certainty that Luther sought. "Luther felt alone in the universe, battered by the demands of God's law and beyond the reach of the Gospel. He doubted his own faith, his own mission, and the goodness of God."[4] He would come to rely on "Scripture alone" rather than on such mediations. In the message of the gospel, Luther found assurance that, through faith and even as a sinner, he could rely utterly on the grace of God for justification.

Luther suffered periods of affliction throughout his life. Making his own diagnosis, he concluded that his tormenter was none other than the very God, encountered in the form of a destroyer. Luther would wrestle with God his whole life. He would emerge from those encounters, like Jacob wrestling all night at the ford of the Jabbock, wounded and yet certain of God's claim upon him. In Luther's interpretation of the story, the threatening stranger is also the Savior, the Christ.[5] Here the etiology of invasion is taken up a notch: God's battle against the devil is being waged throughout earthly life, including in the church and in the soul. Luther was indeed vulnerable, yet not finally to a disordered soul and world so much as to God.

It was not only Luther who was afflicted. He saw faithful Christians who were vulnerable to suffering and hunger; he argued that the true church could be found with them "under the cross." His contrast between a theology of the cross and a theology of glory expressed and informed his radical critique of the church. Luther worried that rituals and structures were taken to be glorious ends in themselves. He believed that such false claims to glory diverted attention from God and suffering humanity. Luther therefore accented both the invisibility of God's glory and the realities of suffering through his paradoxical construal of the relationship of divine power and human life. I will argue that his paradoxical construal ultimately cannot support a robust account of vulnerability and glory. At the same time, Luther offered multiple critical and constructive perspectives that remain instructive for our day.

THE SIGN OF THE CROSS

According to Luther, faith alone is the only sure basis for life before God. Nowhere was this more consistently affirmed than in his theology of the cross and his depiction of the church under the cross. "Faith does not require information, knowledge, or certainty, but a free surrender and a joyful bet on his [God's] unfelt, untried, and unknown goodness,"[6] he explained. The apex of "unfelt, untried, and unknown goodness" is Christ crucified. With the apostle Paul, Luther affirmed: "I . . . know nothing except Jesus Christ, and him crucified" (1 Cor. 2:2). "Christ crucified" was an epistemological key, a decisive test of interpretation, a blade that shaved away presumptive knowledge. Luther asked in effect, "Have presumptions to know God's favor, to be able to gain salvation through the church's or one's own efforts, been surrendered? Have presuppositions been set aside to rely on faith alone?" In the cross, assumptions about the glory of God are overturned, emptied out: there God in Christ is humiliated for the sake of salvation.[7] Similarly, Christians empty out their self-reliance to rely solely on God's Word, favor, and action; human feeling, efforts, and knowledge cannot bridge this distance. Rather, faith surrenders completely to God.

The theme of surrender was also sounded in Luther's teaching that the true church is found "under the cross." Luther believed that the battle for the true church, and the persecution and suffering that accompany it, would only intensify until God's final reformation and ultimate judgment. In the meanwhile, to resist the devil and the captivity of the church was to follow Christ and to become a church whose surrender to God was attested in suffering. A true remnant of the church would be found wherever a suffering communion of Christians steadfastly proclaimed their faith without benefit of privileged status or protection of the powerful.[8] Here surrender is not only an epistemological stance. "Under the cross," like faith itself, is an existential placement that also has moral and practical implications. How does one know which is the true church? Luther answered, look for the people gathered by and beneath the cross; moreover, look for the people who take up their crosses after Christ and likewise surrender themselves to God and, it seems, to suffering.

Luther maintained this view of the church as a suffering communion from his early lectures on the Psalms to the end of his life.[9] In *On the Councils and the Church* (1539), he named suffering or the sign of the cross as the seventh distinguishing sign or possession of a holy Christian people. Both courageous fortitude and passive endurance are entailed:

> The holy Christian people . . . must undergo every misfortune and persecution, all kinds of trials and evil from the devil, the world, and the flesh (as the Lord's Prayer indicates) by inward sadness, timidity, fear, outward poverty, contempt, illness, and weakness, in order to become like their head, Christ. And the only reason they must suffer is that they steadfastly adhere to Christ and God's Word, enduring this for the sake of Christ, Matthew 5[:11], "Blessed are you when men persecute you on my account."[10]

Luther moved to a provocative conclusion: The holy Christian people ". . . must be called heretics, knaves, devils, the most pernicious people on earth, to the point where those who hang, drown, murder, torture, banish, and plague them to death are rendering God a service."[11] Was he stating (overstating, perhaps) what seems to be inevitable for Christians? Was he noting what is not lost in God's economy? Or did he view suffering to be a necessary part of the Christian life?

Luther compared the suffering of the poor, persecuted Christians of his day with the example of Christ and the early church. In another essay he explained, "Our lot is like that of the ancient church, and in this we are beyond measure like it, so that we may well say we are the true ancient church, or at least its companions and copartners in suffering."[12] Luther adopted a rhetorical strategy used by the apostle Paul against his critics. Both shamed their critics, using irony and example to demonstrate the humility and self-evident authenticity of suffering Christians. In 1 Corinthians 4, after employing an ironic reversal of rich and poor, wise and foolish, Paul described how followers of Christ met humiliation with endurance:

> To the present hour we are hungry and thirsty, we are poorly clothed and beaten and homeless, and we grow weary from the work of our own hands. When reviled, we bless; when persecuted, we endure; when slandered, we speak kindly. We have become like the rubbish of the world, the dregs of all things, to this very day. (1 Cor. 4:11–13).

Like Paul, Luther wrote about the devastation of hunger and homelessness and not only about persecution. He contrasted the church's call for fasting with the need of hungry Christians:

> We do not just fast, but (with St. Paul [1 Cor. 4:11]) we suffer hunger. We see it daily in our poor ministers, their wives and children, and in many other poor people, whose hunger stares at you out of their eyes. They scarcely have bread and water, they go about naked as a jaybird, they have nothing of their own. The farmer and the burgher give them nothing, and the nobility take, so that there are only a few of us who have something, and we cannot help everyone. This should be the purpose of monasteries and convents.[13]

In these passages, irony exposes pretensions to holiness. Authentic holiness is evident where Christians persevere in faith despite persecution and the wearying lack of basic necessities such as food, clothing, and shelter.

The sensibility here is to view suffering as a sign of persistent faith rather than to valorize suffering per se. Unless we keep this sensibility in mind, Luther's observation that "the more Christian a man is, the more evils, sufferings, and deaths he must endure"[14] remains both incomprehensible and repugnant. To consent to persecution and suffering as necessary or as an integral part of faith is an idea that is rightly troubling in our day. Too often admonishments to endure have bolstered the powerful and perpetuated oppression. Too seldom have they served to reveal the pretensions of the powerful and to empower the dispossessed.

For Luther, as for Paul, surrender through suffering opened an existential vantage point on the reality of God. "He, however, who has been emptied [cf. Phil. 2:7] through suffering no longer does works but knows that God works and does all things in him."[15] Whatever cautions should be given about the danger of encouraging submission to suffering, Luther's attention to suffering drew a sharp contrast to a triumphant church. He accused his opponents of cheating the masses by selling the supposed benefits of fraudulent relics. Not only were the relics of questionable authenticity; in any case, they also could not produce holiness. He contrasted this pricey exchange of commodified holiness to a Christian people whose holiness was authenticated in suffering. Although they may endure hardship and hunger, the suffering poor are not excluded from the free exchange of grace in Christ. Indeed, their endurance in faith despite persecution is a sign and attestation of genuine holiness.

CAPTIVITY

Martin Luther wrestled as vigorously with the late medieval church as with the alien force that tormented him personally. Mincing no words, he denounced the "Romanists" as "heretics and impious schismatics" whose "innumerable abuses" of the sacrament "turn the holy sacrament into mere merchandise, a market, and a business run for profit." His conclusions pointed the opposite direction from Cyprian's confidence in the episcopal unity of the church: "I saw clearly that the papacy was to be understood as the kingdom of Babylon."[16] Luther gave the problem of ambiguity decisive reformulation. In fact, ambiguity may be too tepid a description for what Luther saw. The problem did not lie with lapsed people or false practices alone, it was systemic. He called it captivity. Virtually every aspect of organized Christianity—doctrine, sacraments, structure, laity, clergy, ethos, mission—was not only susceptible to abuse and deception, but also already captured by evil forces.

Luther saw a church united under false authority. He warned against the dangers of complacency in a church that took its power and security for granted. Such a situation allowed falsehood to breed within the church itself, in its leaders, their sacramental practices, and the doctrines they promulgated. If the church appeared to be triumphant in the world, it was only because diabolical forces were well disguised. Luther viewed the problem in terms of the influence of hostile agents rather than disorder within church and society; moreover, the boundaries were not merely threatened; they had been breached. The papal hierarchy, from its center outward, had been captured by the enemy in this cosmic battle.[17] To switch metaphors, Luther was not describing a vulnerable, "earthen" church but rather a leaky, polluted, and perhaps irreparably damaged vessel.

The thoroughgoing deception that Luther denounced can be compared to the pervasive distortions addressed in various postmodern critiques, but with a notable difference. He attributed much more power to his devil—and to his God—than most postmodern theories attribute to technologies of cultural domination and configuration. Luther joined what might otherwise have been viewed as disparate ills in a systemic diagnosis of interconnected abuse and deception. For such a situation, no piecemeal therapy was possible; thoroughgoing reformation that brought the whole under the authority of the Word of God was required.

Luther found templates for depicting systemic abuse within the Jewish and Christian Scriptures themselves: in psalms and prophetic literature that mourned and denounced the period of Babylonian rule, and also in denunciations of broken covenants and empty rituals. Luther's critical approach was tremendously powerful. Because of that power, it also had dangerous side effects. His denunciations sometimes became vilification, intended and not intended. His critique of laws and rituals gone awry tended toward dismissal of all "external forms"—gospel opposed "the law"; the work of Christ on the cross abrogated all other "work"— and although Luther's blows were directed against powerful Christian adversaries, they often landed on Jews and Judaism. In addition, he adopted Pauline oppositions of law and gospel and of faith and works not simply as templates for leveling thorough critique, but also as central expressions of Christian faith. He typically characterized the problems of legalism and formalism as intrinsic to, even definitive of, Judaism, and as having been overcome in Christ; he charged the "Romanists" with reverting to a form of religion that had been superseded in Christ.[18] Furthermore, Luther seemed to find engaging in anti-Jewish polemics to be perfectly acceptable.

If we stop with Luther's powerful and sometimes deeply problematic denunciations, however, we will miss crucial aspects of his contributions. For Luther also opened up a positive space of reformation with his treatment of "the holy Christian people." He anchored this view in his interpretation of the Word of God, moving from it in dialectics of denunciation and annunciation. In this way he tried to clarify human vulnerability and the ambiguity of medieval Christendom in contrast to the grace and power of God. He contrasted a papal treasury of indulgences to the true treasure of the church, the gospel; the sham relics and supposed holiness of the medieval church to a holiness imparted by the Word and the Spirit; and a church defined by hierarchy and known in external things (such as buildings, vestments, rituals) to a communion in Christ that was "hidden in the cross."

THE TREASURE OF THE GOSPEL

As Martin Luther stated in his *Ninety-five Theses* of 1517 and affirmed throughout his life, "the true treasure of the church is the Holy Gospel of the glory and the grace of God."[19] To hold fast to the treasure of the gospel, to the Word of God alone, was Luther's central response to vulnerability and ambiguity. The Word—the message of God's grace as known in Christ, taught in Scripture, and proclaimed in the church—offered certainty in a volatile, anxious age. "When you have the Word, you can take hold and grasp him with certainty."[20] Luther held to this certainty himself and taught it to others. "Where the Word is, there is faith, and where faith is, there is the church."[21]

Luther's 1539 treatise *On the Councils and the Church* makes it clear that the Word of God is Christendom's foremost treasure. "This is the principal item, and the holiest of holy possessions, by reason of which the Christian people are called holy; for God's Word is holy and sanctifies everything it touches; it is indeed the very holiness of God." The Word creates, transforms, and marks a people. "Now, wherever you hear or see this Word preached, believed, professed, and lived, do not doubt that the true *ecclesia sancta catholica*, 'a Christian holy people,' must be there." Luther was not merely writing about a productive, critical principle of Christian life; wonders are at work. The Word is God's power to create and tear down: it is a balm that brings eternal life and a weapon that drives out devils. "This is the thing that performs all miracles, effects, sustains, carries out and does everything, exorcises all devils, like pilgrimage-devils, indulgence-devils, bull-devils, brotherhood-devils, saint-devils, mass-devils, purgatory-devils, monastery-devils, priest-devils, mob-devils, insurrection-devils, heresy-devils, all pope-devils, also Antinomian-devils." Thus Luther concludes, "It is enough for us to know how this chief holy possession purges, sustains, nourishes, strengthens, and protects the church."[22]

Luther came to believe that the focus ought to be on the treasure of the gospel rather than the vessel of the church and that the treasure ought to shape the vessel rather than the other way around. The apostle Paul had assured the Corinthians that mortal Christians who suffered hardship and persecution were worthy vessels for the gospel of the glory of God. Irenaeus and other theologians of the second and third centuries were concerned with the vitality of the treasure, so they extolled the reliability of the church as a vessel. By contrast, Luther determined that the church of his day was not reliable. He denounced not only indulgences and relics, but also its rituals and structure as pretensions to glory. He contrasted all outward expressions to an inward, invisible treasure, the gospel. The grace and glory of God cannot be assured by the vessel, that is, by the church's structure, rites, or life. Instead, the vessel ought to be shaped by the treasure. "We must therefore restore everything to its right shape—that is, to conformity with the Word of God," Luther concluded.[23] In the course of being taught and proclaimed, the Word effectively creates its own vessel, its own visible manifestations or signs.[24]

THE CREATIVE POWER OF THE WORD

In Luther's view, the Word has power: (1) to call people forth as an assembly of believers, (2) to address them personally (and thus tear down the hierarchy of priests and laity), (3) to mark and shape them, and (4) to unite them in Christ. Enormous creative power is potentially released from constraints of the institutional church into the people of God. The Word goes out into the world and calls forth God's people into new congregations, new vessels.

1. The Word Calls Out Community: An Assembly of Believers

For Luther, the church is an assembly of believers called into being by the Word. It is a congregation who hears, believes, and confesses the gospel. Luther's redefinition of the church as congregation was shaped by the Apostles' Creed and the Bible, and by language of the communion of saints, the people of God, and *ecclesia*, "assembly." The Word of God calls a people into existence and also incorporates them in Christ with one another. The true church is neither a structure nor a hierarchy, but a holy people, a communion of saints, a congregation of the faithful.[25] The church is a gathered people who are interrelated in a common life in Christ; it is neither a superpersonal sacramental agent nor an institutional guarantor of saving doctrine.

To construe the church as a congregation, together with the related notion of the priesthood of all believers, was among the most radical ideas of the Protestant Reformers. Luther's approach suggests something more like a theology of sociality—as perhaps does Paul's trope of treasure in earthen vessels. His interpretation of the church as the people of God and as an assembly or congregation, together with his emphasis on incorporation in Christ, bridge concerns that are sometimes divided between theological anthropology and ecclesiology. The full import of these ideas was not seen until the disestablishment of Roman Catholic and Protestant churches and, arguably, is still being worked out.

2. The Word Calls Every Christian: The Priesthood of All Believers

Luther took another related and equally revolutionary step in formulating the notion of the priesthood of all believers. "All Christians are priests, and all priests are Christians," he explained.[26] Each person stands accountable before God, *coram Deo*, and with other Christians in mutual accountability for support, assistance, and intercession. In formulating the notion of the priesthood of all believers, Luther focused on conveying the plenitude of God's benefits that Christians share in Christ: "The good things we have from God should flow from one to the other and be common to all, so that everyone should 'put on' his neighbor and so conduct himself toward him as if he himself were in the other's place."[27]

The notion of the priesthood of all believers entrusted the authority and dignity of the ministry to the community of believers, rather than to the hierarchy.[28] Luther reasoned that all Christians were charged with proclaiming the gospel. Inasmuch as all ministry involves forms of proclamation, Christians also share the functions of baptism, administration of the Lord's Supper, the power of the keys (binding and loosing from sin), "offering spiritual sacrifices," prayer, and judging doctrine. In his 1523 treatise *Concerning the Ministry*, he construed these "functions" as "common rights" and "common property" of Christians.

The priesthood of all believers could also be expressed as the laity of all priests. This was one of the matters at stake when Luther wrote about vocation, vows, and marriage. His concern was to dismantle sacramental hierarchies. He held that ministry is functionally, not ontologically, distinct from other callings to serve God.[29] The public office of ministry is of vital importance, but it is one vocation among other vocations, and all vocations ought to serve the neighbor. Unfortunately, as twentieth-century theologian Paul Tillich noted, "Protestantism has not always lived up to the greatness and radicalism of this idea." Despite Luther's radical laicism, "a quasi-priesthood of the orthodox doctrine arose, as arrogant as the sacramental priesthood of the Roman church."[30]

The notions of the priesthood of all believers and of ministry as one vocation among others imply an underlying judgment that human life ought not to be divided between "spiritual" and "secular." "Just as there is no priest having a special religious function, for everybody is a layman and every layman is potentially a priest, so there is not religion as a special spiritual sphere," Tillich explained. "Everything is secular and every secular thing is potentially religious. . . . The 'holy' is not one value beside others, but a qualification, appearing in all values and in the whole of being."[31] All life is before God; everything has potential religious significance. To use an image from the Gospels, one to which we will return later, the "holy" may appear on any threshold needing to be welcomed, fed, and sheltered.

3. The Word Marks a Holy Christian People with Distinctive Practices and Signs

Luther himself envisioned not a "quasi-priesthood of orthodox doctrine," but rather a holy people who were marked by distinctive practices and signs. Christian assemblies should be evidenced by public signs, the outward signs of invisible faith. Just which signs or practices are the distinguishing ones and how many there are varied somewhat in Luther's writing, although Word, sacrament, baptism, the power of the keys, and prayer and worship were always among them.[32] He interpreted these signs as proclamations of the gospel; they both result from the gospel and attest to its effectiveness.

In *On the Councils and the Church*, Luther contrasted seven "holy possessions" of the true church to relics, which figured prominently in popular piety. For medieval folk who sought them, the bones of saints, wooden fragments of "the true cross," and other actual and fabricated relics seemed to offer both tangible evidence of saintly lives and special mediation of divine power and favor.[33] Luther rejected such relics as fraudulent bones of dead saints, which could not sanctify even if they were genuine. Yet he presented the seven possessions themselves as decisive artifacts and bearers of holiness that are produced by the Word of God. (*Heiligthum*, the word translated as "holy possession," connotes both "relic" and "sanctuary.") In other words, these seven holy possessions are the authentic "bones" or products of living by faith, the authentic dwelling places of faith. They connote both holy things—true relics, as it were—and practices that can reliably distinguish and effect a holy Christian people. Luther stopped short of calling them sacraments, referring to them in this treatise also as "the seven principal parts of Christian sanctification,"[34] but in any case, he described them as the chosen and effective means of divine agency. Through these means— Word, baptism, the Lord's Supper, the power of the keys, the office of ministry, prayer and worship, and suffering—the Holy Spirit sanctifies and blesses the people of God.

Thus Luther's holy possessions are variously functions of ministry or forms of the gospel, indicators or distinguishing marks by which holy Christian people can be recognized, properties or characteristics possessed by a holy Christian people, artifacts or evidence of holiness produced in holy living, practices through which these characteristics and artifacts of holiness are formed, and means through which the Holy Spirit sanctifies the Christian people. Lastly, they are markers that help to identify the holy Christian people, to know "what, where and who the holy Christian church is."[35]

Luther's expositions served both explanatory and apologetic or defensive purposes. Using the signs, he explained what continuity with the true, ancient church ought to look like. More often he employed them and, by implication, the ancient attributes that they elaborated, to distinguish true Christian holiness from false doctrine and practices, and thus the true church from the false one.[36] See, for example, his highly polemical rejoinder *Against Hanswurst* (1541), where he threw down ten distinguishing practices like a gauntlet, daring his challengers to prove that they are the true church while he "proved" them to be the false church.[37]

Through such signs, Luther asserted, "we know for certain what, where, and who the holy Christian church is, that is, the holy Christian people; and we are quite certain that it cannot fail us."[38] God institutes these signs as the means through which the Word is heard and the Holy Spirit sanctifies. No religious elite controls them, and even these signs do not grant exhaustive knowledge of the true church: "The church is a high, deep, hidden thing which one may neither perceive nor see, but grasp only through faith, through baptism, sacrament, and Word. Human doctrine, ceremonies, tonsures, long robes, miters, and all the pomp of popery only lead far away from it into hell—still less are they signs of the church. Naked children, men, women, farmers, citizens, who possess no tonsures, miters, or priestly vestments also belong to the church."[39] Although the Christian people, humble and privileged alike, will never know the full extent of divine grace and glory, they can be sure that it is hidden in the heights and depths of God, not in the recesses of church hierarchies and ceremonies.

4. The Word Unites Christians in Faith; the Church Is a Spiritual Unity

As the communion of saints, the true church is not only an assembly of the faithful; it is also an assembly in faith, a spiritual unity. Faith is an inward reality, a matter of the soul or the heart. "The essence, life, and nature of Christendom is not a physical assembly, but an assembly of hearts in one faith," Luther argued.[40] No external thing creates Christians or the church. Faith is a gift imputed and imparted by God through which the sinner is justified and the soul united to Christ and other Christians. In their union with Christ, Christians are united with each other, not externally by participation in an institution or its rites, but from the inside out, as it were.

Luther's spiritual unity is first and foremost a unity in faith and in Christ. It is also a unity of love, joy, and hope among Christian souls.[41] We might call it an intersubjectivity in Christ. Luther called it "an abundance of all good things in Christ," a "flow" of God's gifts that connects Christ, the Christian, and one's neighbors. "From faith thus flow forth love and joy in the Lord, and from love a joyful willing and free mind that serves one's neighbor willingly and takes no account of gratitude or ingratitude, or praise or blame, of gain or loss."[42] This flowing, uniting abundance is the sustaining center—"the essence, life, and nature"—of the true church. "Regardless of whether a thousand miles separates them physically, they are still called one assembly in spirit, as long as each one preaches, believes, hopes, loves, and lives like the other. . . . This unity alone is sufficient to create Christendom, and without it, no unity—be it that of city, time, persons, work or whatever else it may be—can create Christendom."[43] The church, then, is this communion, this shared union in Christ. It is given, believed, and shared, not sought, earned, or achieved.

Here we have returned to the theme of the unity of the church so important to Cyprian and Augustine. Does Luther's spiritual unity, an assembly in God's gracious abundance through faith, differ fundamentally from Augustine's vision of unity in the love of God? In many ways, no. Both believed that the sufficiency of grace alone made possible salvation and life before the unfathomably mysterious God. For Augustine, the ultimate unity of the church and society in the love of God was the end of a transformative process of ordering life to God, of healing the soul and history, and of realigning the will and institutions. This ordering, while imperfect, nevertheless partakes of the healing grace of God. To be sure, as we saw in the passage on the church as mother, Augustine's vision of the ultimate order of things was sometimes too readily translated into an affirmation of the institutional, hierarchical church, with faith being reduced to obedient assent to the church's teachings. For Luther, faith, and thus unity, is a gift of God infused into the human heart. It is less an ordering than a participation. The unity of faith is the essence of Christendom, not the end toward which ecclesial and societal processes are ultimately ordered.[44]

Luther employed the Pauline dialectics of an inner and an outer nature (2 Cor. 4:16) and of the spirit and the flesh (Gal. 5:17) to teach that no external thing or work—institutional, sacramental, or moral— can justify. Salvation is personal and comes through grace by faith alone. He developed the dialectic to teach about the Christian life in *The Freedom of a Christian* (1520). In his less famous treatise of the same year, *On the Papacy in Rome*, Luther contrasted "spiritual, inner Christendom" to "bodily, external Christendom." This contrast served both as a critique of the existing church and as an explanation of the mixed nature of all churches. Luther denounced interpretations that limited the church to a visible structure or material entity. Accordingly, he taught that (1) the true church is not an external or structural unity; it is a spiritual communion of one faith; (2) the true church is neither primarily a structure or institution;[45] (3) "external matters of worship," such as vestments, rites, special masses, are not essential to true Christendom; what the Scriptures and the creeds teach is faith alone, which is inward and spiritual; (4) the true church is not built up to the pope as its head; only Christ can be the source of life for the body; and finally, (5) the true church is not limited by the inequalities of material bodies— that is, those who are stronger, healthier, richer, or more powerful are not superior Christians.[46]

This last point was illustrated poignantly in Luther's treatment of the church as a suffering communion, the theme with which we began and to which Luther returned throughout his life. "Under the cross" was one place where he said the true church could be seen. Yet it is precisely there that we are returned to the idea of the invisible church. For, in relation to the cross, Luther makes it clear that the true church, indeed the fullness of life and the glory of God, is hidden with Christ in God and essentially invisible on earth.[47]

PARADOX: THE VISIBLE AND THE HIDDEN CHURCH

Luther's primary strategy for revealing and responding to the torment of uncertainty and the ambiguity of the church was to turn to the Word of God, the revealed and proclaimed message of God's grace in Christ, as the authoritative center of Christian life and practice. He denounced the church of his day for the propagation of false doctrine and the displacement of God's Word. In judging and explicating what conformity to the Word entails, Luther appealed to faith rather than to morals or rituals. Faith alone—not theological speculation, monastic discipline, ritual practice, or ecclesiastical authority—must orient shared life in Christ. Although he found every aspect of the church to be under captivity, he judged false teaching to be the root cause of its moral and religious failings. "To treat doctrine is to strike at the most sensitive point," he explained. "Once we've asserted this, it's easy to say and declare that the life is also bad."[48] To be sure, Luther denounced moral and religious corruption, but his main concern was deception: with how the church offered false certainty or conveyed false doctrine. He was, on the whole, unconcerned with measuring the conformity of the church's moral and religious life to particular biblical precepts. Rather, any distinctive personal character or corporate practices will flow freely from faith in Christ through grace.

Luther distinguished sharply between spiritual power and power that is manifest politically or culturally. The former "rules in the midst of enemies and is powerful in the midst of oppression. This means nothing else than that 'power is made perfect in weakness' [2 Cor. 12:9]." Through faith, Christians participate in "a spiritual dominion in which there is nothing so good and nothing so evil but that it shall work together for good to me, if only I believe."[49] Such power grants Christians considerable freedom to act on behalf of their neighbors through any number of vocations and social institutions. However, although Christians can and must exercise political, social, and economic agency, they ought not assume that they can thereby build the kingdom of God on earth through political and institutional means.

Luther tended to caricature late medieval Christianity as being distorted by material excesses and to polemicize against Judaism as a religion of externals; moreover, he drew a severe line between such externals and the inwardness of Christ's kingdom. He interpreted Jesus' words before Pilate, "My kingdom is not from this world" (John 18:36), to mean that Christendom is distinguished "from all worldly communities as being nonphysical."[50] Christ's kingdom, like faith, is not material and external, but spiritual and internal.[51] Faith, which is the sole basis of Christian righteousness and life, is inward and intersubjective. Neither faith nor Christ's kingdom are visible in society or history; the true church, like them, can at best be glimpsed.

Luther's distinction between the outwardly visible church and the hidden true church served theological purposes similar to Augustine's distinction between the visible and invisible church. Augustine turned to the distinction in order to preserve the sovereignty of God's grace and the unity of the church while yet responding to concerns about the church's perfection. Augustine taught that the transformations that God wrought were more mysterious than could be evidenced by membership in the visible church alone. In words not unlike Augustine's own against the Donatists, Luther observed that "there are many Christians who are in the physical assembly and unity but through their sins they exclude themselves from the inward spiritual unity."[52] For Luther, as for Augustine, the dividing line between the true and the false church cannot be determined simply by membership in the church or by participation in the sacraments, and certainly not by participation in pilgrimages, the cult of saints, or programs of penance. Rather, the church rests on God's grace alone; Christians partake of it by faith alone.

Luther, like Augustine, taught that God's grace confounds human judgment. For Augustine, there was always the possibility that God's irresistible grace might work surprising transformations within the divine drama of creation and redemption. Luther was more concerned about a devil who was wily enough to usurp the glory of the world. And so, he insisted that God's grace did not rely at all on human effort and was even hidden in weakness. According to Luther, the "stumbling block" for human judgment is Christ crucified. The glory of God is hidden or "masked" in the cross; it is known or seen only by grace through faith in the gospel. In his interpretation, Christian life is paradoxical. In a sense, the perspective of faith transforms the ambiguities of existence into the paradoxes of Christian life.[53]

Luther rejected Augustine's metaphysical realism in favor of rendering "invisible" as internal or inward, the soul, in contrast to "visible" as external or material, the body. Moreover, Luther construed the visible church, like individual Christians, to be less a "mixed body" than a paradoxically divided body and soul. In earthly life, Christians are internally divided by lines of faith and sin, and therefore they dwell partly within and partly without the true church. The Christian remains simultaneously a sinner and justified, servant and lord. Similarly, the true church, the communion of saints, is partly visible in the proclamation of the Word and in suffering while yet hidden in God—and distinguished sharply from the visible church in Rome.

Thus Luther reinterpreted the Augustinian distinction between visible and invisible church in adopting it. His concern was to explain how the true church could exist in faith even though the visible church was false. Membership in the visible fellowship in and of itself "does not make a true Christian," Luther explained. "Nevertheless it never really exists without some people who are also true Christians."[54] As we have seen, he articulated the significance of the community of believers who were gathered by the Word. However, unlike Augustine, Luther did not take the visible church for granted as the starting point of transformation. In a 1527 sermon, he used the metaphor of church as bride to underscore how hidden the true church is: "God does not want the world to know when he sleeps with his bride."[55] Augustine assumed that the glorious destiny of the invisible church would be reached in and through the visible church, even though the whole visible church might not participate in it. Luther was suspicious of any claim that God's glory was becoming manifest in the visible church. His reinterpretation led him to a conclusion that Augustine would not have contemplated: that an invisible spiritual unity in faith can exist apart from the visible church.

MULTIPLE STRATEGIES

Contemporary theologian Peter Hodgson has argued that Luther's reformulation of Augustine's distinction moved "in the direction of understanding the invisible church as a *critical theological principle* that permitted quite radical criticism of the church's institutions, dogmas, and practices."[56] There can be no doubt that Martin Luther's theological critique transformed the reality and theology of Christianity in his day and henceforth. His searing assessment found virtually every aspect of organized Christianity to be tainted with falsehood. However, he centered his critique in a reinterpretation of the Word of God, not primarily in a reinterpretation of the invisible church, as Hodgson suggests. Luther turned his attention, and that of subsequent theologians, from the vessel of the church to its treasure, which he defined theologically as the Word of God. He held fast to the treasure of the Word and moved from it in dialectics of denunciation and annunciation.

Luther's theological critique was radical but not simple. He deployed multiple strategies for resituating and reinterpreting creaturely existence before God. Luther routed out pretensions to truth, especially the false claims of authority, by holding fast to the Word of God through faith alone. A fresh interpretation of the gospel as the power of God was his primary weapon in the battle against a church he judged to have been captured by the devil himself. His reformulation of Augustine's distinction between the visible and invisible church was closely related to his use of the contrast between "bodily, external Christendom" and "spiritual, inner Christendom." These, in turn, were often governed by his paradoxical construal of life before God.

The limits of Luther's approach reflect both the intensity of his focus on false authority and dogma and the extent to which he believed deception to permeate creaturely life. When he denounced false pretensions of the papal church, he also stripped human certainty obtained through knowing, feeling, or doing. Only a trusting surrender, a "joyful bet" on God, yields certainty. Such surrender is epitomized by poor and believing Christians who dwell "under the cross": there God's grace and glory are known in their inversion. This paradoxical construal of the relation of divine power to human life offered assurance amid the trauma and travail of historical life. In such a situation, the Word of God provides a critical principle that exposes false authority and also provides assurance that Christians dwell ultimately under spiritual rather than earthly dominion. However, the transformation of souls, churches, and societies was not necessarily evident in history.

That said, Luther offered more than trenchant critique and paradox. As we have seen, he depicted the creative as well as the critical power of the Word of God. The Word calls out and equips a holy Christian people, marks them with distinctive signs, and unites them in faith. That entailed the redefinition of church as a congregation, a functional redefinition of the Christian life in which vocation and practices replace ontological and sacramental distinctions, the use of distinguishing signs or practices to identify the true church, and a retrieval of the theme of the faithful as a suffering communion from the Psalms and Pauline Epistles. These strategies, at least as much as the contrast between visible and hidden church, shaped Luther's depiction of Christian life as vulnerable to suffering and to God's grace and power. Indeed, in his own ministry the emphasis fell on the reconstruction of Christian life through preaching, teaching, establishing congregations and schools, and otherwise attending to practical needs and affairs. As Heiko Oberman observed, Luther struggled "to bring the church of faith back into history, into the reality of his—even without him—unsettled time, back into the reality of his day."[57]

In the face of the economic and intellectual upheavals of his day, the terror of the plague, and personal anxiety, Martin Luther wrestled with God for certainty and assurance. In that wrestling, he found himself and the people of God vulnerable not only to trials and suffering, but also to God. In construing these traumas as external assaults—often by demonic forces, over against which God was understood as a contravening force who would ultimately prevail—Luther remained a medieval thinker. In the next chapter we turn to John Calvin, who famously and infamously depicted the corruption of the will, imagination, and rationality, and also of history and societies. At the same time, in Calvin's theology the church and Christian life enter more fully into history and society, that is, they are interpreted as necessarily historical, social, cultural, and political realities as well as theological ones. With these shifts, which also mark the emergence of modernity, a more robust account of vulnerability to devastation and to transformation begins to emerge. It is not necessarily a more optimistic account of life before God; rather, vulnerability to idolatrous distortion in history and society and possibilities of transformation in social-historical institutions rise into view together.

CHAPTER 3

Calvin on Corruption and Transformation

> God, therefore, in his wonderful providence accommodating himself to
> our capacity, has prescribed a way for us, though still far off, to draw
> near to him.
>
> –*John Calvin*[1]

Most treatments of John Calvin's thought, whether astute or hack-
neyed, convey his dire assessment of the state of human affairs:
"For as a veritable world of miseries is to be found in mankind, and
we are thereby despoiled of divine raiment, our shameful nakedness
exposes a teeming horde of infamies," he observed in the very first section of the *Institutes of the Christian Religion*. Among these miseries and
infamies are "ignorance, vanity, poverty, infirmity, and—what is more—
depravity and corruption" (1.1.1). Yet Calvin was no mere pessimist. He
used these observations to help attune his readers to the "consciousness
of unhappiness" or, as he put it a few pages later, the "anxiety of conscience" (1.3.2), which points beyond human miseries to the contrasting
goodness of God. Calvin's creatures are without a doubt susceptible to
(in fact, plagued with) dullness and corruption, but they are not imper-
vious to a sense of the glory of God. Moreover, Calvin's attention to real
suffering—poverty, despair, hardship, persecution—made him all the
more insistent that transformation toward the glory of God can be and
is being wrought in persons, church, society, and history.

This chapter explores strategies employed in Calvin's *Institutes of
the Christian Religion* to diagnose the corruption of human life and to
depict possibilities of transformation, especially in relation to the purpose and work of the church.[2] While I endeavor to place Calvin's ideas
in their historical, political, and rhetorical context, my primary concern
in this chapter is to identify resources for contemporary theological
work rather than to advance a historical interpretation of Calvin's ideas

and their effects. Some of Calvin's strategies, together with approaches we have reviewed in the first two chapters, can provide resources for an account of life before God as vulnerable to devastation and transformation and, correlatively, of vulnerability as the situation wherein the grace and glory of God may be met.

"HOW GOD'S GLORY MAY BE KEPT SAFE ON EARTH"

Calvin began writing the *Institutes of the Christian Religion* while he was in hiding in 1534. A growing fury against French evangelicals, fomented by the church and monarchy, had forced him to flee France and seek exile. The intensifying persecution hastened his determination to complete the work in order to offer it on behalf of the threatened "poor little church." He prefaced the first edition with an appeal to King Francis I of France to mitigate the "violent heat" of the situation. Calvin pled that the deceitful claims of French clerics and the resulting persecution of faithful church folk were matters of ultimate significance: the very existence of the true church was threatened. Calvin's "Prefatory Address to King Francis I of France" remained in subsequent editions, long after King Francis had died, perhaps because persecution did not wane and perhaps because the French monarchy itself became an agent of persecution. By addressing the king, Calvin tacitly extended the critique of idolatry from ecclesial symbols, practices, and hierarchy to include the political powers that upheld them.[3]

In his plea, Calvin made a crucial theological move. He placed the question of the true church within the broader question of the relationship of God and the world. What was at stake, he contended, was nothing less than "how God's glory may be kept safe on earth, how God's truth may retain its place of honor, how Christ's kingdom may be kept in good repair among us" (11). Calvin saw a vast gap between the glory of God and the lowly state of human life.[4] Yet, he insisted, human lives are lived before God in a world that is a theater of God's glory. The church ought therefore to glorify God and help persons to live rightly before God.

Calvin charged his opponents with giving no thought to the glory of God, but only "to keep either their rule intact or their belly full" (14). Their religious zeal is insincere, and they are consumed with self-interest. Their worst offense is their deceitful doctrine. They misrepresent and misunderstand the church and, in so doing, imperil souls and the church itself. They falsely teach that the church is bound up with

a visible institution and its rites and falsely equate the church with the
Roman order, thus supplanting God's ineffable glory with ecclesiastical
trappings.

They assumed that the visible Roman church was the true church;
Calvin explained otherwise: "We, on the contrary, affirm that the church
can exist without any visible appearance, and that its appearance is
not contained within that outward magnificence which they foolishly
admire." While rejecting his opponents' attachment to institutional
glory as idolatrous, he affirmed a different outwardness as the baseline
of the true church: the proper worship of God as indicated by signs of
"the pure preaching of God's Word and the lawful administration of the
sacraments" (24–25).

Calvin judged the persecuting church to be as corrupt as the one
Luther denounced. Luther, fully a medieval thinker at this point,
described the captivity of the church in terms of a cosmic battle between
God and the devil. Calvin, too, attributed corruption to Satan. By
contrast, Calvin usually portrayed the present situation as a deceitful
betrayal of the divinely instituted order of ministry and, ultimately,
of the glory, truth, and rule of God on earth. Like other humanists at
the beginning of the modern age, Calvin viewed the corruption of the
church, thoroughgoing as it was, as historical.

Calvin interpreted the French situation within a history of idolatry.
He viewed the mixture of corruption and holiness within the community of believers as ancient. Among "the very swaddling clothes of the
church," that is, the patriarchs, there was wickedness (4.1.24). At times,
the situation was so bleak that "no form of the true church remained."
The prophet Elijah complained of a fullscale defection to Baal. In the
fourth century, Hilary of Poitiers protested, "It is wrong that a love of
walls has seized you; wrong that you venerate the church of God in
roofs and buildings; wrong that beneath these you introduce the name
of peace. Is there any doubt that the Antichrist will have his seat in
them?"[5] Calvin found that the "deadly hydra" of idolatry still "lurked"
in his own day.

By explicating a history of corruption, Calvin at once suggested the
inevitable ambiguity of the church and also that true religion ought to
right these abuses in history. He placed his ultimate confidence in God
alone. God's children were always protected, he explained, "for he knew
how to preserve them in the confusion of Babylon, and in the flame
of the fiery furnace." Divine mercy abounded to the patriarchs. Elijah
eventually learned that seven thousand remained who resisted idolatry

(25). And, Calvin implied, God's providence endures. In the meanwhile, he asked King Francis to exercise "judicial gravity" and employ civil authority to keep God's glory safe on earth: "Let not the gospel of God be blasphemed in the meantime because of the wickedness of infamous men" (30).

In turning from Calvin's 1535 "Prefatory Address" to the rest of the 1559 *Institutes*, I focus on a few central features relevant to an account of vulnerability and transformation. These features have already been signaled in his preface: one, idolatry as a diagnosis of human ill; two, divine accommodation as key for interpreting the relationship of the world and God, together with a related emphasis on divine pedagogy; three, the visible face of the church; and four, the marks of right hearing of the gospel and right administration of the sacraments as touchstones and guarantees of the church. I then engage Calvin's views on suffering and the Christian life before offering some conclusions from the first three chapters.

IDOLATRY AND CORRUPTION

For Calvin, idolatry was not merely the problem of the French church and monarch; it was the root problem of human life.[6] When Calvin examined the human situation, from individual consciousness to religious and political life, he made the diagnosis, informed especially by the Hebrew prophets and Deuteronomic law, of idolatry: "Man's nature, so to speak, is a perpetual factory of idols," he explained (1.11.8). Insofar as idolatry is a "common vice" pursued through the ages, the French clerics were no different from everyone else. Calvin had special contempt for them because they, purporting to be guardians of God's truth and salvation, seemed to deceive others on purpose, and because their idolatry seemed particularly perverse: not only did they purvey false doctrine; they also conveyed it with superfluous rituals and a multiplicity of images and relics.

In Book 1 of the *Institutes*, Calvin provided a sort of ethnography of human life and religion. "Each man's mind is like a labyrinth," he observed, "so it is no wonder that individual nations were drawn aside into various falsehoods; and not only this—but individual men, almost, had their own gods" (1.5.12). Calvin mapped the pervasive tendency to worship and to create ways of worshiping. In a backhanded compliment to humankind, he noted that, "man's mind, full as it is of pride and boldness, dares to imagine a god according to its own capacity."

Furthermore, humans fashion images of the gods they imagine in order to provide assurance of divine presence. "Daily experience teaches that flesh is always uneasy until it has obtained some figment in which it may fondly find solace as in an image of God" (1.11.8). Even when the creators of these images intend to distinguish between God and the image they have fashioned for God, the images inevitably limit their understanding of God and effectively limit God. Thus, Calvin indicated an array of inclinations behind the manufacture of idols: sometimes cleverness or pride, sometimes fear, sometimes ignorance, sometimes naïveté, sometimes wickedness, and sometimes sheer perverseness.

Idolatry is rampant, multiform, and tenacious because it diverts energy, so to speak, from the deepest inclination and highest purpose of human life: to know and honor God. Human creatures are labyrinthine, full of multiple dimensions and conflicting desires that do not easily coalesce, even into this deepest inclination and highest purpose. Here Calvin's diagnosis probed further, turning from an ethnography of idolatry and piety to a theological etiology of corruption and conversion. His etiology offers at least the explanatory power of Freud's or Marx's, and his "idolatry critique" is arguably as suspicious.[7]

Why are humans so prolific and tenacious in their idolatry? In short, because they want to worship; it is the characteristic that distinguishes human creatures from all others. Humans bear the indelible inscription of God, Calvin explained. They yearn to know and honor what exceeds and sustains their lives—God, the source of goodness and righteousness—but they are incapable of reaching it on their own. Humanity has "an awareness of divinity" or a "seed of religion" and, closely related, a sense of the distinction between good and evil. These, in turn, incline persons to seek to know and honor the author of all life and goodness. Yet however deeply this sense is embedded, what human creatures sense remains vague and fleeting at best. Often they lose track of the fact of having this sense itself. But whether they are aware of it or not, they fasten their seeking and honor upon something. Because of their incapacities, humans inevitably fall back on more tangible and immediate assurances, on small gods of vindication, comfort, stability, control, privilege, revenge. Whatever they seek and honor unavoidably shapes their lives.

Idolatry, then, is far more seductive and dangerous than false opinion or unjust action. Calvin depicts the human condition as more complexly threatened, damaged, and damaging than invasion or imbalance etiologies suggest. Idolatry is more like a cancer or a HIV/AIDS epidemic than a wound or infection, to use contemporary medical metaphors, and it is exacerbated by both internal and external factors. Humans are not only susceptible to the damaging effects of alien powers and of internal disorder; their own powers and capacities also become co-opted. External powers and internal propensities engage and aggravate each other and, in turn, wreak further havoc on the self and others, thus perpetuating cycles of distortion and corruption.

The struggle against idolatry is not merely a matter of obedience to Scripture, as it was for some of Calvin's fellow reformers, but of striving to know *and worship* God rightly, and correlatively, to know ourselves and live rightly before God. True piety is the opposite of idolatry. Historian Carlos Eire underscores the "enormous significance" of Calvin's dialectic of idolatry and true piety or worship, and of its placement at the center of his account of religion. "Religion is not merely a set of doctrines, but rather a way of worshiping and a way of living," Eire explains.[8] To acknowledge and confess God truly is to align one's entire life to God and to resist competing claims for honor and obedience.[9] On their own, Calvin explained, human creatures can reach neither God's glory nor their own. However, God reaches to them. The corrupted condition of human life can only be countered with help of the rescuing and redeeming power of God. As we shall see in the next section, divine accommodation provides for knowledge and worship of God, and thus enables the faithful to struggle against false gods and false existence.

DIVINE ACCOMMODATION

Calvin taught that while the full glory of God is not yet revealed, and indeed is hidden under earthly corruption and idolatry, God accommodates inability, coaxing and teaching humankind. Divine accommodation provides the benefits of salvation through Christ, the Scriptures, and the "external means of grace." The latter includes the church, the sacraments, and the civil order.

The notion of accommodation, found in classical rhetoric, was regularly employed by the church fathers to interpret the relation of the divine and the human.[10] Calvin, like Irenaeus, Origen, John Chrysostom, and others before him, explained that God communicates to humanity in "baby talk" through the Scriptures and the incarnation:

> For who even of slight intelligence does not understand that, as nurses commonly do with infants, God is wont in a measure to

"lisp" in speaking to us? . . . [To] accommodate the knowledge
of him to our slight capacity, . . . he must descend far beneath his
loftiness. (1.13.1)

Christian theologians regularly turned to the notion of accommodation to interpret differences between Judaism and Christianity. When
they did, they employed the notion to diverse, even opposing, ends.
Sometimes accommodation was used, problematically so, to sever ties
with Judaism by explaining that Christianity was an accommodation that
superseded Jewish law and practice; at other times accommodation was
employed to accent the continuity of divine engagement with humanity from Jewish law through Christ's apostles. Calvin, too, appealed to
accommodation to account for differing forms of God's relation with
humanity. Following Paul's analogy in Galatians 4:1, Calvin contrasted
the "rudimentary teaching" that God provided the Jews with the "firmer,
. . . more manly discipline" provided in Christian teaching (2.11.13).[11]
Calvin explained that God's Word, while conveyed most fully in Christ
and in the apostles' testimony to Christ, remained constant even though
God used diverse forms of teaching in diverse times: the law, the prophets, Christ, and the apostles.

Perhaps Calvin viewed the challenge of addressing the ambiguity of
the church as similar to these long-recognized interpretive challenges,
that is, as a matter of demonstrating the constancy of God despite obvious changes and corruptions among human institutions. In any case,
he went beyond his predecessors' use of accommodation. In effect,
his *Institutes* construed the entire order of creation and redemption—
especially the Scriptures and the incarnation, but also the visible church,
the sacraments, and the civil order—as divine accommodations to
humanity.[12] Calvin's God can be glimpsed across the order of creation
and redemption, as sixteenth-century children might have glimpsed
their own parents encompassing their worlds: talking to them in simple
language, encouraging, instructing, correcting, and exhorting.

Calvin rendered the figure of treasure in vessels in relation to this
notion of divine accommodation. He explained, "To make us aware,
then, that an inestimable treasure is given us in earthen vessels [2 Cor.
4:7], God himself appears in our midst, and, as Author of this order,
would have men recognize him as present in his institution" (4.1.5).
While the full glory of the church remains hidden in God, the visible
church is God's provision for human weakness. Calvin articulated the
premise of his teaching:

> In order that the preaching of the gospel might flourish, he
> [God] deposited this treasure in the church. He instituted "pas-
> tors and teachers" [Eph. 4:11] through whose lips he might
> teach his own; he furnished them with authority; finally he
> omitted nothing that might make for holy agreement of faith
> and for right order. First of all, he instituted sacraments, which
> we who have experienced them feel to be highly useful aids
> to foster and strengthen faith. Shut up as we are in the prison
> house of our flesh, we have not yet attained angelic rank. God,
> therefore, in his wonderful providence accommodating himself
> to our capacity, has prescribed a way for us, though still far off,
> to draw near to him. (4.1.1)

Because of ignorance and sloth, persons need "outward helps" to partake of salvation. Through the church, God's power is accommodated to human (in)capacities.

Contrast Calvin's approach with Luther's view: according to Luther, the church is to be conformed to its treasure, the gospel of the glory and grace of God; for Calvin, God adapts to human capacity through the means of the church. Whereas Luther retained a medieval—high and almost magical—view of the intrinsic holiness and power of Scripture, Calvin viewed the gospel as already "earthen." It is already an accommo-dation to the (in)capacities of creatures. The gospel bears God's grace in a way that is effective for humanity. In short, the idea of accommodation allowed Calvin to interpret the transforming work of God in history rather than in paradoxical relation to it.[13] In considering life before God, this contrast of approaches between paradox and accommodation is *the* crucial contrast between Calvin's and Luther's theologies.

ADVANCING TOWARD HOLINESS

It was not mere rhetorical flourish when Calvin asked King Francis "how God's glory may be kept safe on earth, how God's truth may retain its place of honor, how Christ's kingdom may be kept in good repair among us" (11). King Francis never replied. Calvin fashioned his own response through his writing and ministry. He assumed that some mea-sure of God's truth and justice could be manifest in churches and in civil order. Calvin sought a way of advancing God's glory that neither falsely exalted the church for its own glory nor presumed perfection. He sought a middle way that emphasized reliance on God alone and yet fostered the transformation of earthly life—"till God is purely worshiped by all, and all the world is reformed."[14]

Concern with the good repair of Christ's kingdom thus frames the whole *Institutes* and, by extension, the whole of earthly existence. After the 1536 edition, Calvin kept the address to King Francis as the preface and placed his treatment of civil government as the final chapter. Between these bookends, Calvin focused on the corruption of human life and the transformation that God was working in persons and in history through the law and the gospel of Christ and by means of the church.

According to Calvin, the church is only at the beginning of a process of sanctification and is far from perfection. Under most circumstances, it is the "faithful custodian" of the truth. Despite the dubious results of some church councils, Calvin wrote, "I am quite convinced that truth does not die in the church, even though it may be oppressed by one council, but is wonderfully preserved by the Lord that it may rise up and triumph again in its own time" (4.9.13). In fact, the imperfect holiness of the church provides the occasion for forgiveness of sins within the church. Against any demand for perfection as a prerequisite for participation in the church, the church is to be built up precisely because God's mercy is promised in the communion of saints. As the Lord's Prayer teaches, believers must confess their sins continually and be pardoned continually (4.1.23). The church was advancing toward holiness, but only through a process that proceeded by the grace of God (4.1.17).

Calvin's middle way of transformation is a pedagogical way. To dwell before God is a lifelong process that takes place through the church's help, nurture, and instruction. Teaching and learning were central to his construal of Christian life and his practice of ministry. He understood believers to be under the tutelage of a divine pedagogy. His favored images of the church, mother and school, accented processes of nurture and maturation.

Following Cyprian, Calvin described the intimate correlation of God as Father and the church as Mother to believers. He depicted the church as a mother "into whose bosom God is pleased to gather his sons, not only that they might be nourished by her help and ministry as long as they are infants and children, but also that they may be guarded by her motherly care until they mature and at last reach the goal of faith" (4.1.1). As in Cyprian, the image of church as mother illustrates the necessary role of the visible church in conveying God's benefits of salvation and preservation. The visible church is the church we can know as "mother," Calvin explained. "For there is no other way to enter into life unless the mother conceive us in her womb, give us birth, nourish us at her breast, and lastly, unless she keeps us under her care and guidance. . . . Away from her bosom, one cannot hope for any forgiveness of sins or any salvation" (4.1.4). Calvin's use of the metaphor of church as a nursing and guiding mother assured believers that they were being nourished and prepared for a strong and venturesome faith.

Calvin also wrote about the church as a school for the increase of faith. Although God could perfect the elect instantly, the divine preference is for believers to mature under the church's guidance and tutelage: "[God] prefers to address us in a human fashion through interpreters in order to draw us to himself, rather than to thunder at us and drive us away" (4.1.5). "The ordinary manner of teaching" is the means that God chooses to exercise power. God is a schoolmaster, Calvin explained, who sometimes has to repeat lessons several times. God also provides ministers and public worship as means for divine pedagogy. "Believers have no greater help than public worship, for by it God raises his own folk upward step by step" (4.1.5).

Like the image of church as mother, the image of God as teacher had a long lineage. According to historian William Bouwsma, "That Protestant preaching was truly *teaching* seemed to [Calvin] a major difference between Protestant and papal churches." The image would have also resonated deeply with Calvin's fellow humanists. Bouwsma observes that "Calvin's church was more like a humanist academy than a school of theology, and he imagined God now, looking over the shoulders of his pupils. Scripture, in this context, was a textbook through which God propounded his teachings to his children."[15] I will return to pedagogies, although not necessarily to God as schoolmaster, and to their role in the transformation of vulnerable creatures in chapter 6. First I will resume discussions about the visible and invisible church, the marks of Christian life and community, and suffering and the Christian life.

THE FACE OF THE CHURCH BECOMES VISIBLE

Like Luther, Calvin adopted and modified Augustine's distinction between visible and invisible church, using it to teach that divine election, not the institutional church, provides the assurance of salvation. The invisible church is the church "which is actually in God's presence." It includes "all the elect from the beginning of the world." The church is a necessary means of salvation, but the church does not effect salvation, Calvin stressed. God does. The foundation of the church, and finally the only relevant distinction for who is in the church and who is not, is "God's secret election and inner call." This foundation is so strong that "even if the whole fabric of the world were overthrown, the church would neither totter nor fall" (4.1.3).

Calvin deployed the dialectic of visible and invisible church to explain the necessary role of the visible church in the glorious, yet mysterious, work of God. There is no other way to enter into life than through the visible church; it is a necessary "external means of grace" (4.1.10). "So powerful is participation in the church that it keeps us in the society of God," Calvin explained (4.1.3), offering a variation on Cyprian's assertion that "good men cannot leave the church." Note that Calvin's variation emphasized the power of divine election at work through the church, whereas Cyprian accented the integrity of the institution. Calvin rejected the visibility of the institution, the papacy, or rites and ceremonies, as guarantors of salvation and the determination of the true church. At the same time, against the Anabaptists, he rejected the moral and spiritual perfection of believers as the key to the true church. Instead, he looked to visible marks of the church: the ministry of the Word and the celebration of the sacraments. Thus Calvin redefined the true church as an "external means" by which God accommodates to human incapacity, specifically as the means instituted by Christ in the Word and the sacraments.

Calvin concluded that the Nicene phrase, the communion of saints, "very well expresses what the church is." His view is close to Luther's on this point: the church is a community "united in brotherly love" who share mutually in "whatever benefits God confers upon them." Chief among the benefits is the assurance of salvation. This assurance rests on the knowledge and inner conviction of God's election, union with Christ, and the promises of Scripture. It also rests on the conviction that truth abides in the church. Relative to Luther, Calvin offered a greater emphasis on the sociability and organization of life before God. He believed that, except under dire circumstances, the church *was* a reliable vessel of the grace and glory of God.[16] "[God] ever sanctifies certain vessels unto honor [cf. Rom. 9:23ff.] that there may be no age that does not experience his mercy" (4.1.17).

Calvin offered little speculation about the nature of the invisible church. Rather, he employed the distinction between visible and invisible church to aid believers in keeping communion with the church they could see. Calvin explained that "the Lord by certain marks and tokens has pointed out to us what we should know about the church." What, then, should we know? The essence of the invisible church? The core message of the gospel? Neither of these is the "touchstone" to which Calvin appealed (4.1.11). Rather, God has "set off by plainer marks the knowledge of his very body to us, knowing how necessary it is to our salvation" (4.1.8). When the marks of the ministry of the Word and the celebration of the sacraments are seen, "the face of the church comes forth and becomes visible to our eyes" (4.1.9).

The church's foundation in divine election may be primarily invisible, but its ministry and purpose are primarily visible. Initiation into its membership is by baptism; its unity in doctrine and love is attested by the Lord's Supper; and its ministry is preserved in the preaching of the Word. The visible church consists of "the whole multitude of men spread over the earth who profess to worship one God and Christ." It is, in Augustine's phrase, "a mixed body": "In the church are mingled many hypocrites who have nothing of Christ but name and outward appearance." Therefore, Calvin instructed Christians to believe the true church is visible to God alone, while yet keeping communion with the visible church (4.1.7).

Calvin's theological convictions about divine accommodation inclined him to this emphasis on the church's ministry, as did his anthropological convictions about human proclivities to worship (and to idolatry) and his practical concerns for Christians in his day, particularly for French Protestants who were deprived of the benefits of proper corporate worship because of persecution.[17] Indeed, he suggested that the proper subject matter of theology is the ministry of the *visible* church rather than the invisible church.[18]

Calvin taught that the true church is founded in God's inscrutable will and in Christ's historical institution of the Word and the sacraments. Its divinely instituted ministry exists in history and is susceptible both to corruption and to correction. Thus Calvin construed the relationship of the invisible and visible church dialectically and historically whereas Luther construed their relation paradoxically. This crucial difference—a dialectical versus a paradoxical relationship—relates to different construals of the relationship of God and history and results in different assessments about the possible transformation of religious and political organizations and thus of transformation in history.

Yet if their interpretations of the relation between invisible and visible church differed, Luther and Calvin shared a fundamental similarity in the use of the distinction itself. Neither employed the contrast as the primary strategy for critiquing or reconstructing the church. Both turned to the Word—or the Word and Sacrament—as primary. As we have seen, Luther held fast to the Word, moving from it in dialectics of denunciation and annunciation. Calvin held right knowledge and worship of God to be central to all life. He viewed the Word and the sacraments as the forms of teaching and worship that the church received from Christ. And he moved dialectically from the marks of the Word and the sacraments, using them to assess shared Christian life. How, then, did Calvin employ the marks?

OUTWARD MARKS

Calvin knew the visible church to be an ambiguous institution where immorality, impiety, and falsehood could be found. His chief strategy for distinguishing between the true and the false church was to look for two outward marks: "Wherever we see the Word of God purely preached and heard, and the sacraments administered according to Christ's institution, there, it is not to be doubted, a church of God exists" (4.1.9). When these marks are present, "there . . . no deceitful or ambiguous form of the church is seen" (4.1.10). The outward marks of ministry, not the institution itself, assure believers of right knowledge and worship of God.

Calvin presented the marks as a baseline, a "touchstone," of the church (4.1.11). Simply put, the church can be judged by its ministry. The truth of the church can be judged by whether it possesses the ministry of the Word and celebrates the sacraments, as instituted by Christ and passed on by the apostles. These two means or marks, the Word purely preached and reverently heard and the sacraments rightly administered, constitute the foundational observances of the church's ministry. Their authority resides in Christ, who instituted them.[19] God's power working through them guarantees their effectiveness. "These can never exist without bringing forth fruit and prospering by God's blessing" (4.1.10).

Calvin denounced the medieval papacy for having virtually abandoned the ministry instituted by Christ, as evidenced by the absence of these marks. In one particularly vivid passage, Calvin explained that "the papists" have "extinguished" and "choked" the Word, befouled the Lord's Supper, "deformed" worship, and "buried" and "driven out" true doctrine. In short, they have turned what should be a school of true piety into "schools of idolatry and ungodliness" (4.2.2). For many pages following, Calvin catalogued the nature and extent of the abuses. With biting sarcasm, Calvin described a church of "formless chaos, full of desolation," that was utterly ignorant of the ministry given to it by the apostles and church fathers (4.5.13). Calvin judged the preponderance of doctrine and life—institutional, spiritual, and moral—of the late medieval church to be false. He granted that some sound elements remain in the Roman communion, but quickly added that God's providence, not papal succession, had allowed these vestiges of truth to endure.

At the same time that Calvin rejected papal authority as false, he cautioned against facile rejections of the church's ministry. Where the Word is rightly preached and the sacraments rightly administered, there is "no excuse" for the person "who voluntarily deserts the outward communion of the church." Calvin regarded the two marks not only as touchstones and guarantees, but also as warning signs against rejecting any church where they are found, "even if it otherwise swarms with many faults" (4.1.12).

Calvin undercut perfectionism with his view of history as inherently ambiguous and human knowledge as inherently limited. Consequently, he urged a measure of tolerance: "Since all men are somewhat beclouded with ignorance, either we must leave no church remaining, or we must condone delusion in those matters which can go unknown without harm to the sum of religion and without loss of salvation" (4.1.12).[20] Calvin rejected Donatist-like protests about the purity of the minister or of the members, viewing the authority of ministry to reside in the office of Word and Sacrament rather than in the person called to the office (4.8.2).

Calvin, like Luther, viewed questions of certainty and authority as central issues in the debate about the nature of the true church. Both anchored the authority of the church's teaching and ministry in the authority of the gospel. Both understood the Word, that is, the message of the gospel available through Scripture when rightly proclaimed and taught, to provide clear and reliable knowledge of God. Indeed, Calvin rejected allegorical interpretation and distrusted theological paradoxes because, according to Bouwsma, they make "the teaching of scripture ambiguous and deprive it of all certainty and firmness."[21]

Moreover, both Luther and Calvin understood the Word to be self-authenticating: God's own know God's voice just as sheep know the voice of their shepherd. Calvin contrasted the "unbridled license" of the papacy with the legitimate authority of the church, which is subject to the Word of the Lord and "enclosed within it" (4.8.4). He cautioned that it was therefore "better to keep within the limits" of the Word (4.8.12). The conjunction of the Word and Spirit in the church insures that truth and holiness are preserved in the imperfect vessel of the church.

As we have noted, Luther judged the mixture of true and false doctrine to be the root cause of moral and religious ambiguity. Calvin, by contrast not only with Luther but also with some later Calvinists, did not abide such a separation of "doctrine" and "life." The gospel, he explained, "is a doctrine not of the tongue but of life." For Calvin, true piety contrasted with idolatry and consisted in the conjunction of right knowledge and right worship. The gospel "must enter our heart and pass into our daily living, and so transform us into itself that it may not be unfruitful for us" (3.6.4).[22] In other words, Calvin interpreted the ambiguity of the church within the ambiguity of life and insisted that the truth and falsehood of teaching cannot be addressed apart from all life, work, and worship before God.

For Luther and Calvin alike, the marks both result from and attest to the effectiveness of the gospel. Their redefined marks allowed them to reject a hierarchical, institutional construal of Christianity in favor of an interpretation centered in living and teaching the faith. Luther's marks signaled a holy Christian people, that is, they provided identifying signs of the people who have been assembled and enlivened by the Word and Spirit of God. Luther's marks were the outward signs of inward faith among the people of God, manifestations or artifacts of their shared inward life in Christ. He employed the marks descriptively, pedagogically, and apologetically, in other words, to describe, teach, and defend "what, where, and who the holy Christian church is, that is, the holy Christian people."[23] Although Luther sometimes wrote of seven and more marks, he and Calvin agreed that the two marks of Word and Sacrament were the central ones.

Calvin's *Institutes* backed away from Luther's radical redefinition of the church as a holy people, a congregation, while going beyond Luther in providing a concrete plan for re-forming the church, especially its ministry. Calvin's marks indicated and certified authoritative ministry, the order of preaching and teaching that he understood to have been instituted by Christ. He interpreted the marks as outward signs and guarantees of an effective ministry where Christian faith is nourished and taught. Thus he also employed the marks legislatively.

In his writings and in the city of Geneva, Calvin strove to order the ministry and life of the church rightly. He described the proper offices and right order of ministry in his writings and brought them into being under his leadership. Calvin had defined the church by reference to its proper offices and order of ministry; his Geneva attempted to enact this definition through its laws and in its institutions. The resulting Genevan order and its judgments were sometimes harsh, if arguably no more so than other ecclesiastical and civil authorities in a time of transition from medieval culture and feudal authority to early modernity. In any case, from Geneva's consistory and magistracy arose an ecclesiastical bureaucracy (or at least the beginnings of one) entwined with the civil order.[24]

In our day, any Calvinist drift to a bureaucratic and doctrinaire Christianity must be disentangled from Calvin's affirmation that the mercies of God and possibilities of transformation abide in vulnerable institutions and despite a history of ambiguous relations and actions. It is both possible and necessary to eschew this drift while taking up the affirmation in new ways.

In fact, the effects of Calvin's teaching about an authoritative order of ministry were hardly monolithic. For example, his insistence on the benefits of true worship in communion with the visible church led him to encourage French believers to defy local laws and form secret, autonomous gatherings that would come to be known as "churches under the cross." According to historian Philip Benedict, Calvin and Heinrich Bullinger, like other Reformed leaders, "agreed to disagree on fundamental issues of ecclesiology, for they both believed that the visible church allowed for diversity of institutional forms and worship according to time and place."[25] Because of this adaptability, they effectively encouraged the proliferation of numerous and diverse congregations. Thus the Reformed emphasis on the visible church defined by its order of ministry may actually have been more productive of diverse Christian congregations than Luther's arguably more radical definition of the church as congregation.

At its best, the gap that Calvin saw between divine glory and creaturely existence called forth this sort of practical responsiveness. And more, it called forth venturesome Christians who would live out their faith in the midst of a world that was a theater of God's glory, albeit one distorted by corruption and idolatry. They understood their worship of the God of grace and glory to entail the possibilities of transformed ecclesial, cultural, political, and economic life toward greater goodness, truth, and justice. Some grew impatient with falsehood and injustice and became uncompromising agents of change, as we shall discuss in chapter 7. But other followers of Calvin, fearing God and their vulnerability, came to evade the gap between creaturely existence and God's glory by creating and submitting to authoritarian religious and political regimes.

PATTERNING THE CHRISTIAN LIFE

In Calvin's view, to live before God inevitably involves struggle and suffering. "We toil and suffer reproach because we have our hope set on the living God," he explained to King Francis, using the text of 1 Timothy 4:10. "For the sake of this hope some of us are shackled with irons, some beaten with rods, some led about as laughingstocks, some proscribed, some most savagely tortured, some forced to flee. All of us are oppressed by poverty, cursed with dire execrations, wounded by slanders, and treated in most shameful ways" (14). Although Calvin did not count suffering among the marks of the church, as did Luther, he gave it a prominent place in the Christian life. For him, bearing the cross epitomized the Christian life.

In Book 3 Calvin interpreted "bearing the cross" as a pattern of the Christian life, as an approach to life in which the Christian's pride of self is emptied out and surrendered before a merciful, sovereign God. This orientation levels pretensions to power and reorients the Christian to persist in a grateful, unselfish affirmation of life as a gift of God. "Bearing the cross" also has a pedagogical role: it helps to "promote" one's salvation. According to Calvin, undergoing suffering and persecution teaches trust in God as well as patience and obedience. To bear the cross is "medicine for our salvation" and a necessary discipline. (We can only find problematic his description of discipline as fatherly chastisement for sons, which in turn conveys the "legitimacy" of one's birth as God's child.) Christians can bear suffering patiently because they trust in God's providential care. "In the very act of afflicting us with the cross he is providing for our salvation" (3.8.11). If persons were already suffering persecution, as the French Calvinists were, then Calvin's counsel to bear suffering would perhaps be heard as endowing sufferers with agency and assuring them of divine care, rather than as encouraging active agents to become passive sufferers.[26] Outside of that context, however, it is all too easy to hear these words as promoting passivity and suffering as goods in themselves.

Calvin construed the Christian life as a continual process of turning from one's self and self-glorification to seeking God's will and advancing God's glory (3.7.2). On the one hand, he refuted the assertion that righteousness can be attained simply by following inner inclinations, and on the other hand, the assertion that Christians can attain perfection in this life. In response to the first view, he argued that we are to "depart from ourselves" and express the pattern of Christ's life in our own. To deny one's self and take up the cross means both to follow the example of Christ in the pattern of one's life and to be engrafted into Christ, to be united with Christ as the source of life. In response to the second view, he argued that the Christian life is a matter of the affections of the heart that incline one to the goal of perfection, to which one continually strives. Some progress is possible, but humility must reign. Moreover, given the distorting effects of self-love and pride, persons cannot rely upon their own powers of intellect and affection. Rather, we need to "get out of ourselves," to be grateful for all that God has given us, and to be good stewards of that with which we have been entrusted. "The sum of the Christian life is the denial of ourselves," he paraphrased Romans 12. Self-denial ultimately means surrendering one's self and every possession gratefully and reverently to God, trusting that God alone is the Governor of all life. "We are not our own," he repeated, building to the response, "we are God's" (3.7.1).

For Calvin, to "get out of ourselves" meant to get into the world. According to Carlos Eire, Calvin's diagnosis of idolatry and his call for "confessional integrity" between inward belief and outward worship produced anything but passive sufferers. "To accept the Calvinist credo, body and soul, was to become an agent of change," Eire concludes.[27] Calvin viewed the Christian life as a strenuous, engaged life. He rejected what we could call triumphalist and sectarian views. Like Augustine, he assumed that Christians dwell in the midst of life's complexities, vulnerabilities, and ambiguities, not on the edge of the world.

> In bearing with the imperfection of life we ought to be far more considerate. For here the descent is very slippery and Satan ambushes us with no ordinary devices. For there have always been those who, imbued with a false conviction of their own perfect sanctity, as if they had already become a sort of airy spirits, spurned association with all men in whom they discern any remnant of human nature. (4.1.13)

Christians are no "airy spirits," no angels who live above the world. "The church's holiness is not yet complete." Rather, the church is holy in that God is "daily at work" in it and "in the sense that it is daily advancing" (4.1.17). In the meanwhile, godly persons should rely on God's mercy, give glory to God, name ignorance and falsehood for what it is, acknowledge their own vulnerability and ambiguity, and strive to transform lives and institutions toward the glory of God.

VULNERABILITY, AMBIGUITY, AND TRANSFORMATION

Theologians from Paul and Augustine to Luther and Calvin offer many resources for a contemporary account of vulnerability and transformation. For example, in their endurance of persecution and in their controversies with the Gnostics, early Christian theologians teach us to be suspicious when flesh-and-blood relations are denigrated in favor of "invisible" realities. Augustine advises us to reject understandings of the church that attempt to preserve its holiness by withdrawing from the "world." He instructs us to advocate for complex and dynamic strategies for transforming communities and societies while being located in their midst. With Luther, we learn that no aspect of human life, not even the church, is exempt from the possibility of corruption. His thoroughgoing denunciation of the misuse and abuse of institutional power and privilege, and his corresponding conception of the church as congregation, a people gathered by the Word, rather than as institution, remain as relevant today as ever. Calvin chastens our judgment about what is possible and what is necessary for salvation and thereby informs practical engagement toward historical transformation.

We have found depictions of and responses to creaturely vulnerability and the ambiguity of the church that are far more varied than a student of modern theology might expect to find. The dialectic of historical existence and ideal essence, transmuted from that of visible and invisible church, becomes central to modern theology in a way that the visible/invisible distinction never was in Luther or Calvin. Although Calvin gave it some prominence, his central approach was to rely on the marks of the church. Similarly, Oberman argues that Luther scholars and later Protestants have disregarded Luther's "declaration of loyalty to the Church as the communion of saints." According to Oberman, "As long as the Protestant tendency to play off the invisible church of the faithful against the visible institutional church has not been overcome, this declaration will make no impression."[28]

In Luther and Calvin, the distinction between visible and invisible church is but one part of their depiction of Christian life and community. We have found other strategies, for example, appeals to holiness tested in persecution and the use of the marks of the church, whether as indicators of a holy Christian people or as a baseline guarantee of the true church. An array of other dialectics, such as mortality and glory or the hidden and revealed, complicated and sometimes subsumed the antithesis of visible and invisible. Various figures of Christian life and community—such as vessel, treasure, body, mother, word, communion of saints, martyrs, people of God—were interpreted and reinterpreted in these considerations.

Contemporary theologians can still be instructed by Luther's multiple strategies of critique and reconstruction and Calvin's call for transformation in personal, ecclesial, and public life. At our peril we neglect their accent on daily living, the deployment of a theological principle of critique, the interpretation of the church as a people rather than an institution, and the articulation of distinguishing signs or practices of a holy people. We must still heed Luther's critique of institutionalism and be instructed by his construal of the creative power of the Word at work in the world, congregating and shaping a people. Shared life before God is rightly interpreted as more intersubjective than institutional, more as an ethos than as a structure of authority. Nevertheless, no simple recuperation of Luther's or of Calvin's thought is sufficient for our day. Luther's paradoxical approach undercuts attention to the social-historical and cultural-ideological dimensions of vulnerable life and, correlatively, of devastation and transformation. Calvin's historical sensibilities and his appeal to divine accommodation suggested human capacities for transformation as well as for corruption. Yet at the same time, his focus on the offices and order of ministry contributed to bureaucratic and doctrinaire forms of Christianity.

An account of personal and communal life before God as vulnerable and capable of transformation must avoid the dangers of dogmatism, legalism, and institutionalism. To do so returns us to questions of suffering and salvation similar to ones that Calvin and Luther faced, but we must engage them while also rejecting any valorization of suffering as such. We will take up these questions in part 2.

The next chapter argues that an adequate account requires several shifts, including a shift from the focus on the relation of the divine to the human in the church, usually thematized as the dialectic of invisible and visible, or as renovated in modern thought, the dialectic of ideal and historical. It argues for the necessity of moving beyond strategies of stabilizing "the church" or "the Christian life" to a view of the ongoing transformation of life before God.

CHAPTER 4

Modern Treasure?

The problem is avoided by not admitting its premise, namely, that a
suprahistorical or essential nature of the Church is more real, purer, or
of greater value than its changing social character.
                                                —*James M. Gustafson*[1]

In the nineteenth century, theologians transmuted the distinction
between the visible and invisible church into the contrast between
Christianity's historical existence and its ideal essence. This antithesis
provided the dominant logic of modern ecclesiology[2] and arguably of
theology, where it converged with a modern restatement of Chalcedon's
two-natures Christology. The nature of the church and of God's relation to the world were both interpreted in terms of the relation between
historical existence and ideal essence. The antithesis and the relation
between its terms provided a way to formulate the nature of Christian
unity, the holiness of the church, the relation of church and world, and
ecclesial authority. It also provided a means for elaborating the relation
of church and other symbols of Christian faith, especially Christ, salvation, providence, and election. With this transmutation and consolidation, what had been one interpretive strategy among many became a
master model that decisively configured theological reflection.

AN INADEQUATE APPROACH: THE ANTITHESIS
OF VISIBLE AND INVISIBLE CHURCH

At their best, the Augustinian-Reformation dialectic of visible and
invisible church and the modern dialectic of historical institution and
ideal essence allowed for relatively nuanced and dynamic portrayals of
the relations among churches and cultures. They also served as powerful principles of criticism. Yet, when this dialectic became the master

model to the exclusion of other approaches, it proved to be inadequate for several reasons. First, it is unable to thematize diversity and change as strengths.[3] Second, it is inadequate to the complex vulnerability of communal and personal life. Neither the processes of common life nor diverse forms of shared life, work, and worship were made intelligible theologically. Third, in evading such diversity and complexity, the dominant model came to evade vulnerability and ambiguity themselves. That is, rather than clarifying threats to and possibilities of transformation present in personal and shared life, theologians in effect defined vulnerability and ambiguity away.

Finally, the use of the antithesis tends toward a problematic dualism. The definition of the true church has proceeded by way of separating human from divine aspects in the church. The relation of human and divine has often been interpreted in hierarchical and dualistic patterns. In these interpretations, the human is correlated with visible form or historical existence and is subordinated to the divine, now interpreted as invisible, ideal, or essential. The true church is aligned with the latter. It becomes disconnected from how Christians actually work and worship together, and from the problems and possibilities of actual communities. Furthermore, human social existence is sometimes construed as the source of falsehood. Dualistic interpretations tend to exclude from theological reflection Christianity's complacencies and complicities and also its contributions to human flourishing.

The use of the antithesis as a master model proved to be inadequate to the complexity of creaturely life, resulted in doctrinal reductionism, tended toward a problematic dualism and finally, evaded the problem of ambiguity. It provided a strategy for a dogmatic or essentialist defense of "church" in comparison or contrast with "the world." Whether the relation of church and world was interpreted as synthesis, contrast, or paradox, the logic was to capture the whole in two terms and to secure their relation as a stable dyad. Such strategies failed to acknowledge vulnerability, clarify ambiguity, or support transformation in historical, social life.

In the mid-twentieth century some theologians rejected the adequacy of the dominant logic and tried to move beyond strategies of invulnerability. The Swiss Reformed theologian Emil Brunner argued that theology should begin with the intrinsic relation of fellowship and faith, rather than with the relation of visible and invisible church. He rejected an understanding of faith as mediated through institutional forms and practices; indeed, he suspected all outward and organized forms of ecclesial life. However, by framing the central problem as the proper relation of the (effectively invisible) fellowship in faith and (visible) institutional Christianity, Brunner's proposal nevertheless partook of the dominant logic, albeit critically so.

A group of Protestant theologians working in the United States offered a more fruitful alternative. Like Brunner, Joseph Haroutunian, the Chicago theologian and scholar of Calvin, critiqued the institutionalism and individualism of modern Protestantism.[4] He emphasized the communion of believers and their witness in the world as a means of grace. Haroutunian, H. Richard Niebuhr, James Gustafson, and others in this North American strand of theology insisted that the social, historical character of Christian community is intrinsic to its nature and indeed is the means of divine interrelation with the world.[5] In doing so, these theologians stood in continuity with Calvin's themes of divine accommodation and historical transformation while downplaying the framework of the relation of the visible and invisible church. James Gustafson's *Treasure in Earthen Vessels* exemplifies this orientation. Gustafson argued that the nature and purpose of Christian communities ought to be interpreted in relation to, rather than in segregation from, shared human needs and processes. This strand offers crucial insights for our account.

Similar themes emerge in the late twentieth-century work of feminist and womanist theologians. For example, Rosemary Radford Ruether avoids many of the problems that these mid-twentieth century U.S. thinkers identified. She rejects a simple church-world opposition, resists the reduction of theology to Christology, and directs attention to shared experiences of redemption rather than to institutions and doctrines. Yet Ruether's own interpretive framework is not without problems that again relate to the dominant logic.

The chapter engages the work of Brunner, Gustafson, and Ruether as it eschews the dominant logic. In contrast to strategies of invulnerability, I call for a dynamic account of life before God as vulnerable to devastation and transformation, which in turn fosters ongoing conversion toward the glory of God.

BRUNNER'S COMMUNICATING COMMUNION

Emil Brunner worked in the flurry of ecclesiological reflection and ecclesial realignment associated with mid-twentieth-century ecumenism.[6] He referred to the problem of the proper relation between fellowship in faith and the institutional church as the "unsolved problem of Protestantism." Brunner thought that Luther alone of the Protestant Reformers grasped the intrinsic relation of faith and fellowship with his personalistic understanding of a Christian holy people. By contrast, he charged that Calvin's use of the distinction between visible and invisible church made fellowship extrinsic to faith, and that Calvin had a "fundamentally individualistic" interpretation of faith.[7] Luther, despite "his intuitive grasp of the New Testament message of faith," failed to work out the relation of fellowship or spiritual unity to the institutions known as churches. Brunner turned his attention to this relationship.

According to Brunner, "the New Testament message of faith" involves neither consent to true doctrine nor an act or event of faith.[8] When properly understood, it is neither institutional nor individualistic. Rather, faith is "the most inward form of existence that we know." It is "created by the self-communication of the divine life" and consists equally in "a being moved by" and "a being moved toward" God. At present the glory of God remains concealed in the cross, in a "conflict-burdened, paradoxical form." In the not-yet-known form of glory, both the earthen vessel of our present existence in faith and our knowledge of the treasure that it bears will be transformed.[9]

For Brunner, fellowship is an intrinsic part of faith. "*Ekklesia* happens, takes shape by necessity, where the Word of salvation in Christ is received in trust and obedience," he explained. "If we belong to Christ, then we belong to the *Ekklesia*."[10] He took Paul's understanding of the *Ekklesia*, or more precisely, an understanding of shared participation in Christ that Brunner viewed as concomitant with Paul's teaching about the gospel, to be the authentic and definitive *Ekklesia*. With a stunning confidence in his ability to discern the true Paul, Brunner claimed, "Paul's teaching on the *Ekklesia* is the same as ours."[11]

The *Ekklesia* is neither an invisible church nor the existing institutional church, but rather a "spiritual organism." It is a "proclaiming existence," a "form of life which has its origin in Jesus Christ and in which God's self-communication is constantly active."[12] The *Ekklesia* is both means and place of personal encounter with God's Word of salvation. We might call it *an immediacy* in which and through which the Holy Spirit mediates the work of Jesus Christ to contemporary human existence. Jesus Christ is the historical Mediator, God's self-communication in history. Importantly, Brunner argued that the mediation of the gospel of Jesus Christ is intrinsically social. Thus his *Ekklesia* is also *a shared subjectivity*, or in his own language, a "world-embracing brotherhood." He explained, "The *Ekklesia* is a thoroughly uncultic, unsacred, spiritual brotherhood, which lives in trusting obedience to its Lord Christ and in the love to the brethren which he bestows, and knows itself as the body of Christ through the Holy Spirit which dwells in it."[13]

Brunner acknowledged that the New Testament includes diverse and even "fundamentally irreconcilable" conceptions of Christian community. He held Paul's teaching about the *Ekklesia* to be the plumb line against which other perspectives ought to be measured, and he judged them to be lacking. He discounted the views of Jewish followers of Jesus who "never really understood Paul's doctrine of justification; much less . . . appropriate[d] it." He rejected the authority of the Pastoral Epistles in which "the office of the bishop is portrayed and eulogized in a manner unthinkable in a genuinely Pauline community."[14] Finally, he dismissed the community of mutual aid and shared possessions portrayed in Acts 2–5 for being "too direct a translation of *agapē*."[15]

Brunner's objection to the directness of the Acts community indicates his suspicion of social organization. He viewed the spontaneous, interpersonal working of the Spirit to be at odds with enduring social structures. The *Ekklesia* is a "body," a fellowship; moreover, "it is not ordered by the will and law of men, but simply and solely by the Spirit."[16] It is as if Brunner took a structural-functionalist model of social cohesion as the basis for his understanding of fellowship, and then substituted the spontaneous working of the Holy Spirit for the binding function of social mores and norms. His *Ekklesia* is an intersubjective immediacy, a communicating communion, that is created by the mediation of the gospel of Jesus Christ and sustained by the work of the Holy Spirit, neither of which Brunner interpreted as occurring through social or cultural processes. Instead, he distinguished sharply between the working of the divine and the working of human social life. "The *Ecclesia* knows nothing whatever of a sacred polity. It is no institution. Therefore a church can never *be* the *Ecclesia* either by purification or recreation."[17] Churches can never become the *Ekklesia*; at best they can serve as provisional forms, "shells," that help—or at least do not hinder—its growth.

Brunner insisted with Luther that the church, rightly understood, is neither an institutional guarantor of salvation nor a suprapersonal sacramental agent. Luther interpreted the church as a people called out, equipped, and united by the gospel. Brunner focused more narrowly on communion with Christ and others through the gospel and corrected for overly institutionalized and individualized interpretations of life in Christ. He rightly emphasized its intersubjective nature, but he allowed this intersubjectivity no enduring character of its own. Brunner's

Ekklesia was "a personal life flowing from beyond the temporal world; God's own life sharing itself with men through the Mediator."[18] Note that Brunner's "flow" comes only from God; it does not originate in human motivation or action. By contrast, Luther himself taught that a holy Christian people came, through their proclamation of the gospel and their associations over time, to evidence certain patterns or marks of a life together in Christ.

One must understand Brunner's suspicion of institutional and cultural forms of Christianity against the background of his day. Like Karl Barth and other contemporaries, Brunner protested the inadequacy and even complicity of "culture Protestantism" in the face of a vicious and rising totalitarianism. Against this, they emphasized a God who could not be controlled, a Spirit whose movement ought not be constrained, and a gospel of Christ that offered certainty. After World War II, Brunner, with other Protestants, Orthodox, and Roman Catholics, reached for a way to bridge divisions within Christianity—and to some extent, among humanity—that yet remained critical. Thus Brunner rightly refused to privilege what he called "churchiness" or any one particular organizational structure as the true form of Christianity. However, he wrongly suspected organization or polity in itself. His *Ekklesia* not only lacked social processes, patterns, and forms; it was essentially without them.

Brunner admitted that, under the imperfect conditions of human life, the *Ekklesia* needed a "form," but the less structure or organization involved, the better. He shared Luther's dream of a "truly evangelical church order" in which Christians would meet in private homes rather than as a public institution.[19] Similarly, the twentieth-century Japanese *Mukyōkaishugi* (Non-Church movement) captured his imagination. Brunner explained: "'The word alone will do' is their principle, taken over from Luther and out of the Bible, to which they strictly adhere. No institution, no outward and visible structure, is to hamper the free action of the Word of God and the Holy Spirit. Therefore, *Mukyōkai*—Non-Church."[20]

In our day, information technologies provide opportunities for institution-less communion that Brunner never imagined. Would he have celebrated the minimal structure and shared immediacy of faith-based Internet "communities" and social networks? Would he have embraced these new "non-church" expressions, or would he have distinguished the personal mediation of the Spirit and Jesus Christ from the impersonal mediation of technology? At issue here is not information technology per se—arguably it has already altered contemporary culture and religion as much as the printing press did in early modern Europe—but rather that it is impossible, and in my judgment undesirable, to segregate "Christian life" from the patterns and processes of shared human life. No simple equation ought to be made between the authenticity and the "invisibility" of Christianity.

Brunner judged that Calvin, Zwingli, and subsequent Reformed theologians, unlike Luther, failed to grasp the intrinsic relation of faith and fellowship. In his view, their use of the distinction between the visible and invisible church contributed to a "misunderstanding of the church," and then modern Protestants pursued "false solutions" in reinterpreting the distinction through Enlightenment models of historical development.[21] Such approaches perpetuated an individualism and institutionalism that was foreign and indeed opposed to the New Testament *Ekklesia*. Only when the nature of the *Ekklesia* is properly understood can the problem of its relation to the institutions we know as churches be resolved.[22]

Brunner's approach addressed Protestantism's individualism and institutionalism and rightly emphasized the sociality of life before God. The transforming reality of God cannot be constrained to the structures, dogma, or morality of Christianity. But neither does it appear other than in historical-cultural patterns and processes. Such patterns and processes offer means for distortion *and* transformation. Like twentieth-century culture Protestantism, twenty-first-century Christianity also evidences systemic failings, such as clergy sexual abuse and institutional complicity. Institutions have harmed or at least failed to protect persons. However, no view of life before God that treats processes and organization as indifferent can respond adequately to these possibilities and failures.

Can churches be means of saving and realigning life with others before God? Christians face and answer such questions, if at all, with their whole life, work, and worship. For the most part, they give what answers they do in their cumulating existence—in particular practices and attitudes that accumulate as tendencies of response, patterns of organization, and pervasive sensibilities. They answer not in one encounter or one choice, but with many responses that are interrelated with each other and with a communion of saints through time. Moreover, their answers are composed in relation with the world of which they are a part, and in response to a creating, redeeming, and sustaining God. Christianity is not only a communicating communion, it is also a movement—a series of interrelated conversations over time and across cultures that are never ceasing and always changing. Such patterned relations bear possibilities for harm and for healing. Shared life before God may be minimally structured or highly organized—at issue is not the particular polity, but rather the need for patterns and processes that enable accessibility and responsiveness to persons, cultures, and God. These patterns themselves remain "earthen"—shaped in particular situations, changeable, and susceptible to damage—while yet providing the means by which persons and communities come to bear the grace and glory of God.

Brunner's work also indicates the reductionism of much modern theology. Despite his own call to leave the dominant antithesis behind, his contrast between provisional institutional forms and the *Ekklesia* partook of the antithesis. At best, Brunner held patterns of human life and life in Christ (the *Ekklesia*) in paradoxical relation. At worst, he viewed them as opposed, even inimical. Thus his work inadvertently demonstrated the dominance of this logic and its reductionism. To the extent that he portrayed organizations and shared efforts as intrinsically opposed to divine purposes, he also perpetuated a view of salvation as an event that breaks into a contaminated world where God does not dwell, rather than as a paradigm of God's ongoing relationship with a struggling, sometimes glorious, and always vulnerable creation.

GUSTAFSON'S *TREASURE IN EARTHEN VESSELS*

The force of James Gustafson's 1961 book, *Treasure in Earthen Vessels*, is that an adequate interpretation of the reality and work of the church will account for human needs and historical processes. "The Church is *earthen*—of the stuff of natural and historical life. The Church is a *vessel*, it is useful," Gustafson explained.[23] Churches are human communities; they are historical, social, political, language-bearing and -borne communities. Furthermore, churches do not merely have social, political, interpretive, and historical dimensions; they exist in and through these processes.

Ambiguous as such processes may be, they are the means of divine engagement in human life and, correlatively, of human participation in divine purposes. For example, churches address human needs. They offer practices and interpretations that place human life in a broader framework of significance. They can bestow recognition, a sense of belonging, an assurance of the ultimate rightness and goodness of things, integration with and differentiation from society, socialization, and sanctions for behavior.[24] Rituals such as baptisms, weddings, and funerals mark life's transitions—we are born, we come of age, we die—and locate these transitions within the Christian life. The social function of such rituals does not lessen but rather contributes to their theological significance. To give another example, that nourishment is a basic human need does not diminish but rather enhances and indeed makes possible the powerful symbolism of breaking bread.[25] Similarly, churches can be interpreted as political communities and as communities of language, of interpretation, of memory and understanding, and of belief and action.[26] What matters theologically is not, for example, whether churches are "spiritual" in contrast to "political," but whether their organization and patterns of relating are ethically responsible and theologically responsive.[27]

Theological oversimplification and distortion result when interpreters fail to value social, historical processes as necessary means by which communities of faith exist. "Doctrinal reductionism [such as Brunner's] refuses to take seriously the human elements in the church's life or, if it acknowledges them, it does not explore or explicate them except in doctrinal language."[28] Gustafson also argued against sociological oversimplification. Interpretations that rely exclusively on biblical-doctrinal language or on political and social thought without reference to the other are inadequate. Such "closed circles" of theological and social interpretation should be broken open.

What, then, might an adequate social and theological interpretation look like? Gustafson noted the implications of his approach for further theological work. His conclusions are instructive for our account.

First, "the historical and social relativity of the church is part of its essential character."[29] In effect, Gustafson reaffirmed Calvin's teaching that the church exists in history and has a historical nature. He expanded Calvin's insight by affirming also that the church exists in culture, language, polity, and socioeconomic life and that its nature is also cultural, discursive, political, and socioeconomic. Theologians ought to assume churches' historicity, sociality, and so forth and take as part of their own task "to make theologically intelligible the human forms and processes that can be understood and interpreted from a social perspective."[30]

Second, "the human processes of its [the church's] common life are means of God's ordering, sustaining, and redeeming his people."[31] This affirmation stands in continuity with Calvin's accent on divine accommodation to human capacities. "The incarnation," Gustafson explained, "is a testimony to the power of God to use the human as a means of his disclosure and action."[32] Furthermore, Christians are not merely fated to sociocultural, historico-political existence; they can be confident of the ultimate significance of social, historical processes. Divine purposes are accomplished through human processes and, correlatively, the church in its humanness, sociality, and historicity "is in the power of God."

Accordingly, Gustafson affirmed that "social adaptiveness is a strength rather than a weakness." That churches can adapt forms, language, expression of beliefs, and practices in different contexts is necessary and good. Indeed, "failure to adapt means failure in its mission."[33] The power and effectiveness of churches depends upon their "human social character" rather than upon overcoming this character. Implicitly he counters the pervasive tendency to equate what is human with what is sinful in a simple manner. To reject this equation does not entail denying that these processes are contingent, relative, ambiguous, and distorted by sin. It does mean rejecting "docetic" views and also claims about the divinization, inerrancy, or sectarian perfection of the community of believers.

Third, common life is not less theologically significant than unique ideas and singular events. "Uniqueness *per se* is not a quality of Christian life," Gustafson observed. The distinguishing aspects of Christian life lie within a continuum of human processes. Theologians do not have to explain away the processes of human life as "less theological"— or alternately, more sinful—in relation to a "more theological" ecclesial essence or spiritual community.[34]

Fourth, an adequate interpretation requires more than rebalancing the dialectic of church as historical institution and church as ideal or essence. The dominant logic must be overthrown inasmuch as it always opposes social, historical, political, and discursive dimensions of Christian life as "less theological" relative to a "more theological" essence. According to Gustafson,

> The problem of the believer, then, is not how to reconcile the social and historical character of the Church with a suprahistorical or even historical essence. The problem is avoided by not admitting its premise, namely, that a suprahistorical or essential nature of the Church is more real, purer, or of greater value than its changing social character.[35]

Defining the church doctrinally and in contrast to the world precludes adequate attention to sociocultural, historico-political, and hermeneutical character of Christian life, and with it, an adequate understanding of churches. The old logic is inadequate to the concerns of believing persons as well as to the realities of churches.

Finally, neither Christian life in particular nor human life in general can be interpreted adequately in exclusive relation to Jesus Christ, but must be understood in a broader context of "God's ordering, sustaining, and redeeming activity." When churches are viewed in the context of a created and inspired world, supposedly "less theological" aspects— social, cultural, historical, political, and interpretive processes—are seen to be no less potential means of grace than supposedly "more theological" aspects. Moreover, the fundamental opposition between church and world is overturned.

H. Richard Niebuhr made a similar argument in his essay "The Church Defines Itself in the World," written in the mid-1950s. He observed that when the church is defined in opposition to the world, the result is a tendency "to ignore or deprecate the 'worldly' character of the church and 'churchly' character of the world." It becomes more difficult to recognize aspects of common life that "relate positively to the world" as "agencies through which the grace of God as well as the power of sin may manifest itself." The likely result is an ideal church that is "invisible to our time" and, for all practical purposes, separated from the world.[36]

Gustafson, Niebuhr, and others in this North American strand insisted that Christianity's social, historical situatedness is inherent to its reality and indeed is the means of divine interrelation with the world. This insistence was a matter of theological method and an affirmation of God's continuing relation with the whole world as creator, redeemer, and inspirer. As Niebuhr wrote after the devastation that culminated in World War II, "The church is not responsible for the judgment or destruction of any beings in the world of God, but for the conservation, reformation, redemption, and transfiguration of whatever beings its action touches."[37]

RUETHER, REFORMATION, AND REDEMPTION

The call to avoid both triumphalism and sectarianism and for a dynamic depiction of shared life before God rather than a static or defensive dyad of church and world, has been sounded from Augustine and Calvin to the present. It echoes in James Gustafson's admonishment to avoid theological and sociological reductionism and to recognize the theological significance of human patterns and processes; it is found in H. Richard Niebuhr's reminder that the church's responsibility is transformation, not damnation. The call resounds with new poignancy and urgency in the work of feminist and womanist theologians.[38] They argued, in effect, that sexism, misogyny, and violence against women are not "less theological" matters over against some "more theological" essence of church. Rather, God's grace and glory are made manifest in communities of faith where such destruction is resisted and where safety, joy, and flourishing are shared.

Struggles against sexism, racism, and other forms of disregard and degradation, and for freedom and flourishing, are often intensified in churches and in relation to Christian theology and practice. For example, theologian Mercy Amba Oduyoye, an Akan native of Ghana, has denounced the aloofness and muteness of churches in Africa in the face of civil wars and humanitarian crises. She finds these churches yet more problematic for African women: even churches that engage biblical and prophetic traditions to denounce oppression have used other strands of Christian teaching to reinforce women's subordination. Such churches often have depended upon women as their obedient consumers. Oduyoye insists, "The church must shed its image as a male organization with a female clientele whom it placates with vain promises, half truths, *and* the prospect of redemption at the end of time." At the same time, despite churches' sexism and oppression, women sometimes experience inspiration, empowerment, and redemption in them. As Oduyoye observes, "Women have stayed in the church against all odds," for these churches have also been means of healing and sustenance.[39]

In North America, triumphalist theologies have functioned to preserve a clerically controlled, male-dominated ecclesiastical hierarchy or bureaucracy. Sectarian theologies with closed systems of dogma and practice have functioned to constrain the freedom and agency of "outsiders" and to disengage Christians from the plights and possibilities of the wider world. In this section, we look at Rosemary Radford Ruether's call for a feminist reformation of churches,[40] and then we turn to her underlying treatment of liberation and salvation. The latter discussion moves us toward a more dynamic interpretation of life before God as a field of tensions and conversions.

Oduyoye, Ruether, and other feminist and womanist theologians raise questions not unlike those faced by sixteenth-century Reformers. Does Christianity have anything to say to a world struggling with oppression and brutality? Where are the communities that strengthen women's well-being and ensure their freedom from domination and sexual violence? Must they be created outside of historical churches or on their margins? These are not only sociological and strategic questions, but also existential and theological ones. Sixteenth-century theologians assumed that there was no salvation outside the church, but they found the existing institution to be rife with deception, corruption, and idolatry. They therefore debated the nature of the true church. Ruether argues that redemption includes "overcoming all forms of patriarchy."[41] While "existing institutional churches do not have a monopoly on the words of truth or the power of salvation,"[42] redemption nonetheless requires mediation by communities of faith and struggle.

Ruether protested the clericalism and institutionalism as well as the sexism of historical churches. Clerical and institutional control of ministry, doctrine, and sacraments constrains the Spirit and expropriates ministry, doctrine, and sacramental life from the people by fostering a "false faith in the spiritual efficacy of material acts."[43]

In her 1985 book *Women-Church*, Ruether deployed images of exile and exodus to encourage flight from the "land of patriarchy." She argued for the creation of autonomous feminist communities within and on the edges of existing institutions. "We are not in exile, but the Church is in exile with us. God's Shekinah . . . is with us as we flee from the smoking altars where women's bodies are sacrificed, as we cover our ears to blot out the inhuman voice that comes forth from the idol of patriarchy."[44] Her polemics are almost as fierce, if not nearly as extended, as Luther's denunciation of the Babylonian captivity of the medieval church. Through images of idolatry, she suggests a perverse inversion of Christianity: devastation and sacrifice reign where healing and redemption ought to be found. Yet Ruether cautioned against "a sectarian rejection" of the institutional church. She rejected a "radical Protestant" or Reformation paradigm of change insofar as it represents a call to an original truth or pristine church that ignores the intervening history and bypasses tradition.[45]

Ruether reenvisioned church as a "matrix of regeneration": as a dynamic context that supports liberation and healing by reinterpreting God and the world, by ritualizing processes of transformation, by creating new patterns of relationship, and by directing social protest and change. A feminist gathered community, like Luther's congregation, should not be distinguished by its structures of authority or by the sacraments that it safeguards, but rather by the message of liberation around which it assembles and by its contribution to the flourishing of all life.[46]

Ruether called for "spirit-filled" gathered communities to engage a "creative dialectic" with institutional churches. Her formulation is instructive for avoiding both triumphalism and sectarianism—although, I will argue, finally inadequate. Historically, prophetic, spirit-filled movements (for example, Quakers, Shakers, camp meetings, and revivals) have served to renew institutional Christianity.[47] However, charisma is "unstable" as a basis for lasting change. Institutions have systematized and rationalized the insights of spirit-filled communities and in this way have borne the history of renewal and change until new movements arise. Yet, this routinization of charisma, to use Max Weber's term and not one that Ruether herself employs, has also muted and expropriated the contributions of spirit-filled movements. It often has served as a means whereby hierarchical institutions have asserted control over and appropriated the power of the Spirit and of the people, especially of women. Nevertheless, in optimal situations historical institutions "create the occasion for the experience of the Spirit, which always breaks in from a direct encounter of living persons with the divine."[48] In addition, historical institutions allow for communication with the broader culture and through time.

At its best, Ruether's creative dialectic offers a dynamic picture of degeneration and transformation that avoids reduction into a church-world duality.[49] Yet Ruether's dialectic can also be reductionist.[50] Despite her insistence on the necessity of both historical institution and spiritual community, she tends to treat the former as falsely directed and the latter as more true, as evidenced in the image of the Church—capital *C*—going into exile with the women-church. At this point Ruether seems ready to embark on the ecclesiological road taken by Emil Brunner, albeit not prepared to travel as far as Brunner's dissociation of *Ekklesia* (essence) and church (instrument and provisional form or "shell") took him.

In fact, Ruether's interpretation of redemption is more complex than her dialectic suggests. When she treats redemption, which is a major theme in her work, she underscores the dynamism of *multiple* tensions and transformations. As she rightly argues, liberation/redemption in a world of personal, social, and ecological interdependencies cannot mean merely the proclamation of an individual's existential freedom before God. Ruether explains, "We cannot split a spiritual, antisocial redemption from the human self as a social being, embedded in sociopolitical and ecological systems."[51] Liberation and salvation require a communal context that can address the ambiguity and transformation

of personal, sociopolitical, and ecological existence with symbols, rituals, and patterns of relating that are adequately complex and resonant.[52]
Additionally, the theological-symbolic resources of Christianity cannot
be abandoned but must themselves be engaged critically and thereby
transformed. Liberation in its fullest sense involves ongoing conversion
or regeneration in multiple dimensions of existence.[53]

Taken as a whole, Ruether's interpretation locates the heart of a
liberating Christianity neither in the church as institution nor in an
autonomous feminist community, but in a "matrix of regeneration" that
becomes manifest between and among communal forms and between
and among various dimensions of existence. As I have noted, such a
reading is sometimes contradicted by her presentation of the "creative
dialectic." In addition, Ruether sometimes seems to focus dynamism in a
center of energy, "God/ess as Primal Matrix," at the expense of historical
transformation.

Ruether's contributions, nevertheless, underscore the importance
and difficulty of creating a middle way between triumphalism and
sectarianism. This middle way cannot be attained as a static position
or construed as a paradoxical juxtaposition; it will not be a completed
synthesis or a goal reached in a Hegelian overcoming, but rather will
consist of ongoing interactions and conversions. Creatures and communities constantly face threats and possibilities and thus are always changing and being changed; moreover, they dwell before an always creating,
redeeming, and sustaining God.

BEYOND STRATEGIES OF INVULNERABILITY

What is needed is not a surpassing of vulnerable life, but its conversion.[54] For good and for ill, life before God cannot be segregated from
the rest of creaturely existence. It ought not be. As Calvin said, Christians are not "airy spirits." Christians and their churches are formed of
the same stuff as the rest of earthly life; they remain vulnerable, mortal,
and fallible. What is needed is not an overcoming of earthness, but
the strengthening and restoration of vulnerable creatures by the grace of
God. Attempts to preserve an invisible, ideal, or essential church by separating it from vulnerable shared existence are theologically inadequate
to the harm and the good that humans do and also to a living God.

Transformation toward the glory of God does not mean to defeat
present existence or to revert to some original uncompromised state.
Rather, it involves the reorientation and reconstruction of multiple

dimensions of personal and shared life. The old language of conversion conveys this thoroughgoing transformation: it is conversion rather than evasion of our earthen situation and situatedness; it is being turned toward the grace and glory of God and turning toward greater integrity and richer relatedness with others and God. This transformation occurs in receiving and radically reinterpreting life as a gift of God. Thereby selves and communities (including relations, knowledge, affections, and actions) are resituated before God as gracious and glorious.[55] Thus conversion is an intensely personal and yet necessarily communal process of being turned and becoming "something else"—of becoming creatures who receive and bear life as a good gift of God to be shared and enjoyed with and for others.

Human creatures, that of Christians and their churches included, are not only vulnerable, they are also ambiguous. Persons, communities, cultures, and environments are not only susceptible to harm and devastation, they have already been injured and altered. At the same time, they are not only vulnerable to healing and transformation, they have already been strengthened and changed. They are complexly vulnerable to harm and to healing, and as a result of those vulnerabilities, they become ambiguous mixtures of creativity and destruction, of holy and demonic, good and ill, true and false. Furthermore, these vectors of transformation and devastation cannot be divided easily into intra- or extra-Christian realities. Strategies that focus on defending Christian institutions, dogma, or morality are inadequate to such vectors of devastation and transformation. Such strategies of invulnerability tend to focus on removing the ambiguity of churches and ensuring the salvation of Christians at the expense of transformative engagement in the vulnerable, ambiguous, and sometimes glorious world of which Christians are part.

By situating Christian life not only before God but also with others in the midst of earthly existence, the vulnerability of personal, social, and ecological life, rather than the ambiguity of churches, becomes the focus of concern. Or rather, it *returns* as a focal point, albeit in a new way. As we have seen, the ambiguity of the church was not a pressing practical problem for the earliest communities of Christians. What I have referred to as "the problem of ambiguity," that is, ambiguity within churches, emerged over Christianity's first five centuries. Paul wrote of a vulnerable, "earthen" ministry that, despite afflictions, conveyed the grace and glory of God. Second- and third-century theologians, including Irenaeus, addressed how Christians and their communities might be strengthened to bear God, given the threats of persecution and heresy. The problem of ambiguous churches becomes evident when the dominant culture tolerates Christians and their communities; it pervades churches when Christianity gains a privileged status in culture. Cyprian and Augustine endeavored to explain the unity of the church—that is, the stability and integrity of its salvation—despite its "mixed" nature. A thousand years later, Martin Luther judged the medieval church to be corrupt, in fact, systemically so. He decried its "captivity." God alone grants salvation, he insisted; the church does not control it, especially not the institutional church that he saw. Yet neither Luther nor any of the other parties in the sixteenth-century debates ever assumed that salvation existed outside the true church.

In our day, there is no privileged cultural or religious assumption that "salvation" answers the ambiguities of life, let alone that such an answer is found only in Christian churches. There may be pervasive undercurrents of yearning for greater justice, meaning, connection, satisfaction, or spirituality, but there is no general assumption that churches, or anything their God grants, will answer these yearnings. And so when, due to their complicities and corruptions, churches fail to "save" and even perpetrate harm, their ambiguities are relativized in the ambiguities of life. To relativize the ambiguities of churches is not to minimize their failings—Christian anti-Judaism, racism, homophobia, sexism, and other degradation has taken vicious forms, and damage has been enduring. Nor does it mean to minimize churches' capacities for fostering healing and hope. Rather, the "mixed" nature of churches cannot and, more importantly, ought not to be separated from the "mixed" nature of all life. As H. Richard Niebuhr wrote, "We stand with the rest of the world before God as that part of the world which, sharing in the world's unbelief, hopelessness and self-love, has begun to believe, to hope, and to love God."[56]

Building on the contributions of feminist and womanist theologies and of the North American theological strand that we have considered in this chapter, we can offer a more complex view of the relation of vulnerability and the transforming reality of God than was possible within the dominant logic. With Gustafson, Niebuhr, Ruether, and others, this account is formulated in relation to a creating, redeeming, and sustaining God as opposed to a narrow christocentrism or christomonism. It emphasizes community and ethos rather than institution,[57] while yet being suspicious of attempts to denigrate actual, "visible" loyalties and relations in favor of "invisible realities." Note, too, that the patterns and processes of life, work, and worship before God rather than doc-trines about the church and the Christian life become the focus of interpretation.

There are other resonances with these thinkers. I list them below and, for the time being, without further elaboration. With this American strand, this account recognizes the sociality of human life and the felt yearning to be reconciled to an encompassing community of life. At the same time it affirms the value of complex individuality and the necessity of attuning individual conscience and affections. It views social pro-cesses and historical patterns as necessary matrices for the creation of complex individuality and community, and therefore rejects the notions that communities are created by individual choice alone or that per-sons can exist without communities. This account assumes that diverse communities will necessarily offer competing visions of life before God and also that truth and value are not constrained to one specific set of religious experiences and practices. At the same time, this account remains dissatisfied with the limitations of actual communities of faith. It requires a rigorous accounting of the use (abuse) of institutional and interpersonal power/privilege, both to temper idealistic evasions of concrete conditions and to sharpen a vision of what exactly reconcilia-tion entails and justice requires. Finally, with a chastened judgment of both what is possible and what is necessary, this account contributes to practical engagement toward transformation.

PART 2

Transformation and Devastation

CHAPTER 5

A Field of Tensions and Conversions

Faith in God involves us in a permanent revolution of the mind and heart, a continuous life which opens out into ever new possibilities. It does not afford grounds for boasting but only for simple thankfulness. It is a gift of God.

—*H. Richard Niebuhr*[1]

Threats of damaging change figure prominently in contemporary discourse. International efforts attend to globalized threats from climate change, compromised technology, financial instability, international transmission of disease and viruses, and terrorism, among other things. In these efforts, the language of vulnerability, risk, and resilience has become a technical vocabulary. For example, the work of the United Nations International Strategy for Disaster Reduction (UNISDR) recognizes the relationship among disaster reduction, sustainable development, and poverty eradication; it seeks to "reduce the vulnerability of societies" and "build the resilience of nations and communities to disasters."[2] Other analyses indicate how social, cultural, and ecological vulnerabilities may aggravate and complicate physical, psychological, and interpersonal vulnerabilities.[3]

What is striking about this contemporary narrative, and especially insofar as it also suggests the tenor of our times, is that damage and loss have a force of inevitability. The narrative depicts a world permeated by risk and threat. In official UNISDR terminology, vulnerability is "the characteristics and circumstances of a community, system, or asset that make it susceptible to the damaging effects of a hazard."[4] The countervailing term is "resilience": the ability to repel, absorb, or recover from the effects of a hazard—an immunity of sorts. Very present threats and recent disasters drive this narrative, which in turn directs the formulation of crucial policies and action that can mitigate disasters and lessen harm to persons and environments. The questions at hand are how to assess risk, whether risks can be minimized, how to enhance resilience (say, through earthquake-resistant construction), and after the fact, what capacities will be relevant for responding to the damage. Note, then, that in this contemporary literature definitions of vulnerability stay close to the word's Latin root of "wounding": persons, communities, systems, and nations are depicted as being vulnerable to severe and lasting damage by disasters and hazards.

With this narrative of the seeming inevitability of risk and damage and with older theological accounts of the inevitability of sin, I take susceptibility to damaging change—indeed susceptibility to corruption—to be a basic feature of human existence. Due in part to that risk and damage, human creatures are inevitably ambiguous. The account of vulnerability that I have been developing also accents possibilities of transforming change. Vulnerability signals not only the capacity to suffer harm and to be damaged, but also capacities implied by contrast: to be kept safe and whole, to have integrity and dignity, and to be healed and lifted. Human creatures are complexly vulnerable to harm *and* to healing and, as a result, their lives and communities are necessarily ambiguous mixtures of creativity and destruction, holy and demonic, good and ill, true and false.

This account focuses on life before God and its susceptibility to damage and transformation rather than on the risks and threats themselves. Vulnerability is a basic aspect of creaturely existence and a situation wherein the grace and glory of God may be known. It is not a condition to be overcome. To use the images of creation that the apostle Paul appropriated, humans are creatures made of earth and breath and fashioned from the bones of others. Vulnerability and transformation are built in from the beginning, as it were; new creatures and vessels are formed from other valuable and changeable things. While human creatures are embodied and situated, their vulnerability is not caused by their embodiment or emplacement. God is always forming and re-forming the mundane, vulnerable stuff of creaturely existence, breathing life and glory into it. Of course, inextricably related to these images are stories of fall and expulsion that tell how change can also result in damage, loss, and suffering. The close relation of these susceptibilities is conveyed in Paul's image of treasure in clay jars: humans are earthen vessels, capable of being shattered and also of bearing great treasure, the grace and glory of God. Human creatures have been transformed and damaged and *remain* vulnerable, that is, susceptible to and capable of being changed—changed in ways that may be destructive or transformative.

Finally, this account affirms a living God who moves through a creation that can be called good, who strengthens and redeems vulnerable creatures, and whose glory crowns rather than defeats the earth and its creatures. This is in no way to dispute the reality of threats and risks that permeate a globalized world. No shield of invulnerability—be it a dogmatic, ecclesial, or moral strategy for preserving the true faith, the true church, or the true identity—can secure personal, social, and ecological existence from possibilities of damage and devastation. Moreover, such defensive strategies are theologically inadequate to the harm and the good that humans do and also to a living God.

This and the next chapter consider transformation and devastation in relation to theological themes of discipleship and conversion and of bearing suffering and the cross. In this chapter, I begin with the Gospel stories of sending disciples and receiving good news and healing. In these texts, Jesus and his disciples are portrayed as vulnerable to rejection and to welcome; healing and good news are offered in everyday places, where some witness and others welcome. Building on that picture as well as on previous chapters, salvation is situated and interpreted in the midst of life. Finally, H. Richard Niebuhr's treatment of Christianity as a movement informs a depiction of life before God as a field of tensions and conversions.

CALLING AND SENDING

Then Jesus called the twelve together
and gave them power and authority over all demons
    and to cure diseases,
and he sent them out to proclaim the kingdom of God
    and to heal.
He said to them, "Take nothing for your journey,
no staff, nor bag, nor bread, nor money—not even an extra tunic.
Whatever house you enter, stay there, and leave from there.
Wherever they do not welcome you, as you are leaving that town
shake the dust off your feet as a testimony against them."
They departed and went through the villages,
bringing the good news and curing diseases everywhere.
(Luke 9:1–6; cf. Matt. 10:1–15; Mark 6:7–13)

This story about Jesus calling and sending his disciples takes us from contemporary experiences of vulnerability into the heart of the Christian Scriptures, where such experiences may find sympathetic resonance and create critical distance. These texts depict—or rather offer layered and intersecting depictions of—the vulnerability of persons to rejection and indignity, to hunger and homelessness, to violence and suffering, to diminishment and death, and also to sometimes surprising possibilities of salvation, healing, and welcome. They depict the complexity of vulnerability, the space of life before God, and the transforming reality of God. Our historical and cultural distance from these ancient texts and times may help us to recognize analogous realities and possibilities in our day.

Each of the three Synoptic Gospels tells the story of Jesus' commissioning and instruction of his disciples. The Twelve are sent to proclaim the good news of the reign of God and to heal. They are to go without the most meager provisions: no spare coins, nothing to eat, no change of undertunic. They are to take nothing; they are also to expect nothing. They are to accept whatever hospitality is given to them, yet to beware that some places will not welcome them at all and indeed will spurn them. When that happens, they are to shake the very dust of that place from their feet and move on.

The Twelve who are sent are to rely only on the power and authority given them by Jesus. With the power they are given, they are to be signs of the reign and realm of God, authoring its reality in their preaching and healing. (Here preaching and healing are nearly synonymous.) This is the same power and authority, the story's contexts make clear, that was indicated in John the Baptist's ministry and that is evident in Jesus' own preaching and healing. It is an authority and power in which the Twelve share, not their own authority. Moreover, they are not to assume that they can or ought to compel others to yield to this power. However, when others welcome them, then God's reign may be made real through their proclamation and healing.

The Synoptic Gospels juxtapose this story to John the Baptist's imprisonment and death. While the Twelve are out in the villages, each Gospel uses the lull in the action to segue to John, and thus to place Jesus' commission of the Twelve in broader perspective. John the Baptist announced the kingdom of God and prepared for Jesus, now Jesus prepares the Twelve for the work of proclamation and healing. Thus John, Jesus, and the disciples are presented as successive generations in a line of prophets of the reign of God. Each generation will be marked by suffering. The violence of the Baptist's death also foreshadows Jesus' own death and the persecution that Jesus' followers will inevitably undergo: "From the days of John the Baptist until now the kingdom of heaven has suffered violence, and the violent take it by force" (Matt. 11:12).

When the Twelve return to Jesus, at least in the versions of Mark and Luke, five thousand men plus uncounted women and children gather as well. They share in a miraculous feast of loaves and fishes. Humanity, creation, and history seem to converge on Jesus at this moment. Yet the crowd is fed not so that they can linger, but so that they can disperse. They are returned to their homes and villages from this nexus, having been taught and fed and thus prepared.

After the throng departs, twelve baskets of broken pieces of bread and fish remain, one for each of the twelve disciples. Having equipped the Twelve with a commission and with loaves and fishes to share, Jesus provides further instruction about discipleship. His instructions are placed differently in the three Synoptic accounts, but the central teaching about the cost of discipleship is nearly the same in each: "If any want to become my followers, let them deny themselves and take up their cross daily and follow me. For those who want to save their life will lose it, and those who lose their life for my sake will save it. What does it profit them if they gain the whole world, but lose or forfeit themselves?" (Luke 9:23–25).

Interestingly, none of the Gospels narrate the work accomplished by these Twelve after they are sent out. Not one of the Gospels tells us, for example, who James and John heal or which demons are cast out by Simon and Andrew. What matters here is that they are sent out. They preach, heal, feed, and rely utterly on God; they face possibilities of rejection and reception, of losing and gaining life. Taking a poor and humble form, they are emptied out into the world, a *kenōsis* of divine possibility.

By the time this story—or rather these amalgams of narratives and sayings—was put into written form, those who preserved it would have recognized it as a story by which to interpret and judge their own discipleship. They would have known themselves as generations descended from the prophets to John the Baptist to Jesus and Jesus' followers. Indeed, these accounts are as much about the life, work, and worship of these later generations as those of John, Jesus, and the Twelve. In telling and recording these stories, these later disciples reaffirmed the charge to bring good news and healing to the world, the practice of sharing a meal, and the mark of suffering. They reaffirmed the reality of God as the mobilizing and authorizing power of their life, work, and worship.

To approach these texts in this way—from an imagined vantage point of early followers of Jesus, from the perspective of communities who themselves were only a generation or two removed from the Twelve—foregrounds continuities of calling and ministry.[5] This story may be heard as testimony to the astonishing divine possibilities that previous generations have borne to them and as establishing the marks of authentic discipleship for their own time. Otherwise, what registers in our contemporary ears is discontinuity: there are demons to be cast out, spare tunics (or lack thereof), and dust to be shaken off while suffering cannot be. We tend to read the commission and instruction to the Twelve like the "hard sayings" of the Sermon on the Mount, that is, not to take the severity of the instructions too literally. We're not going to be sent out without basic provisions, to rely on the hospitality of strangers and miraculous meals, anymore than we're literally going to pluck out a sinful eye or cut off a sinful hand.

Yet in another way, this Gospel story is not discontinuous with our day. To be dispersed into the world with nothing but the clothes on one's back, to be emptied out into the world with no guarantee of welcome or success or safety, happens every day to refugees and poor, hungry people. In our day, the reality of God continues to be poured out in the villages of the world, in the streets of its cities. It tries to slip across borders; it sleeps in alleys and searches for daily bread in trash bins; it seeks safety from violence and shelter from the streets. In this *kenōsis*, too, there is suffering and real risk of rejection and death. Life—God present in human lives—bleeds and suffers and starves and yet endures, resists, rises.

"WHOEVER WELCOMES . . ."

In first–century Palestine, Jesus' commission to the Twelve might have sounded familiar, if nonetheless rigorous. Strict Jews, itinerant Cynic philosophers, and some rabbis followed many of these practices in their travels. For instance, the Mishnah prohibits carrying various objects— namely, staff, wallet, sandals, and the dust on one's feet—into the temple precincts.[6] The historian Josephus wrote about similar practices by the Essenes. He reports that they "carry nothing with them on a journey except arms as a protection against brigands. In every city there is one of their order expressly appointed to attend to strangers, who provides them with clothing and other necessities."[7]

The *Didache*, a late first- or early second-century manual about the Christian life, assumes that the commission and instructions for the Twelve still apply to the itinerant apostles and prophets of that day. However, its teaching is directed to non-itinerant followers of the way of Jesus. Here is its relevant instruction:

> Now about the apostles and prophets: Act in line with the gospel precept. Welcome every apostle on arriving, as if he were the Lord. But he must not stay beyond one day. In case of necessity, however, the next day too. If he stays three days, he is a false prophet. On departing, an apostle must not accept anything save sufficient food to carry him till his next lodging. If he asks for money, he is a false prophet.[8]

Note that the disciples whom the *Didache* addresses are not the ones being sent out, but rather the ones who already live in the villages, the ones who receive. They are instructed in hospitality and discernment rather than in how to travel. These disciples are already in the villages, as it were, where some are arriving and others are dwelling.

As Jesus charges the Twelve in the Synoptic Gospels, so the *Didache* provides a corollary for village-dwelling disciples. Jesus tells the Twelve to bring no money or provisions; the *Didache* turns this charge into a means by which the villagers can discern true from false prophets. "If he asks for money, he is a false prophet." In the Lukan account, Jesus tells the Twelve to shake the dust off their feet when leaving villages that do not welcome them. The *Didache* instructs the villagers effectively to do the same with false apostles: to turn them out of their dwellings. These later disciples are recognizable not only by the message they bear but also by their ability to discern and to welcome the reality of God. They are distinguished by the power of proclamation and healing and by the power of reception and hospitality.

These dual powers of Christian discipleship are already hinted at in the Matthean version of the sending of the Twelve. On the one hand, the gospel of Matthew anticipates a primarily hostile reception to the Twelve: "See, I am sending you out like sheep into the midst of wolves; be wise as serpents and innocent as doves" (Matt. 10:16). Matthew depicts the way of discipleship as also the way of alienation from parents and children, the way of violence, and the way of martyrdom. Yet Matthew portrays the power of genuine reception as well. Persons who throw open their doors to receive the good news and its messengers are disciples, too. At the conclusion of the Matthean account, Jesus says, "Whoever welcomes you welcomes me, and whoever welcomes me welcomes the one who sent me." He continues, "Whoever welcomes a prophet, . . . whoever welcomes a righteous person, . . . whoever gives even a cup of cold water to one of these little ones in the name of a disciple . . ." (Matt. 10:40–42).

Matthew's "whoever" acknowledges the power of right welcome: the capacity to receive the good news from surprising persons, including from hungry, poor prophets who have only the clothes on their backs. These instructions about "whoever" anticipate the Great Judgment passage to follow: "'For I was hungry and you gave me food, I was thirsty and you gave me something to drink, I was a stranger and you welcomed me, I was naked and you gave me clothing, I was sick and you took care of me, I was in prison and you visited me. . . . Truly I tell you, just as you did it to one of the least of these my brothers, you did it to me'" (Matt. 25:35–36, 40, mg.). The commission to "whoever," like the commission to proclaim the reign of God, is another charge received from the Prophets. Isaiah 58:6–7 asks, "Is this not the fast that I choose: to loose the bonds of injustice, to undo the thongs of the yoke, to let the oppressed go free, and to break every yoke. Is it not to share your bread with the hungry, and bring the homeless poor into your house; when you see the naked to cover them, and not to hide yourself from your own kin?" Like the Prophets, Matthew suggests that the reality of God has already been poured out into the world; it is already standing on village thresholds, needing to be freed, fed, sheltered, clothed, and welcomed. Whoever welcomes these visitors, welcomes Jesus, the very life of God.

The Gospel of Luke likewise teaches about right welcome in the parable of the Great Banquet (14:15–24) and, above all, in the parable of the Good Samaritan (10:29–37). This parable also concerns a man on the road. He, too, is without extra clothing and coins, but this time because they have been stolen from him. He has been beaten and left "half dead." Sheer human need—and neither unexpected good news nor healing—await the person who might welcome this traveler. In fact, on the dangerous road to Jericho, any prudent traveler might have expected the possibility of ambush. The priest and the Levite, perhaps fearing for their own well-being, cross the road and ignore the man. They avoid danger and also the wounded man's need to be healed, sheltered, fed, and clothed. A foreigner, a Samaritan, perhaps someone from the very village that would not receive Jesus (in Luke's previous chapter, 9:51–56), risks safety and does everything he can to respond to the traveler's need. The Samaritan binds up the traveler's wounds, brings him to shelter, and provides for his care. In this story, it is now the welcome more than the traveler that is truly unexpected.[9]

As if to underscore that right welcome entails genuine receptivity to the other more than generosity in itself, Luke follows the story of the Good Samaritan with the story of Mary and Martha (10:38–42). In it, Mary's attentiveness to Jesus' teaching and a simple meal prepared by Martha—right hearing and right welcome—are preferred to a lavish welcome. The point, it seems, is not who is the better host, but rather how attention to basic needs—simply to be fed and to be received and heard—coincides with receptivity to God.[10] In this story, generosity nearly gets in the way. Attention to what is enough allows Jesus' teaching and person to be welcomed rightly: neither too much nor too little is asked.

What is enough attention, enough welcome? Not a lavish meal but sufficient food, a cup of cold water, as it were. Three days of accommodations are too much to ask, but one *is* needed. Right welcome requires attention to the genuine need and dignity of fellow creatures, to the children of God who arrive on the world's doorsteps. These unexpected visitors may be prophets and teachers, even Jesus himself.

SITUATED IN THE MIDST OF LIFE

Through the ages, theologians and churches have located themselves differently in relation to the narratives of sending and receiving (or effectively so). For example, the magisterial church has understood itself as continuing the work of Christ by calling and sending new apostles. Congregationally ordered churches have viewed themselves primarily as the disciples who are sent out and who are marked especially by preaching and sharing bread and wine. The emphasis on receiving "the least of these" (Matt. 25) has been crucial for liberation theologies.[11]

In our day what does it mean to take up the calling of Jesus, John the Baptist, and the prophets? To be marked by suffering and struggle? To welcome rightly? Where are contemporary disciples sent to bring good news and healing? What would be good news and healing for this day? What might it mean to receive messengers in contemporary dwelling places?

In a sense, the stories of sending and receiving have already located their readers and hearers. Their redaction and retelling assume that readers of these texts are already in the villages, where some disciples are sent and other disciples receive. These texts also situate us, their contemporary readers. They situate us neither above nor apart from everyday places and needs, but in the midst of life's vulnerability and ambiguity. They situate us there where true and false prophets traverse, where healing and hope are desired, there where, as these texts tell us, the reality of God has already been poured out. Perhaps we have been sent there, dispersed by the overflow of God. Or perhaps we live in those villages, where true prophets and false prophets arrive and depart. Doors are opened to welcome, meals are shared, good news and healing are received. Some doors are barred; unwelcome visitors are cast out. Some true prophets move on, leaving villages behind; some false prophets linger. In the villages, in the midst of life, lie the possibilities that the humble unexpected ones who have been poured out into the world as the *kenōsis* of God will be welcomed rightly, and that good news, healing, liberation, sustenance, and shelter will overflow in the abundance of God's grace and glory.

To be situated in the villages, as it were, suggests that persons cannot live before God by withdrawing from the rest of the world. To be sure, the villages of our day are more likely to be suburbs, paved in grass and concrete, or throbbing cities, alternately shining and devastated, than dusty hamlets. To begin in the villages, in the midst of daily living, underscores the entwined personal, social, and ecological vulnerabilities of daily existence. Promise and peril appear in mundane places and needs: on the villages' thresholds, on the road to Jericho, and in every hungry, thirsty, wounded, or homeless person. Figuratively if not literally, we meet true and false prophets, we receive good and ill at our doorsteps, and we find good news and healing as well as fear, resentment, greed, and destruction.

What should be resisted? What should be welcomed? Jesus' disciples have to answer such questions again and again. To receive and bear God is no simple matter of once and for all shaking off the world and closing the door on false teachers. It's not as simple as once and for all affirming ancient Christian teaching, belonging to the true church, or achieving Christian "identity." Such approaches fail to attend to the possibilities of grace and transformation that emerge in unexpected places, say, on the dangerous road to Jericho or on a segregated bus in Montgomery, Alabama. To be situated in the midst of life, in the crossroads of our day, is to dwell in ever-shifting, coercing, and enticing spaces. Messages and images flow ceaselessly, relentlessly, through the spaces of our dwelling. Promise and threat itinerate through global media and marketplaces; moment by moment persons choose to reject or to welcome unexpected persons and information. Moreover, to be situated in the midst of life is not only a matter of acknowledging vulnerability, the capacity to be harmed or to be healed; it is also a matter of confronting ambiguity, the mixture of good and ill, that is there.[12]

TURNED TOWARD THE GLORY OF GOD

As Paul and Irenaeus affirmed, God dwells among perishable, vulnerable creatures, strengthening them to bear the glory of God. To receive and bear the glory of God cannot mean somehow to deny vulnerability or to escape ambiguity. Salvation does not entail the defeat of human vulnerability and perishability, but it does involve real and ongoing change—conversion, repentance, empowerment, healing. In classic terms, salvation encompasses justification and sanctification and assumes that receiving and bearing the glory of God involves ongoing processes of conversion and regeneration.

Paul wrote that "the whole creation has been groaning in labor pains" and that "we ourselves . . . groan inwardly" (Rom. 8:22–23). He conveys the ambiguous breadth and depth of creaturely existence, and the related sense that possibilities for transformation are intermingled with the pain that creatures undergo. We creatures feel constraint and anticipate freedom; we are tinged by suffering even as we yearn for "the glory about to be revealed to us" (8:18, 21). The feeling of constraint and the anticipation of freedom sharpen each other; a horizon of glory and the reality of suffering illuminate each other.

In our day, the cosmos and its creatures still groan in affliction. What the earth suffers with global climate change, destruction of environments and cultures, warfare, and terrorism is more like pangs of death than labor pains. Its people suffer brutality and impoverishment. Persons suffer, too, from internalized corruption that can grow and debilitate like a cancer or an autoimmune disease. Patterns of domination and subordination, habits of deceiving and being deceived, and traces of hatred and fear reduplicate in language, practices, and psyches. Moreover, as individuals and as collectives, we are often incapacitated in various ways: we may become fragmented, disempowered, fearful, deluded, greedy; we may suffer moral dullness and inattention; we may lack generosity, courage, and imagination. Paul's diagnosis has this right: from its inmost depths to its vast interdependencies, creaturely existence is in need of repair, reorientation, and even rescue.

Salvation, then, concerns how God dwells among vulnerable, perishable creatures and lifts and strengthens faltering, fallible creatures to receive and bear grace and glory. Jesus and his disciples offered transforming words and acts that made the reign of God manifest at the thresholds of everyday needs and places. The grace and glory of God are made manifest within vulnerable life, transforming but not overtaking it.

Salvation addresses the integrity and destiny of individuals in their solitariness and interdependence and also the integrity and destiny of communities over time and across relations. In solitude, persons may most profoundly encounter the limits of their hearts, minds, and strength—and also possibilities for freedom and re-creation that were previously unimaginable. A man, wounded and helpless by the side of the Jericho road, confronts the viciousness and rejection of others, and the possibility of death. He also meets the limits of convention when a Samaritan, who has every practical and cultural reason to stay on the other side of the road, answers his cry for help. Blandina and early Christian martyrs faced the limits of their powers against the determinations of torture; Augustine's scrutiny ran to the edges of his self and memory; Luther wrestled with abysmal guilt and fear—these instances suggest vulnerability to God at the limits of existence. At the point of inescapable aloneness and the possible oblivion of individuality, these persons found creaturely existence to be limned and lifted by the grace and glory of God—by the luminous source of value and the vivifying power of existence.

The grace and glory of God—attested in creation, witnessed by the Prophets and the Law, praised in the Psalms, taught by and glimpsed in Jesus, shared in Christ, empowered by the Spirit, and mediated by the mercies of others—enable endurance, resistance, and enjoyment to be fashioned from "earthenness." The limits of perceptions, judgments, and imagination are met before the glory of the righteous, living God. Manifestations of grace and glory cause persons to regard their selves and world with new clarity, to realign vision and action. Faith emboldens us to resist diminishment and to persevere against fear, to enjoy and share life as a gift of God, to dare and dwell in a sturdier justice and a widening love. Forgiveness releases the burden of failures and faults, enabling us to straighten our backs, as it were, against the weight of tragedy and pain—our own, that of our time and place, that of other times and places. Love lifts us, binding us to God and one another, to the well-being of neighbors and strangers; it turns us around in reverence; it compels us to reach out in compassion, stretching beyond fears and self-absorption.

Salvation does not only concern individuals in their solitariness. Persons are accountable for the powers that they have been granted by the grace of God through the fates of history, economy, society, and family, and for their use of these powers together with others. Individuals cannot account for their own existence or act responsibly outside of their situation and their relations—whether relations of cooperation, acquiescence, or resistance—to the various historical, social, and global powers that determine and make possible a given life. Thus, in addition to addressing the individual in his or her solitariness before God, salvation must address the interdependence of human and earthly life, and their integrity and flourishing in God.

The Gospel stories of sending and receiving suggest that life shared with others before God is more like dwelling within a multidimensional field of ongoing tensions and conversions than a once-and-for-all transaction between an individual and God's authoritative representative. "Salvation" ought not be constrained to an intra-ecclesial process, and certainly not to a clerically centered transaction between individual and institution, sacrament, or dogma. Salvation is lived more than possessed and cannot be ensured by defending "the church" either dogmatically or institutionally. Moreover, it is the ambiguity of life, not finally the ambiguity of churches, that is at issue. It is not churches that need to be safeguarded, but rather possibilities for the integrity and flourishing of life before God. As the stories of sending and receiving suggest, God's grace and glory are made manifest in the midst of life—met on the Jericho Road, offered in a cup of cold water, shared as a meal, proclaimed in words of witness and acts of healing. The transforming reality of God is made present though neighbors and strangers, close at hand and afar, in local choices and larger connections. Salvation is offered in the midst of everyday life, *outside* the church, as it were. Recall that the multitudes are fed not so that they can stay with Jesus, but so that they can disperse back to their villages, where they too teach and feed. Liberation, hope, the overcoming of evil and sin, and possibilities for life's flourishing need not and ought not to be guarded and hidden inside the church or deferred to another world, but must be accessible in shared life and relevant to creaturely plights and possibilities.[13]

However, one cannot live, work, or worship before God apart from the companionship of others or from social patterns and processes. Moreover, persons cannot dwell *together* before God without shared language, action, traditions, and organizations. Through such shared means, healing and hope can be offered to a world that has suffered damage and continues to be at risk. In this manner, we can reaffirm the ancient teaching "no salvation outside the church" while questioning any particular institution's monopoly over the power of the gospel or over sacramental means of salvation.

We cannot save ourselves. By this I mean to express both the priority of healing and reconciling grace and its necessary mediation through shared life, work, and worship. Communities of faith do not grant grace or glory. Finally, God alone does. But we creatures depend upon the mercies of others to mediate the grace and glory of God. Patterns and places of shared life may provide means for facing anxieties and failings and through which acceptance and mercy are offered. They may become means by which the ambiguities of relationships and efforts are diagnosed and burdens of guilt and shame are lifted. They may empower resistance, grant freedom, and extend love. They may enable life to be received as a gift of God to be used, shared, and enjoyed with and for others. In any case, neither the Christian life nor the church should be construed as a bulwark against the world or an armistice zone from struggle and change. Rather, life before God is an ever-moving field of tensions and multiple conversions.

CHRISTIANITY AS CONVERTING MOVEMENT

When life before God is situated in a world that is threatened, damaged, and yet affirmed as a place of God's creating and renewing, neither a triumphalist nor a sectarian approach will suffice. In Christianity's first centuries, there was neither a simple convergence nor a simple opposition of "church" or "Christ" and "culture"; rather, there were diverse and shifting interrelations. Moreover, the complexity was in Christian teaching as well as in its interactions. Christians worshiped God as creator, who fashioned life from the earth and pronounced it good, while they also relied upon God as savior and healer of their threatened, damaged lives, and while they pressed on toward an even greater glory. Augustine offered the contrast between visible and invisible church to convey the ambiguity of present forms and the mystery of ultimate reality. Later theologians, especially Luther and Calvin, developed Augustine's contrast. However, as we saw in chapter 4, modern uses of the logic of the relation between visible and invisible, usually transmuted into dialectics of historical and ideal or of existence and essence, tended to prize invulnerability and stasis to the neglect of actual communities and possibilities of harm and transformation. The ongoing conversion of life with and for others before God cannot be theorized adequately as an opposition between two terms, a hierarchical ordering of two terms, or a static synthesis of two terms, whether those terms are defined philosophically or sociologically.

Some postmodern theorists and theologians contend that dialectical thinking in itself is the problem. For example, one feminist theorist has argued for the need "to get beyond, not only the number one—the number that determines unity of body or self—but also to get beyond the number two, which determines difference, antagonism, and exchange."[14] However, while a paradigm of difference may be able to depict multiple, shifting personal-cultural relations, it will not necessarily generate and support a critical complexity beyond the avoidance of essentialisms and dualisms and the celebration of indeterminate possibilities. Literary critic Hazel Carby charges: "The theoretical paradigm of difference is obsessed with the construction of identities rather than relations of power and domination and, in practice, concentrates on the effect of this difference on a (white) norm."[15] Similarly, theology can ill afford to obsess with constructing Christian ecclesial identities while denying vulnerability and evading ambiguity. If theology fails to address suffering and indignity—and the idolatries and ideologies that give rise to and perpetuate these conditions—because it focuses instead on the construction of identities, it will also fail to address the need for liberation and salvation that these conditions bespeak.

To thematize the transforming reality of God moving among creaturely existence, theology must be able to depict multiple tensions and conversions. H. Richard Niebuhr proposed a fully dialectical pattern of theological thinking in which contrasting positions neither simply oppose each other, nor readily resolve into each other, but continue to convert and generate among themselves. Such a tensive, ever-converting, generative approach yields a basic picture of life together before God as a field of tensions and conversions.

Niebuhr understood Christianity primarily as a movement, neither first as an (outward) institution nor as an (inward) bond of ideas or doctrine. It is a dynamic movement of relation and response among a living God and a living creation. The social reality of Christianity, the church, is present and yet emergent. It emerges through ongoing processes of conversion—processes that involve forgiveness of individual sins and reconciliation of persons, and also reconciliation across social, racial, economic, national, and religious groups. Conversion also involves reconciliation through history and toward the reign and purposes of God.

Conversion, Niebuhr insisted, is not substitution, say of divine *agapē* for human *eros*, or of the "church" for the "world." Neither is it transubstantiation, which likewise overtakes the integrity of finite existence. Rather, conversion involves reconciliation and restoration: "The gospel restores and converts and turns again; it does not destroy and rebuild by substituting one finite structure of life or thought for another."[16]

Niebuhr's depiction of conversion and of Christianity as a movement of ongoing conversion resonates with the account I have been developing, as well as with Paul's earthen vessel, with Irenaeus's notion of restoration, and with the best of Augustine's and Calvin's insights. It contrasts with triumphalist aspects of Augustine, with Luther's paradoxical view, and with sectarian options in ancient days and in our own. We can take a next step by looking at Niebuhr's method, which assumes this picture of Christianity as a dynamic, converting movement through history and across cultures, and as a present and yet emergent reality that is propelled and impelled by the creating and reconciling work of God.

According to Niebuhr, this movement cannot be represented adequately in terms of synthesis of God and the world (including Thomistic and Hegelian types), which assumes progress, or of dualism (either polarization or paradox), which implies stasis.[17] The best-known version of his argument is found in his 1951 book, *Christ and Culture*.[18] There his descriptive effort employed generalized constructs to group typical features of actual positions into "ideal types." It took Ernst Troeltsch's magisterial *The Social Teaching of the Christian Churches* as an implicit point of departure.[19] Whereas Troeltsch used two ideal types, "church" and "sect," to track the changing theological and moral ethos of Christian churches, Niebuhr presented a continuum of five ideal types. In effect, Troeltsch's church-type is represented in Niebuhr's spectrum of types by "Christ of culture" (accommodation) and "Christ above culture" (synthesis), while "Christ against culture" (polarization) and, to a lesser degree, "Christ and culture in paradox," correspond roughly to Troeltsch's sect-type. Note that the synthetic and paradoxical types already move beyond a church-sect dyad and thus are better described as mediating types. Niebuhr then mapped the very middle with a fifth type, "Christ the Transformer of Culture" (conversion). This type represents the best insights of Augustine and Calvin and is closest to Niebuhr's normative view.

In the opening and concluding chapters of *Christ and Culture*, Niebuhr referred to the dialectic of Christ and culture/s as an "infinite dialogue" that is constantly producing culture/s and "Christian answers" (that is, actual communities and expressions of Christian life and thought). "Infinite dialogue" signals a conversation that both goes on for the foreseeable future and also engages multiple and potentially unlimited perspectives. The book's approach was descriptive rather than normative: it conveyed rather than judged the nature and breadth of the dialogue. However, in another sense that approach already favored a conversionist stance, insofar as the dialectic or dialogue between Christ and culture is understood to be productive of numerous and changing answers (at least five typical answers that themselves point to "infinite" concrete answers), rather than a static opposition or paradox on the one hand, or a unitary synthesis or accommodation on the other. Although the terms of his analysis are two-fold—Christ and culture—the dialogue between them also constantly shifts the terms themselves. Numerous and emerging cultural and theological realities are always affecting each other. Niebuhr elaborated this approach elsewhere as the "method of polar analysis."

Through his method of polar analysis, Niebuhr attempted "to do justice to the dynamic character of that social reality, the Church, by defining certain poles between which it moves or which it represents."[20] Niebuhr viewed certain polarities, such as past and future or subject and object, as giving decisive shape to human life and thought.[21] By definition, neither term of the polarity is thinkable without the other. For example, subjects imply contrasts and relations with objects, likewise selves imply others and God implies a relation with the world or humanity. Polarities are not to be confused with polarizations. In effect, Niebuhr's own position destabilized polarizations of Christ and culture, God and world, self and others, by demonstrating the "infinite dialogue" between and among the polarities. Not all dyads are polarities, however. Niebuhr observed that life and death, God and Satan, being and nonbeing, good and evil, are *not* "true polarities" because one can think of life apart from death, God without Satan, and so forth.[22]

According to Niebuhr, the church and theology are dynamic realities that are generated among the (true) polarities of God and the world, selves and others, past and future, thought and action. In his 1957 book, *The Purpose of the Church and Its Ministry*, written in collaboration with James M. Gustafson and Daniel Day Williams, Niebuhr identified a series of six polarities relevant to the reality of the church: subject (social-historical reality) and ultimate object (divine reality, the realm and rule of God), community and institution, unity and plurality, locality and universality, protestant and catholic, and church and world.[23] The six sets of poles represent different sorts of relationships: for example, some like the subject-object and protestant-catholic polarities are more theological, while the community-institution polarity is more sociological. Thus there are intersecting relations between and among the poles, and the resulting multidimensional interaction is more like an ocean with changing tides and currents than like a channel flowing one direction. Existing between and among the poles requires constant "rebalancing."[24] Niebuhr depicted nondualistic, mutual tensions between each pole and among the other poles that continuously reshape themselves. This was more exactly how he conceptualized Christianity as a converting movement, a "permanent revolution."

Niebuhr's approach found perhaps its keenest theological expression in his treatment of radical monotheism. "Faith in God involves us in a permanent revolution of the mind and heart, a continuous life which opens out into ever new possibilities,"[25] he wrote. He described this faith as "radical monotheism" and depicted its revolution as being generated by dual movements toward iconoclasm and sanctification. On the one hand, as the prophets and Puritans affirmed, God alone is holy: "no special places, times, persons, or communities are more representative of the One than any others are." Radical monotheism rejects all claimants to truth except God alone and relativizes all values in relation to the One source and center of value. On the other hand, Christians have also affirmed "the sanctification of all things": all places, times, persons, or communities—indeed, all being—are created, and as such, good.[26] Radical monotheism finds holiness in all being and requires that all beings be "met with reverence" because they have value. Iconoclasm and sanctification can be compared to the polarity of protestant and catholic, or protestant principle and catholic vision.[27] The protestant pole moves "away from the world that is not God," rejecting "all that is little because God is great." The catholic pole moves toward the world, affirming "the apparently insignificant because God is its creator, redeemer, and inspirer."[28] Note that "protestant" is more than the negation of "catholic"—it involves affirmations of its own—and "catholic" is not merely an antithesis of some sort of apostolic Christianity that gave rise to a greater "protestant" synthesis.[29] I will offer a variation on Niebuhr's depiction of iconoclasm and sanctification, connecting them also to the themes of witness and welcome.

As the stories of sending and receiving suggest, the intersections and interactions of life before God involve "infinite" possibilities of devastation and transformation. Human creatures are not only vulnerable, but also ambiguous; neither progress nor regress is inevitable. Strategies of defense or invulnerability are inadequate to this reality. Life before God is rather a field of multiple tensions and conversions—before God, in the midst of life, with and for others, between God and creaturely existence, between past and future. In this ever-converting movement, the glory of God is present and yet emerging in vulnerable creaturely existence.

The phrase "life before God" already conveys the constitutive relation between creaturely life and God. Creaturely life is placed before God, and God is present in the midst of life as a living God who creates, redeems, and inspires creaturely life. Life before God is a moving space that is created and re-created by navigating between triumphalism and sectarianism, by attending to the actual and emerging realities of shared life with others before God, and by witnessing and welcoming the creating, redeeming, and sustaining work of a living God. The depiction of life before God as a field of tensions and conversions allows recognition of threats and possibilities. It also allows an affirmation that all earthly existence is before God and of God as creator, redeemer, and sustainer of all that exists. Yet earthly existence is also ambiguous. The next chapter explores what vulnerability means in a world that is already marked by suffering and devastation. I return to the relationship (often problematically construed) among undergoing suffering, being vulnerable, and living before God. I argue that life before God must "go through" suffering—neither valorizing suffering nor denying its reality—while resisting the degradation of life and of the living God, and while enjoying God and life as a gift of God.

CHAPTER 6

Vulnerability in a World Marked by Suffering

In spite of everything, there was in the life I fled a zest and a joy and a capacity for facing and surviving disaster that are very moving and very rare.

—*James Baldwin*[1]

In 1983 a group of Salvadoran *campesinas* met to "reflect on the word of God and to see what it was saying to us and what we could do in our communities."[2] Soon other groups of women joined them; they became known as the Congregations of Christian Mothers for Peace and Life. They organized their communities against the decimation of war. They started schools and literacy programs, collectives for food and health care, and sewing workshops. They confronted the army to demand their rights and, in doing so, mobilized entire communities to "defend life always." In the face of daily devastations, their response offered a means by which the people could "insist on deciding, until their last breath, how to live."[3] The Christian Mothers made no sharp distinction between "more theological" and "less theological" in their work and witness: the struggle for human rights, dignity, and survival was a matter of social and theological significance, of political existence and existence in faith, and of life and death.

Salvadoran theologian Jon Sobrino argues that when a community persists in works of love and justice despite repression, they recover the deepest sense of the *kenōsis,* or sacrificial self-emptying, of God.[4] Here we are close to what Luther meant by the sign of the cross as a sign of a holy Christian people. When the Christian Mothers chose to face persecution, even death, by organizing against a repressive regime, they attested to the reality of an encompassing power of goodness and justice. In their harsh existence, annihilation was possible, yet there, too, God was manifest. "Life is already present in death; the resurrection in the crucifixion; and fear need not paralyze but can be transformed into boldness through the Spirit," María Pilar Aquino explains. "The divine presence is felt within this tension between life and death, oppression and liberation."[5]

In our day, after death squads in El Salvador, after the organized brutality of slave trade, death camps, killing fields, and more, and in the face of ongoing torture and terrorism, we must reject any notion that suffering in itself can be a positive sign of the church or of human existence. Yet the fact of suffering is part of the witness of those who face and resist devastation; it cannot be disregarded. In this chapter I argue for a more complex interpretation of the relationship between suffering and life before God, one that focuses on vulnerability to destruction and to transformation in a world that can itself be understood to be marked with suffering. This interpretation reengages Luther on the sign of the cross and Calvin on suffering, and it suggests the need to train attention, imagination, and action to the presence of God and to creaturely need in a suffering yet glorious world.

A WORLD MARKED BY SUFFERING

With the Christian Mothers, we have come full circle to the passion of early Christian communities. The apostle Paul wrote, "We are afflicted in every way, but not crushed; perplexed, but not driven to despair; persecuted, but not forsaken; struck down, but not destroyed; always carrying in the body the death of Jesus, so that the life of Jesus may also be made visible in our bodies" (2 Cor. 4:8–10). In this passage the subject who bears affliction, perplexity, persecution, and death is a "we"—bodies plural and a collective body. Their trials already unite them and mark their common life. Their collective body also bears suffering in a way that attests to and bears God. We are marked, Paul writes, "so that the life of Jesus may also be made visible in our bodies." Irenaeus and other second-century theologians asked "how the frail mortal body might become a reliable container for the Spirit of God."[6] Irenaeus insisted that Christians "gradually become accustomed to receive and to bear God."[7] In twentieth-century El Salvador, where repression threatened destruction, the Christian Mothers practiced domestic arts that re-created their world. Like their forebears in faith, they were marked by survival wrought from adversity, by a confrontation with forces of destruction that became a testimony of the grace and glory of God. They became, in Renny Golden's phrase, "the crucible of communal survival."[8]

As we have seen, Luther and Calvin also wrote about Christians who were afflicted and persecuted for their faith. They contrasted the suffering of modest Christians to the abuse of wealth and power by civil and ecclesiastical authorities, while also reinterpreting Christian existence in relation to Christ's cross and God's glory. Although they sometimes veered toward the valorization of suffering, neither Luther nor Calvin construed the Christian life as involving a passive acceptance of suffering. They assumed that churches would have critical, transforming relations with the cultures of which they, for good and for ill, were part. They employed the sign of the cross to interpret and pattern those relations.

Can the mark of suffering or the sign of the cross have any significance for our day? Does it serve only to indicate vulnerability to devastation? Can it also be understood as pointing to the possibility of transformation for vulnerable, often ambiguous creatures? When persons and even the earth itself are scarred by enslavement, impoverishment, torture, and genocide, no simple answer will do.

A series of aerial photographs by Yann Arthus-Bertrand, taken in the corners of every continent, witness a world "marked" in graphic ways.[9] (A few years ago, huge enlargements of his photographs—think of small billboards—were displayed in public squares from Chicago to Kraków.) Many of his photographs depict a lush world, altered and inhabited by all manner of living things. A patchwork of Turkish rugs dry in an open field, a river of changing colors cuts a dramatic swath through trees, sun-soaked naturists populate a French beach. Viewed from the photographer's distance, many of these subjects appear in patterned images. The pattern that emerges in some of his work is, speaking theologically and in language that Arthus-Bertrand does not himself employ, the sign of suffering and brutal death on the spaces of earthly habitation. His photographs reveal an evidently "mortal" world that has suffered damage. One photo shows an impoverished mud-and-stick village, one- and two-room dwellings collapsed together in row after row; in another, cattle carcasses are strewn across a rooftop slaughterhouse, while their blood-stained butchers look up, surprised by the camera. In yet another view, B-47 fighter jets, painted in camouflage and angle-parked in precision, make a herringbone design across the Arizona desert. In other photographs, there are places of ecological devastation, places of forced evacuation, places of forced incarceration, places scarred by warfare and violence.

When the earth itself seems to be marked by affliction and brutality, what could it mean to affirm that life before God is marked by anything resembling the ancient sign of the cross? First and foremost, it ought to mean neither that Christians alone bear suffering nor that all trauma and brutality can somehow be comprehended, gathered up, in the cross. Rather, any reengagement of that ancient sign and its theological heritage must begin by acknowledging that Christian life is always situated, in fact but also constitutively, in the midst of a highly ambiguous world—one that is sometimes glorious and sometimes vicious, sometimes unfathomably so.

If no place in the world is left unmarked, some places are more affected than others. Arthus-Bertrand's project suggests that we humans must train our eyes—and minds, hearts, and strength—to the vulnerability and glory of earthly existence. His photographs serve to tutor attention and to nurture a range of responses: wonder, delight, compassion, sorrow, horror, guilt, outrage.[10] They help to attune us to brutality and beauty, to alert us to threats and possibilities, and thus to elicit appropriate relationships and response. As I shall argue next, a world marked by suffering requires not only recognition of vulnerability and accounting for damage that has been done, but also moral and theological attention to threats and possibilities that circulate in global interdependencies.

REENGAGING THE SIGN OF THE CROSS

When theologians write about suffering as a mark of Christian life and community, they take yet another step. They claim, in effect, that sites of suffering demand special attention—have a privileged place—as keys to interpreting the transforming reality of God. For example, Martin Luther trained his attention to vulnerable children and poor preachers, finding that their plight clarified the purpose of the church.[11] Suffering, epitomized in Jesus' death on the cross and manifest in the hungry poor, provided an epistemological key to reality: bringing the cross into central focus enabled a perspective that "calls the thing what it actually is."[12]

We can step back for a minute to reflect on "marks" and "signs" in contemporary cultures. Consumer cultures are pervaded by them, often very different ones from Luther's sign of the cross. Persons mark themselves with corporate logos and brand-name swooshes, body piercings and tattoos, wedding bands and clergy collars; they declare affiliations on hats and shirts. These marks clamor for attention, claim possession and belonging. Such marks can distinguish a person while also submerging that person in a group identity. We might say, "Sara's the one who always wears a pink ribbon," at the same time that the ribbon tells us, "Here is one of millions who have been affected by breast cancer." These marks can also indicate value. Dollar signs, four-star ratings, American flags, pink triangles, red crosses, and labels like "pro-life" and "fat free" offer interpretations of what has value and what does not.

I met a man in central Los Angeles who had "Florence" tattooed across his forehead, over his skull, and around his neck. He was literally marked as belonging to one particular L.A. neighborhood, to one particular tribe, if you will. His forehead bore a threat: any disrespect shown to him was to be understood as disrespect for his hood, and subject to violent retaliation in the prevailing culture of honor and shame. Tags marked the physical boundaries of his neighborhood as well, creating a realm of power—often violent power—within relative economic, interpersonal, and political powerlessness. Outside the neighborhood, his tattoos subjected him to the power of opposing realms, that is, marked him for death.

The equally vivid "tattoos" of some religious elite—tonsures, miters, flowing robes—and "tags" of restricted cloisters and corridors signal the power of an otherworldly realm. Consider, too, how a well-cut suit, precise haircut, and gated access may indicate expansive realms of economic, political, and social power.[13] Martin Luther said, in effect, that attention to such marks of power distorts reality. He charged that when theology attends to "glory"—that is, to pretensions of power, not the rightful glory of God—and neglects suffering, it will misconstrue reality and call "evil good and good evil."[14] Luther rejected such signs and argued for the cross as a more adequate point of reference for knowing what really is good and what really is evil.

In reinterpreting the mark of suffering and the sign of the cross, we are considering such a point of reference—an epistemological key—by which to orient judgments of what is creative and destructive, good and ill, holy and demonic, true and false. As we saw in chapter 2, the focal point of Luther's theology of the cross was surrender of pretensions to glory and knowledge more than suffering per se. "Christ crucified" indicated, among other things, the surrender of human feeling, efforts, and knowledge to God's favor, action, and word. As we have also seen, Luther called attention to the hungry poor of his day[15] and supported relief efforts. Ultimately, for him, it was the extent of their reliance on God alone, not the fact that they suffered hunger or poverty, that made them exemplary signs of the cross. Therefore, Luther's paradoxical view of the relation of divine purposes and human existence could negate the use of human capacities for responding to God, and thus could vitiate response to hungry people and naked children as such.

Any reinterpretation of the sign of the cross must direct attention to such devastation rather than diverting it to some supposedly "more theological" reality. Pain, want, and diminishment in themselves demand response from fellow creatures. In sites of greater, or at least more evident, suffering and oppression, life cannot be said to flourish. Persons may go hungry, ill-clothed, homeless, destitute, sick, and weary; they may be demeaned, victimized, tortured, or struck down. Other living things and environments may be endangered as well. Suffering ought to be encountered as a cry for mercy and justice that beseeches fellow creatures and indicts passive bystanders, as well as the powers that be. Figurative and literal cries for mercy show suffering as suffering and unmask brutality, tyranny, and indignity as such. In Luther's phrase, these situations "call the thing what it actually is" and necessitate theological thinking together with acts of mercy and justice.

Yet suffering is not always evident. Moreover, the problem is not only lack of attention to its reality. Symbols of power typically increase the perception of power, if not actual power—likewise for symbols of value. Pain, however, resists communication. Intense pain reconfigures the felt world of the person who suffers it, demanding the center of attention and shrinking all else along the peripheries. That reconfigured world may become incommensurable with the worlds of those outside the pain. When others suffer something that we ourselves do not, we may try to touch our fingers to their wounds and to enter the reality of their pain, but finally we are asked to believe or disbelieve the reality of their pain. Here Luther, following Paul, Jesus, and the prophets, was right to associate profound suffering with questions of epistemology and faith. As Elaine Scarry observed and we discussed in chapter 1, intense pain not only resists expression; it also "actively destroys" language. Pain is certain to the person who is suffering it, even if it cannot easily be shared with another. "For the other person," she explains, "it is so elusive that 'hearing about pain' may exist as the primary model of what it is 'to have doubt.'"[16] When the pain of others becomes believable, it can become the basis for collective response.[17]

Building on Scarry's work, we observed how early Christians "domesticated" torture's weapons by insisting on the agency of torture's victims till death and on the lasting power of memories of the martyrs for the church. The church became the artifact made by articulating and confessing the unmaking that reigns in torture and by preserving the agency of victims (martyrs), and in them the agency of the early church against the action of Roman authorities. Early Christians believed the terrible reality of suffering and torture; they also believed in the power of God to create and restore over against the claims of the empire to determine life and death. They affirmed the church as a place where vulnerable lives could be strengthened to receive and bear the power of God. Similarly, Luther, in writing about the suffering of poor Christians, claimed it as a "holy thing (*Heiligthum*)"—as an artifact, sanctuary, and defining practice that makes manifest, sanctifies, and forms a holy people.

Centuries earlier, the Hebrew prophets had interpreted the demand for response to suffering as none other than God's own call. Deutero-Isaiah offered these words as God's own: "Is this not the fast that I choose: to loose the bonds of injustice, to undo the thongs of the yoke; to let the oppressed go free; to break off every yoke. Is it not to share your bread with the hungry, and to bring the homeless poor into your house; when you see the naked to cover them, and not to hide yourself from your own kin?" (Isa. 58:6–7). Response to human need is the means by which divine presence is made known in sites of suffering. Sites of suffering are therefore also potential sites of restoration and thus of revelation and redemption. When resistance and compassion are offered, then human life is restored and renewed, and, Isaiah says, God draws near and is made known: "Then your light shall break forth like the dawn, and your healing shall spring up quickly; your vindicator shall go before you, the glory of the LORD shall be your rearguard. Then you shall call, and the LORD will answer; . . . Here I am" (Isa. 58:8–9).[18]

Like the prophets before him, John the Baptist proclaimed the presence of the Lord in places of oppression and devastation. The Baptist's calling of Jesus signaled Jesus' continuity with the prophets. Jesus' ministry with the poor and outcast proclaimed God's healing, vindicating presence. The cross—Jesus' crucifixion by imperial powers and the rise of courage and faith among his followers—can be interpreted within this ancient prophetic calling so that it signals the presence of the living, transforming God in the midst of persecution and oppression.

When the reality of suffering is believed such that diminishment and need are met with compassionate response, then situations of suffering may become places where God's grace and power are made manifest. Interpreted in this way, the sign of the cross can be understood as pointing to transformation that comes through the recognition of pain and response to it, rather than as a sign of divine favor for suffering or resignation. For instance, let us look again at south-central Los Angeles, not as viewed by rival powers, but directing our attention to places where the violently imposed definitions of warring gangs are resisted. I met the man, whose tattooed forehead signaled threat and marked him for death, at an agency that helps persons face and reject the definition of their lives and worth by gang culture. Through that organization's ministry, he came to reject a deadly economy of honor and shame. An alternative community that fostered dignity and responsible interdependence with others and that afforded experiences of love and forgiveness helped to reconstruct his sense of self and vocation. At the same time, he was literally changing the signs that marked him: he was having his tattoos removed through months of treatments that effectively involved second-degree burns.[19]

The sign of the cross can serve, then, as an acknowledgment that suffering is real, even if its depths are unfathomable, but that suffering itself is neither the purpose nor the determinative feature of earthly existence. Vulnerability *is* a basic feature of human existence, that is, vulnerability to devastation *and* to transformation is a basic feature. Human creatures remain open to being damaged and open to being transformed because they remain susceptible to being changed by others—whether the "others" are neighbors, strangers, or enemies, communities, economies, or the flow of media. These others, in turn, may become means through which God's grace and glory are made manifest. Even at the point where humans are most vulnerable to the deadliest organized brutality of fellow creatures, they remain susceptible to restoration and healing. To underscore this point, we can revisit and reformulate the affirmation of the second and third centuries, "*caro salutis est cardo*: the flesh is the pivot of salvation,"[20] as "*vulnerability* is the pivot of salvation." Not suffering—or "the flesh" or embodiment or emplacement—but vulnerability is the creaturely opening to God's grace and glory. It also opens the possibility of devastation.

This reformulated affirmation implies the necessity of a stance of critical consciousness that enhances moral agency in a world marked by suffering and that alleviates brutality rather than a stance of passivity or victimization in the face of suffering. Interpretations of the Christian life and the church that define them passively by the fact of suffering or oppression should be rejected. Moreover, important as it may be to acknowledge the suffering and threat that mark our world, that is not enough. Neither is solidarity with those who suffer. The claim heard in suffering must be heard as "call[ing] the thing what it actually is": an epistemological opening to the reality of indignity and degradation known as such in the gap before the transforming reality of God. The glory of God is made manifest in the restoration of creaturely integrity and dignity, and made possible through acts of recognition, mercy, and justice.

Suffering, brutality, and devastation are evident and yet hidden throughout the world. We creatures and the cosmos itself are vulnerable to harm and devastation. How will Christians situate themselves with others and before God in a world marked by suffering? Will they be distinguished by their efforts to dignify creaturely life and tend earthly flourishing? At stake is a proper sense of human capacity, agency, and responsibility before God and with and for fellow creatures on the earth. In the next section, I explore to what extent Calvin's interpretation of "bearing the cross" can help to train attention, imagination, and action.

GOING THROUGH SUFFERING

In interpreting the mark of suffering in relation to the transforming reality of God, I have been threading two challenges. First, I have rejected the notion that suffering is good or salvific in itself, while yet acknowledging the sometimes complex relationships among perception, valuation, revelation, and suffering. Second, I have accented attentiveness, responsibility, and agency in the face of suffering and rejected passivity and victimization, while yet recognizing that human powers are limited and that, ultimately, grace alone enables persons to bear the weight of their lives.

A third challenge meets us along with these other two. Can persons acknowledge life as not only vulnerable but also profoundly ambiguous and yet receive it as a gift of God? And, how are human capacities and incapacities entailed in receiving and bearing the grace and glory of God? Note that the challenge before us is not theodicy per se—to justify God's action in relation to suffering—but rather whether suffering and susceptibility to suffering ought to characterize or constitute life before God.

Our lives are not fully under our own powers and control. Persons may come to believe that their lives, rimmed as they are by brutal and glorious mysteries, are encompassed ultimately in an abundance of just and merciful power that they dare to call God. In believing, they may receive their lives, and the mercies that allow them to bear the joys and burdens of their lives, as gifts of God to be shared and enjoyed. However, Christians and their communities ought neither to presume power to evade suffering and struggle, nor to pretend the ability to master suffering—whether through mortification, submersion in the wounds of Jesus, or thoroughgoing rebellion against "the world." Rather, persons and communities must "go through" suffering, neither denying nor avoiding it but acknowledging its reality.

John Calvin sought a way of existing before God that neither falsely exalted the church for its own power and glory nor assumed its moral and spiritual perfection. To confess reliance on God alone, Calvin taught, neither placed persons triumphantly above "the world" nor removed them from it. In fact, to live before God in a corrupted and yet glorious world inevitably involves suffering and hardship. Calvin distinguished such struggle from striving somehow to obtain one's own salvation, in other words, from what might be called works righteousness.

Triumphalism and sectarianism take new forms in our day. We cannot merely recuperate Calvin's approach. However, his map between these tendencies remains instructive.[21] A middle way between triumphalism and sectarianism involves "going through" suffering—that is, neither immersion in suffering nor evasion of it, but acknowledging vulnerability as basic to creaturely life. To "go through" suffering involves resisting powers of degradation and indignity. At the same time living before God involves affirming God as gracious and glorious, fostering gratitude for life in its vulnerability and glory, and enjoying God and the life that God grants. Such joy and enjoyment, in turn, offer sustenance even while persons struggle to survive and flourish in the face of devastation and evil. This approach—through suffering, against the diminishment of God and life's integrity, and toward the grace and glory of God—can avoid triumphalism and sectarianism.

With these challenges in mind, we now return to Calvin's notion of bearing the cross, following it to its most problematic and its most promising insights. My intent is to explore vulnerability and transformation in relation to Calvin's thought, not to rehabilitate a divine pedagogy of suffering. However, training of attention and response is needed. I call for "going through" suffering by moving away from idolatry and indignity, in the calling and testimony of resistance, and moving toward the grace and glory of God in an itinerary of delight and gratitude.

CALVIN ON BEARING THE CROSS

Calvin did not instruct Christians to welcome suffering and to pursue martyrdom. Rather, he described sorrow and affliction as already part of human life. He rejected impassibility as an appropriate response to the afflictions that humans inevitably suffer, and therefore he opposed the Stoics of his day.[22] "We have nothing to do with this iron philosophy which our Lord and Master has condemned not only by his word, but also with his example. For he groaned and wept over his own and others' misfortunes."[23] Calvin's Christians also "groan":[24] they suffer disease, poverty, persecution, and loss, and "shall weep the tears that are owed to our nature."[25] It may be of immense human significance to sense that one's deepest sorrows somehow also register in the depths of the divine, but perhaps not enough. At least Calvin thought not. He was unwilling to leave history framed by fate. He taught that these very real afflictions, which in themselves may be brutal and evil, must be understood within a horizon of divine order and care. The real ambiguity of history, including Christ's suffering and death, ought to be viewed within, rather than outside of, the scope of divine providence. "Whether poverty or exile, or prison, or insult, or disease, or bereavement, or anything like them torture us, we must think that none of these things happens except by the will and providence of God, that he does nothing except with a well-ordered justice."[26] In effect, Calvin's instructions were: rest assured that your afflictions are not the travails of death but the birth pangs of a well-ordered justice, a divine order that extends beyond history as mortals can know it.

Is there more to life than to weep and to hope? Yes, according to Calvin. Even in the midst of profound suffering, God restores and teaches humanity. Christians who suffer "harsh and difficult conditions" that are in themselves "adverse and evil" nonetheless can know this as sharing Christ's sufferings. "By communion with him the very sufferings themselves not only become blessed in us but also help much in promoting our salvation."[27] Calvin elaborated a divine pedagogy of suffering by which God's people are tested and trained in humility, patience, and moderation. He instructed Christians to bear affliction patiently—that is, to bear patiently the pain and brutality that they already suffer, not affliction that they somehow seek—and to trust that "with the cross" God is indeed "promoting for our salvation." Calvin not only counseled patience, he also portrayed Christians as patients of suffering, and correlatively, portrayed suffering as a divine pedagogy and "medicine." In bearing suffering, he concluded, "we consent for our own good," and "the bitterness of the cross [can] be tempered with spiritual joy."[28] Note that joy comes not from suffering but despite it, from confidence in God's mercy.

Is this exactly the sort of acquiescence to and valorization of suffering that I have eschewed? Yes and no. Calvin rejected impassibility and absolute passivity while construing patience itself as a distinctive kind of agency. In contrast to the Stoic cultivation of apathy, Christians must constantly "train," "keep," and "pursue" patience in face of real sorrow and pain. He referred to the exercise of patience, moderation, and humility in the face of suffering as "bearing the cross." As we saw in chapter 3, Calvin interpreted bearing the cross as a pattern of living in which pride is emptied out and surrendered before a merciful, sovereign God. Christians are to "depart from themselves," to be united with Christ as the true source and power of their lives, and to express the pattern of Christ in their lives. Calvin's notion of bearing the cross can be understood, then, as a certain kind of consciousness and agency that is patterned in and empowered by Christ. However, it appears to be a relatively passive "agency," having to do mainly with taking one's place in the divine drama and with consenting ultimately to the mysteries—or vagaries, as it seems to many readers of Calvin—of divine providence.

The background against which Calvin developed this picture of Christian life must be noted. He contrasted Christian life that was intentionally patterned by bearing the cross to a clerically driven, institutionally controlled penance system that undercut individual responsibility and response to God. From Calvin's perspective, "it makes a great difference whether you teach forgiveness of sins as deserved by just and full contrition, which the sinner can never perform; or whether you enjoin him to hunger and thirst after God's mercy to show him—through the recognition of his misery, his vacillation, his weariness, and his captivity—where he ought to seek refreshment, rest, and freedom; in fine, to teach him in his humility to give glory to God."[29] We are inclined to ask how great a difference it really makes whether persons learn that they can never be contrite enough to extricate themselves from the wages of sin or whether they learn, through divine judgment and punishment, how miserable they are and finally seek mercy. But if we set these suspicions aside for a moment, a matter of great significance comes more clearly into view: Can divine mercy be known within vulnerable, ambiguous human life? Correlatively, can human capacities, fallible and faltering as they may be, be reoriented to the goodness and glory of God? It matters greatly for Calvin, as for our day, whether theologies support responsive, responsible life and its flourishing before God.

The optimal effect of Calvin's teaching was to counter self-deception, to dethrone false gods and tyrannical powers, to enable persons to receive life as a gift of God, and to orient the right and joyful use of God's gifts for the benefit of others. Despite our "puny capacity," Calvin taught, we *are* being transformed; though we cannot attain perfection, we "should strive and struggle" toward the fullness of God's glory.[30] At the heart of his vision of the Christian life was the conversion of the self and transformation of social relations through divine grace, restoration, and instruction. Conversion entailed a thorough destabilization and reorientation of consciousness and agency. According to Calvin, the first step in conversion is a confrontation with one's "puny capacity" to avoid sin and seek the good. Only when pride and undue self-concern are disrupted do persons come to the reorienting awareness that "we are not our own, we are God's."[31]

Without a doubt, profound suffering destabilizes selves and communities, disrupts expectations, and disturbs assumptions about God and the world. In itself, such suffering cannot be understood as creative, holy, or good, even if, in the broader scheme of things, pain and loss may serve other purposes and tragedy may be accepted as an inevitable part of creaturely and cosmic existence. That does not make pain and suffering constitutive of life before God. It is not bearing the cross but rather resistance to idolatry and indignity—resistance that involves the risk of being harmed—as well as delight and gratitude that ought to orient life before God. That said, to receive and bear God will sometimes take a cruciform pattern, lead through brutality, and end in death, as it did for early Christian martyrs and for Salvadoran martyrs, and for the hungry poor in Luther's day and in our own. In this sense, life before God may still be epitomized by "bearing the cross"—but then the cross is understood to mark not suffering itself, but rather, the transforming reality of God manifest at the point of need and pain.[32]

ALTERNATIVE PEDAGOGIES?

A focus on bearing the cross could have the effect of subduing human agency, of overaccenting human incapacities and thereby vitiating response to God and others. In interpreting the meaning of bearing the cross, Calvin emphasized training in patience, moderation, and humility. By contrast, I will emphasize resistance to idolatry and indignity and call for attending to delight and gratitude.

Calvin's accent on Christian patience and emptying out of pride correlated with a strong sense of divine providence and a strong confidence in the authority of Scripture when rightly proclaimed. Such hardy confidence may appear as overconfidence in a world marked by brutality, oppression, and more mundane threats and sorrows, and may become zealous religiosity that fuels the flames of intolerance and viciousness. A world marked by suffering suggests the need for more modest claims about divine pedagogy and power than Calvin presumed, yet also the need for caution about assuming that persons therefore teach themselves salvation. At the same time, the vulnerability of creatures and cosmos requires a greater accent on human responsibility and on collective response than Calvin articulated.[33]

Calvin's discussion of bearing the cross related to his doctrine of providence as well as to his teaching about the Christian life and redemption. He reformulated this doctrine partly in response to scientific discovery, rapid change, and the traumas of his day, as well as to his study of the Bible, especially the Psalms, and of classical philosophy and theology. For instance, he joined the doctrines of creation and providence, and he set aside the distinction between general and special providence. Without right knowledge of God as creator and redeemer, persons "can hardly avoid entangling themselves in inscrutable difficulties." Lacking such knowledge, he observed, persons might conclude that God is arbitrary and "throwing them about like balls," or they might not take their own responsibility and freedom with due seriousness; persons might be overwhelmed with adversity; they might feel "menace" instead of "joyous trust" in existence.[34] Similar questions persist today: Is there a good order to the universe? How free and responsible are human creatures? How can suffering be endured? Are joy and trust possible in life?

When suffering is subsumed under a divine pedagogy, theology risks mocking God and both the real devastations and transformations of creaturely life. The picture of a god who teaches by punishing—whether God is father or mother, benevolent or severe—is not adequate to the best insights of the Jewish and Christian traditions, including of Calvin's own thought, or to contemporary existence. Moreover, Calvin's pedagogy of bearing the cross arguably ought not be read as a theodicy—that is, as a justification of God's goodness in the face of evil and suffering—but rather as an account of how Christians who were already suffering persecution can be strengthened to persevere toward God's truth and righteousness. Notably, Calvin drew the line at seeking speculative knowledge about God's being and at defending divine goodness. His primary interest was the significance of the doctrine of providence for earthly existence: how it might enable persons to live with a sense of certainty and trust rather than a sense of arbitrary fate, so that they might use their freedom well, be responsible and fair in their relations with others, and refer their lives to God's care. (He devoted more pages of the *Institutes* to writing about the salutary effects of the doctrine for daily existence than to its exposition.) Calvin approached the "inscrutable difficulties" of his day by offering practical guidance for living rightly before God.

Calvin himself suggested that the Christian life was shaped in more ways than through a pedagogy of suffering. The *Institutes* itself is a pedagogical text, as was the Bible for Calvin: both texts clarify right knowledge of God and self and thereby elicit conviction, contemplation, understanding, and action. As we have seen, Calvin construed the church as a mother and a school of life, and God as a benevolent but strict father and teacher. Calvin's God was always tutoring and disciplining, and Calvin's interpretation of divine accommodation made teaching and learning central to the whole order of creation and redemption.

In his teaching about providence and about the Christian life, Calvin also outlined what might be called a pedagogy of gratitude and enjoyment. Human life may indeed be harsh, filled with pain, and disfigured by deception. Nevertheless, Calvin contended, it can reflect the glory of God and, through Christ and the Spirit, be united with God as the source of goodness. Human existence does not need to be bolstered by the accumulation of power and embellished with possessions. Rather, when all that we are and all that we have are offered gratefully and reverently to God, then self, others, and the goods of life are given their proper place and stature in relation to God. God's mercy shows where "to seek refreshment, rest, and freedom" once proper place is given to God. Human life, work, possessions, and relations can be received rightly as gifts of God and governed rightly through proper stewardship.

Right use of these gifts involves a persistent, other-directed impulse. "All the gifts we possess have been bestowed on us by God and entrusted to us on the condition that they be distributed for the neighbors' benefit."[35] Enjoyment and gratitude inform care for others and for common life. Others should not be regarded with contempt, and neither should their worth be judged. Rather, Christians ought "to look upon the image of God in them, which cancels and effaces their transgressions and with its beauty and dignity allures us to love and embrace them."[36] Other-regard was more than a matter of viewing others "as if" they were the image of God, attributing to them dignity and beauty that they do not actually possess. According to Calvin, the flow of love and regard is not merely directed "through" the other to God. Rather, "a sincere feeling of love" will guide Christians toward the well-being of others. Feelings of love and kindness toward fellow creatures attest to the intrinsic value of life. The perception of the goodness of what God provides in turn informs how Christians share these benefits with others.

Calvin did not limit the inclination to gratitude and fellow feeling to interactions with human beings. The entire creation evokes delight, offers enjoyment, and deserves proper attention. "Now if we ponder to what end God created food, we shall find that he meant not only to provide for necessity but also for delight and good cheer. . . . Did he not, in short, render many things attractive to us, apart from their necessary use?" At the same time, Calvin cautioned against abuse of these created goods. He warned about overindulgence in culinary pleasures, when "the smell of the kitchen or the sweetness of its odors so stupifies others that they are unable to smell anything 'spiritual.'"[37] These last observations suggest that true enjoyment may contain its own limits, a sense of what is "enough" and what is "too much." In addition, proper proportion and integrity are gauged in relation to God's own "sweetness"—one of Calvin's favored descriptions of God's goodness.

Profound joy can attune creatures to each other, the cosmos, and God; it can foster gratitude and inspire worship. Delight and gratitude can thereby serve to integrate and bind creatures with each other, creation, and God. By contrast, profound suffering destabilizes selves and communities, disrupts expectations, and disturbs assumptions about God and the world. One can reject the construal of divine action as fatherly punishment that accompanies Calvin's pedagogy of bearing the cross and the precedence he gives to this pedagogy, and yet agree that destabilization and reorientation are necessary for the Christian life. Moreover, indignation, sorrow, and anger experienced in the face of suffering may attune persons to injustice, falsehood, and evil. "A chief evidence of the grace of God—which always comes to us in, with, and through each other—is this power to struggle and experience indignation," Beverly Wildung Harrison observed.[38] A sense that all is not well can animate resistance to harm and brutality and lead to critical consciousness of vectors of destruction and transformation, which can then further inform what and how to resist. When indignation or sorrow demands attention and leads to resistance, it can also disrupt self-preoccupation and undue pride—but with less danger of vitiating human capacity and responsibility than a pedagogy of patience in suffering.[39]

For Calvin, the central dynamic of the Christian life was, first, to "depart from" or deny one's self and, second, to seek God's will and to advance God's glory.[40] Calvin addressed suffering primarily in relation to this dynamic: bearing the cross (undergoing suffering) provides training in patience, humility, and moderation that enables self-denial. In a world already marked by suffering, attention must necessarily shift to how Christians will be responsive to devastation and to possibilities of transformation in such a world. The valorization of suffering must be rejected and distinguished from the acknowledgment of vulnerability. Life before God must "go through" suffering. However, it does not require a pedagogy of suffering. Rather, attention and action can be directed by indignation and resistance on the one hand, and by delight and gratitude on the other. The final chapters develop these themes while leaving behind the language of pedagogy. They depict *ways* of living before God: a call and testimony of resistance and an itinerary of delight and gratitude. This depiction does not reject learning as important to life before God; rather, it signals distance from Calvin's portrayal of human creatures as relatively passive students in a world determined by a teaching, disciplining God.

WAYS OF LIVING BEFORE GOD

Properly understood, Calvin's approach was not a theodicy; rather he provided practical wisdom for living amid suffering and before God. This account of vulnerability and glory is likewise not a theodicy; it concludes by developing and depicting ways of living with and for others before God. In this chapter I have argued for reinterpreting the sign of the cross as pointing to vulnerability as the "pivot," open to both transformation and devastation, and as the situation where God may become manifest. Living before God involves going through suffering, moving in indignation and resistance and toward delight and gratitude. The final chapters develop these two ways.

The call and testimony of resistance, considered in chapter 7, and the itinerary of delight and gratitude, depicted in chapter 8, evoke the ancient ways of *knowing* God, the *via negativa* and the *via affirmativa*, but as ways of *living* before God. They draw together practical arts of living, working, and worshiping rightly with others before God. Like Calvin's pedagogy, these ways of living before God can destabilize privileged presumptions and attune attention to others and God. They train persons to recognize and to respond to what tears down God and creaturely dignity and to what restores and renews life as a good gift of God; they can place human (in)capacities in their proper proportion to God and to others. Resistance and delight/gratitude are closely related to the religious impulses that H. Richard Niebuhr referred to as iconoclasm and sanctification, and they can also be articulated in relation to early Christian practices of right witness and right welcome.

The call and testimony of resistance and the itinerary of delight and gratitude are interrelated ever-converting ways of living with and for others before God. They are, to use (and shift slightly) Niebuhr's formulation, polarities that cannot be lived without each other. These formulations assume each other; they are not options to choose between. I organize my presentation of each of these ways around depictions of individual lives: the way of resistance and testimony is explored in relation to the seventeenth-century Calvinist Marie Durand, and the itinerary of delight and gratitude is depicted in relation to novelist Paule Marshall's character Avey Johnson. These figures point to lived realities beyond their particular historical and fictional existences, such as to later Reformed resistance against anti-Semitism and Christian anti-Judaism, and to African American culture, respectively. Thus, in some ways, use of these figures also serves to ground and test the ways of living before God in historical struggles and patterns. That said, Marie Durand and Paule Marshall's character are not presented as exemplars; neither do they represent either/or choices. Rather, in the next chapters, these historical and fictional figures and their struggles offer means for cumulating metaphors and perspectives from previous chapters, and for portraying more vividly the interactive contrasts and relations among ways of living before God.

There is yet another pattern that informs the interpretation and interrelation of the two ways: the Protestant marks of the church. These ways of living before God align the Protestant Reformers' insistence on right proclamation of the gospel with the testimony and call to resist idolatry and inhumanity, and also align the emphasis on right worship with corporate practices that foster delight in and gratitude for the good gifts of life. In a world marked by suffering and in which creatures are vulnerable to devastation and transformation, such testimony and resistance and such delight and gratitude may provide a baseline for living with others before God.

Finally, by depicting vulnerability and transformation in terms of an ongoing tensive negotiation of multiple dimensions of existence—affective, moral, religious, and epistemic—I want to indicate that no aspect of existence should be understood to be "outside" of or unengaged by Christian life and community. All existence and every dimension of existence is before God. Every human creature is vulnerable to transformation and to devastation, although some, by virtue of privileged social and economic situations, may be less at risk to damage and/or better able to recover from devastation.[41] In a world marked by suffering, life before God ought also to be distinguished by attention to and care for vulnerable creatures and not merely by the fact of suffering. There is no secular exclusion: no creature ought to suffer cruelty, brutality, and indignity.

PART 3

Living before God

CHAPTER 7

Always Reforming, Always Resisting

This is the disciple who is testifying to these things and has written
them, and we know that his testimony is true.

—*John 21:24*

"Résister." She carved the word into the stone. Marie Durand, an eighteenth-century French Calvinist, etched this word into the chamber of the fortress in southern France where she was imprisoned for her faith. Resist—resist tyranny, it implied. She was not, herself, a political insurgent. Rather, Marie Durand was an activist in the sense that it took the full force of her life to resist powers that would bind her conscience and constrain worship of God. During thirty-eight years of captivity, she never stopped singing the Psalms, studying the Bible, and writing to secure provisions that she and the other women prisoners needed for their survival.[1]

In the mid-twentieth century, other French Protestants took "Résister" as a rallying cry. In a 1935 address, writer and antifascist activist André Chamson took up Durand's call in relation to the threats of his time and challenged church leaders to resist Nazi tyranny and their own anti-Judaism.[2] Subsequently, remote mountainous areas of France that once sheltered French Calvinists from religious and political persecution again provided shelter: this time to French-born and refugee Jews who fled Nazi brutality. Freedom fighters in the Cévennes, the stronghold of the French Reformed Church, sang of defying the German occupiers and writing "Résister" across the flags of France.[3]

Violence and viciousness persist in the twenty-first century, often wrought in the name of religion or ethnicity. Although most regimes and cultures can be measured in terms of more or less tolerance of religious, racial, caste, and cultural differences, few if any are exempt from some brutality. Even so, what is faced today is seldom so massively and exactingly a matter of life and death as what was met under the Nazis' systematic program of extermination.

However, tyrannies and idolatries have by no means been eradicated from twenty-first-century lives. We consume them, conform to them, are implicated in them by what we take for granted and fail to question. Any sense of the glory of God is already shaped by global financial realities and, almost inevitably, becomes entangled with the promotion of consumption as a dominant way of engaging the world. Any notion of God's truth is already shaped by the global flow of language and images and, almost inevitably, becomes appropriated and spun into byte-sized, media-ready information. Any construal of a well-repaired kingdom of Christ is already shaped by the patterns of relation and order in which we live and, almost inevitably, becomes distorted by grotesque rifts in wealth and entrenched patterns of power and privilege. The effects of tyrannies and idolatries often cumulate quietly, for example, in climate change and in inadequate health care, housing, and schools. The effects are deadly in dispersed ways, such as in pressures to consume and keep up, and in contaminated food, water, and air. Indeed, the questions of what and how to resist may be more difficult to answer in our day.

For Marie Durand and the twentieth-century freedom fighters, "Résister" was a testimony of faith, a testimony to how faith is sparked and oriented by resistance. It is marked by protest against the debasement of God and creaturely life, a protest that seems to surge from the depths and that reorients life and worship. To resist was also a call, a summons to transformation. By pushing back, resisting creates a sheltering space for vulnerable life. Resistance can therefore be understood as the corollary to the increase of love of God and of neighbors, strangers, and enemies. It opens a space of freedom where dignity, love, and justice might survive and grow.[4] In this chapter, Durand and the twentieth-century resisters stand in for countless and nameless others who have struggled in dire circumstances for survival, dignity, and flourishing. They serve as icons through whom we can gain and organize insights more than as paradigms against which to measure either other lives or effective social action. Drawing on their lived faith and on insights from the ancient *via negativa*, the chapter depicts resistance as a calling and a testimony to a gracious living God who appears in the midst of vulnerable life.

MARIE DURAND: "RÉSISTER" AS TESTIMONY

In 1730 Marie Durand was arrested by the French authorities for professing the "so-called Reformed Religion." She was not yet twenty, newly married, and living in her family home in Bouchet-de-Pranles, a hamlet just west of the Rhone River and about halfway between the cities of Lyon and Avignon. The year before, her father had been arrested and imprisoned. Although professing the Reformed faith was reason enough to be imprisoned indefinitely under French law, ecclesial and civil authorities were especially interested in the Durand family: her older brother Pierre was a Reformed pastor.[5]

The Royal Declaration of May 1724 had called for the execution of all preachers, the imprisonment of all who professed the Reformed faith, and the seizure of their property. Moreover, any parents whose children were baptized or married in the "so-called Reformed Religion" and anyone who attempted to comfort a dying person with it were subject to the galleys—to forced labor and life in chains aboard a ship—or to life imprisonment. Louis XV's advisers thought this decree would finally extinguish the Reformed religion in the kingdom. Instead, it inspired resistance.[6] In 1726 Pierre Durand was ordained at the first National Synod to be held in France in sixty-six years. He preached, administered the Lord's Supper, and performed four hundred marriages—all in homes and outdoor gatherings in secluded places, since all Reformed temples had been demolished or forbidden. When he eluded the authorities, they arrested his father, then his sister, and finally his mother-in-law. In 1732, after a sizeable price was put on his head and he was betrayed, Pierre Durand was arrested. At his trial he explained that he thought the Declaration's prohibitions pertained only to "those who foment revolt, against which I have always preached." He continued, "I do not believe it was ever the king's intention to forbid his subjects to worship God according to their conscience."[7] He was sentenced to death and is reported to have walked to his execution while singing the Psalms.[8]

To resist, for Marie Durand as for her brother, was not to revolt but to defy idolatrous encroachments on a person's faith in God, including those sanctioned by civil and ecclesial authorities. To resist was part of ordering one's life in response to God, for to worship God in all one's days and with all one's powers required eschewing false authority and worship. To resist was also to persist in seeking to live rightly before God despite persecution and threat of death.

Persecution was not new to the Durand household. Every French Protestant lived under threats of imprisonment, forced labor, and death, especially after the 1685 Revocation of the Edict of Nantes. Marie's father, Étienne Durand, marked one doorway in their house with the plea "Have mercy upon me, Lord God, May 1694." Two years later, he engraved "Praise be to God" over the kitchen fireplace. The Durand family grew up literally under the plea for mercy and the praise of God. In 1719, when Marie was not quite eight years old, soldiers raided a neighbor's home where a group had gathered to worship in the forbidden faith. The house was destroyed. Her mother was taken away, never to be heard from again, as were an uncle, cousins, and family friends. Her brother Pierre, who was probably leading the service, managed to slip away; eventually he would study for the ministry in Geneva. Soldiers occupied the Durand home for the next three weeks. After they left, Marie and her father made a life together. He would retrieve the Bible from its hiding place in the wall and teach Marie about Scripture, prayer, and the Christian life. He told her the story of the persecuted Calvinists. She memorized psalms of exile and learned to make the language of the Bible her own.

From her father, Marie Durand received a better education than most of her fellow prisoners would receive (two-thirds of the women did not know how to sign their names); indeed, she was probably better educated than most people of her time. Apparently she was also an indomitable spirit. She taught a child who was imprisoned with her mother and led others in singing the Psalms and reading Scripture. She corresponded with Paul Rabaut, a pastor in Nîmes, and with the Walloon church in Amsterdam, securing the prisoners' survival with needed funds and supplies. From that smuggled correspondence, as well as extant letters to her niece, we know more about Marie Durand's persistent faith. Biblical images and language suffused her letters, as did a sense of God's merciful providence, even when she suffered bitter disappointment.[9]

The plea for God's mercy and the praise of God's beneficent power that marked the Durand family home were written across the whole of Marie Durand's life. The editor of her letters, Étienne Gamonnet, comments that she "subscribed perfectly" to Calvin's sense of God as the fountain of all truth, knowledge, goodness, justice, judgment, mercy, power, and holiness.[10] Perhaps he was overly eager to portray her as an epitome of Reformed faith. Then again, perhaps we can better understand the sustaining source of whom Calvin wrote through Marie Durand's testimony. Unrelenting tyranny, confinement, suffering, as well as sometimes fleeting health and not-so-fleeting despair, stripped her life of all but the essentials. They did not, however, separate her from God, to whom she prayed for mercy and deliverance, even when she lost the capacity to hope in it, and whom she praised as the source of all that is, even when her own existence was nearly unbearable.

Yet what Marie Durand inscribed in the fortress tower was neither a plea for God's mercy nor praise of God. After these inscriptions she added another: "Resist." Resist what is not of God or of the reign and justice of God. In her testimony echoed John Calvin's protest that "we are not our own, we are God's" and Martin Luther's thundering "God alone." This sensibility of fundamental protest is one of the wellsprings of Protestant faith. It is more than revolt, more than negation, more than a political stance; it is an undeniable conviction, an orienting religious experience. "Résister" testifies to the surpassing glory of God and calls for the alignment of life in response. At its best, Christian life is oriented by these interrelated sensibilities of protest, mercy, and praise: to resist encroachments upon God and creaturely dignity, to rely upon the mercies of God and others, and to find life's fullness in glorifying and enjoying God.

In Marie Durand's lived testimony, the conviction of the grace and glory of God was inseparable from the conviction of human dignity. To put it differently, she confronted the violation of *both* tables of the commandments, the violation of the double command to love God and neighbor. She resisted both idolatrous presumptions about God and tyrannous distortion and disregard of human life. As Gamonnet explains, "To annihilate being is the law of all tyranny; to crush all intellectual and religious life that rises up, to break hearts at the same time as spirits and wills. It is against this attempt by the authorities, more than for survival or safeguard of heritage, that Marie Durand had to 'resist.'"[11]

A CALL TO RESIST IDOLATRY

To resist is not merely to revolt from authority, constraint, or human frailty. It is to push back against evil and harm, rejecting the sovereignty of "alien powers" and repelling destructive constrictions of self, others, and world. The call to resist is threefold. Marie Durand's word can be connected to John Calvin's diagnosis of idolatry and compared to the German Confessing Church's 1934 Barmen Declaration. "Résister" also calls for the denunciation of indignity and degradation, and thereby the diminishment of God as the source of life and center of value. Mid-twentieth-century French Protestants took up the call to resist as an expression of love of neighbors and strangers, specifically of persons who were subject to extermination as Jews. Finally, to resist requires that theology itself be subject to ongoing reformation.

Marie Durand's testimony exemplified the counsel that John Calvin had given two hundred years earlier: "See that you take courage to separate yourselves from idolatry and from all superstitions which are contrary to the service of God, and to the acknowledgment and confession which all Christians owe to him, for to that we are called."[12] As we have seen, protest against idolatrous political power dates to the beginning of Calvin's work. His 1535 preface to the *Institutes of the Christian Religion* addressed "a very great question" to King Francis I of France, namely, "how God's glory may be kept safe on earth, how God's truth may retain its place of honor, how Christ's kingdom may be kept in good repair among us."[13]

Calvin's polemical address to Francis I was itself already a response to the king's brutal retaliation to the affair of the placards in late 1534. (Whereas Luther nailed one copy of his Ninety-five Theses on Wittenberg's cathedral door as a call to public debate, this French group, working clandestinely under the cover of night, posted placards condemning the idolatry of the Roman mass throughout Paris and north-central France. Legend has it that the coverage was so thorough that the king awoke to find a placard posted on his bedroom door.) Francis responded to the affair of the placards as a political problem, a matter of anarchy, as well as a religious problem, a matter of heresy. Three months after the affair, in a grandiose spectacle that involved a procession of relics and the sacrament through Paris and high mass at Nôtre Dame, the king denounced the protesters and oversaw the public burning of six of them. Persecution intensified after that, causing Calvin to flee France.[14]

Calvin essentially agreed with the placards, namely, that the sacrament had become an idol and the Roman mass was false worship, and went on to say that the Roman church itself was false and its prelates greedy and self-absorbed.[15] In addition, by addressing the king with the question of safeguarding God's glory, Calvin tacitly extended the critique of idolatry from the church's worship and order to the political powers that upheld them. In his writings and through Geneva's consistory, academy, and magistracy, Calvin eventually provided his own answer to the "very great question" that he posed to the king. He showed how persons, churches, and the civil order can "advance toward holiness" by adhering to the gospel.[16]

Calvin found idolatry to be rampant not only among French clerics, but also across all human existence. As we discussed in chapter 3, for Calvin, worship is the characteristic that distinguishes human life. Although idolatry is the opposite of true piety, it shares an underlying dynamic: humans are prolific and tenacious in their idolatry because they want to worship. Humanity has "an awareness of divinity" or a "seed of religion," and closely related, a sense of the distinction between good and evil; in turn, these incline persons to seek to know and honor the author of all life and goodness. Yet however deeply this sense is embedded, persons' awareness of it remains vague and fleeting at best. Consciously or not, they fasten their seeking and honor upon something. Whatever they seek and honor unavoidably shapes their lives.

To acknowledge and confess God truly entails aligning one's entire life with God and resisting competing claims for honor and obedience. On their own, Calvin explained, human creatures can reach neither God's full glory nor their own. However, God reaches to humanity, accommodating its inability through the witness of Scripture, the gospel of Christ, the work of the Spirit, and the work of the church. While confessing reliance on God alone, Christians are to take responsibility for eschewing idolatry and aligning every dimension of their lives with God.[17] It was this notion of idolatry's tenacity and its dialectical opposition to true piety that lay behind Calvin's counsel to French Protestants that they separate themselves from idolatry and render due acknowledgment, confession, and service to God.

After Calvin's death, the French situation seemed to regress from holiness—at least by Protestant or humanist standards. Thousands of French Protestants were killed in the 1573 massacre of St. Bartholomew's Day.[18] Perhaps not surprisingly, the next generation of Calvinist leaders argued explicitly for political resistance to Catholic monarchies. "Instead of being called to overturn statues and altars," historian Carlos Eire explains, "Christians were now being called upon to overturn governments."[19] The relation of Calvin and Calvinists to political resistance and revolution has been much debated by historians and political theorists; it cannot even begin to be summarized here. Nevertheless, two basic observations have particular relevance for contemporary life before God. First, "Résister" must be heard as a call to engagement, not a political program or polity. Second, this call assumes an underlying diagnosis of idolatry.

At their best these Reformers offered a call to resist idolatry with confession and political engagement, not a program for political transformation.

The call to resist poses anew Calvin's "very great question" about safeguarding God's glory, honoring God's truth, and keeping Christ's kingdom. By contrast, the assumption of an unchanging polity or political theology is fraught with peril. Theocratic ambition has too often arisen within Calvin's own tradition: when Reformed authorities have sought to rule church, society, or state as though they had sole purchase on the rule of truth and righteousness, they themselves have become tyrannical. Witness harsh condemnations of outsiders, witness the restriction of women to spheres of domesticity, and, more particularly, witness Calvin against Servetus, Puritan witch trials, and South African apartheid. These instances are perhaps easy and even over-cited targets of criticism, but they nonetheless serve as sobering cautions. Calvin's "very great question" cannot be answered for once and for all; it must be asked again in every age and situation. Each new situation requires Christians to take their place in history seriously, to take responsibility for the power that they have, and to work for justice and truth within the institutions and relationships of which they are part.

Four hundred years after the affair of the placards, the German Confessing Church renewed the call to lived confession with their 1934 Theological Declaration of Barmen, issued amid the rise of National Socialism.[20] They declared the independence of the church from "any alien voice" and proclaimed its "sole dependence" on God and on the Word of God as the source of truth. Barmen repudiated the idea that the state "should and could become the single and totalitarian order of life" and thus usurp the church's vocation.[21] That the Confessing Churches understood themselves to be resisting the alien voice and illegitimate claims of National Socialism and the Reich Church was obvious enough, if never explicitly stated—obvious enough that Barmen became a rallying point for the churches' struggle against Hitler and obvious enough to mark the signers of the declaration in the eyes of the secret police.

According to Confessing Church theologians Karl Barth and Dietrich Bonhoeffer, to confess the gospel and the lordship of Christ entailed an active, uncompromising stance. Under a totalitarian regime that demanded ultimate loyalty, Confessing Church members eventually faced the same alternatives that the persecuted French Protestants had: either to flee or to remain and resist false worship, even at the cost of one's life. The option that both groups rejected was to avoid persecution by professing inner allegiance to what they understood to be the true faith while outwardly appearing to be faithful to the "alien" power.[22] As Carlos Eire explains, "Calvin would admit no separation between private belief and public behavior." For Calvin's political heirs, "this principle of confessional integrity went beyond mere passivity: It also called for an aggressive public rejection of the many social norms that supported 'idolatry.' "[23] This Reformed principle helps us to understand the power of Barmen's confession as well.

Yet for all of its power to orient courageous protest, the Barmen Declaration had serious shortcomings. Its protest remained church-centered, focused on the constriction of the church and Christian conscience. It evaded explicit condemnation of Hitler and Nazi totalitarianism and, as Bonhoeffer and later Barth acknowledged, it did not even approach the so-called Jewish question. It failed to protest the most heinous aspect of the Nazi regime: its propagation of virulent hatred of Jews and other "outsiders," a propagation that would escalate, horrifically and relentlessly, in a few short years into a massive, systematic program of extermination. We must ask, albeit with the clarity of hindsight, whether Barmen's understanding of idolatry was broad enough, whether its theology effectively removed God from history, whether it truncated the moral heart of Jewish and Christian traditions by emphasizing the first table of the law to the diminishment of the second, and to what extent its focus on hearing the Word of God alone hindered its ability to hear the claims of suffering humanity. These questions lead to the second aspect of the call to resist.

A CALL TO RESIST THE DENIAL OF HUMAN DIGNITY AND THE DEGRADATION OF LIFE

The call to resist must be understood as a call not only to defy encroachments upon God, but also to resist the denial of human dignity and the degradation of all life, and thereby the distortion of God as the source of all that is and the center of value. The Nazi regime was not merely idolatrous because its "alien power" contravened the authority of God and the church, but also because it presumed to determine the worth of life, to define what was worthy of worship and honor, and to judge between life and death. The death camps represented, among other things, a pernicious and thoroughgoing denial of human dignity and thus a denial of the God of life.

The commitment to the worth and dignity of creaturely existence ought not to be separated from the confession of the grace and glory of God. Each commitment must correct and extend the other: resistance to idolatrous limitations of God must inform an expansive notion of earthly integrity, and resistance to hatred and indignity must likewise shape a capacious understanding of God. Marie Durand resisted both idolatrous presumptions about God and tyrannous distortion and disregard of human life. She confronted the violation of *both* tables of the commandments, the violation of the double command to love God and neighbor.

The full import of "Résister" is suggested by the French Reformed who rallied to the call in the mid-twentieth century. They resisted the power and values of the Nazi (and Vichy) regime and also its degradation of human life and dignity. Furthermore, their solidarity with the persecuted Jews led them to deepen their understanding of the love of neighbor, to address love of enemy by defying the destruction of life, and to confront the limitations of their own faith.

As I noted at the beginning of this chapter, in 1935 writer and antifascist activist André Chamson took up "Résister" in relation to the threats of his time, calling the Reformed Church in France to resist both the Nazi threat and the scourge of Christian anti-Judaism. By the early 1940s, remote mountainous areas that had once sheltered French Protestants from persecution were defying Vichy rule to shelter French-born and foreign-born Jews. As Nazi atrocities multiplied, Reformed pastors and people intensified their efforts and joined with other persons of goodwill to make the region of the Cévennes, the population center and historic stronghold of the Reformed Church, an area of refuge.

In and around the Cévennes, the struggle and faith of the French Protestants under persecution are remembered vividly, not only within the Reformed Church, but also in the culture in general. According to historian Philippe Joutard, this memory resulted in "an instinctive solidarity" with the persecuted, particularly with the Jews. He views this sense of solidarity as "the decisive phenomenon" behind fairly widespread Cévenol efforts to shelter Jews from capture and likely death.[24] Many in the isolated Cévennes had never met a person of Jewish faith or ancestry; they knew the Jews rather as the people of the Bible and as those whose psalms of suffering they had sung as their own. But with knowledge of deportation centers as near as Lyon and Toulouse and with word of the death camps, "the Jewish question was no longer simply a biblical question, but a reality," one Cévenol pastor explained, a reality that addressed their consciences.[25] We might call the profound recognition of human vulnerability and dignity and the deep revulsion at the persecution of the Jews "an awareness of divinity" and a testimony of conscience.

Felt solidarity was decisive, but there were other factors that inclined the Cévenol pastors and people to resist. These factors are instructive for any adequate response to the call to resist. First, the Cévenols obtained the best information possible about the nature of the threat: information channeled through Switzerland told them of Hitler's "final solution" before many others knew of it or were prepared to believe it. Second, their leaders, especially Marc Boegner, President of the Protestant Federation in France, kept up the call to resist from the mid-1930s to the end of the war. Third, congregations, neither funded by the state nor subject to a vast ecclesiastical hierarchy, were autonomous enough to pursue resistance activities at their own initiative, without need for authorization from a bureaucracy or hierarchy, and with needed secrecy. Fourth, they had some time, and they used it to prepare themselves: already by 1933 they started to address the Nazi threat and the so-called Jewish question and did not come under Vichy rule with its censures and deadly sanctions until 1940. Most of all, they deepened their "instinctive solidarity" with biblical study and theological reflection and, through these, readied themselves for active solidarity and resistance.

Biblical texts were engaged freshly in light of the situation, and much of this engagement served to unmask Christian anti-Judaism. Among the texts that figured prominently was the parable of the Good Samaritan with its question of who is my neighbor. North of the Cévennes, in the village of Le Chambon that would shelter hundreds, possibly thousands, before the war's end, the Protestant temple had "Love one another" inscribed across its doorway. Pastors Éduard Theis and André Trocmé preached that nations and individuals must resist evil (le mal, which also connotes "harm") with all their power, and particularly the hatred and destruction that the Nazi regime represented. Philip Hallie explained that "the sermons did not propose a neat blueprint for fighting hatred with love." Rather, beginning in the late-1930s, Theis and Trocmé preached "an attitude of resistance and of canny, unsentimental watching for opportunities to do something in the spirit of that resistance." The village's mayor and a dozen other parishes in the area were also attuned to the threats and to the moral challenge to respond that loomed on the horizon. And "opportunities soon came" as Hallie elaborated in his account of Le Chambon's resistance, *Lest Innocent Blood Be Shed*.[26]

Pastors in the Cévennes deepened their felt solidarity and readied themselves for active resistance also by thinking theologically about tyranny and by examining underlying theological and cultural assumptions.

Articles in the *Revue du Christianisme social,* a journal well circulated among Reformed pastors, had addressed the German situation and Christian anti-Judaism regularly since 1933, as had a more popular church publication. Karl Barth's prophetic "No" was much admired and his writings widely read, but they were also met with vigorous critique. At dispute was never the denouncement of Nazi tyranny, but the theological grounds for doing so. French theologians questioned Barth's "métaphysique de l'Intemporal," his "disdain of history," his construal of God as "pure will" who is seemingly "a rigid vertical line that nothing can bend," and an apparent "misanthropy," in the strict sense of a distrust of all people.[27] In contrast to Barth's revelationism, these theologians and pastors engaged the Bible and theology to immerse themselves in the events of the day, struggling to wrest meaning from and wage resistance to the hatred and inhumanity that were so evident around them.

In our day, after the death camps, after the formal end of global colonialism, and in the face of ongoing torture and terrorism, we must continue to cultivate a sense of solidarity with suffering humanity, to deepen it by critical biblical and theological engagement, and to sharpen it not only through a Calvinist "idolatry critique," but also through the use of contemporary critical theories. This felt solidarity is perhaps the "awareness of the divine," the testimony of conscience, that is most relevant in our day. But, unlike approaches that foster distrust of deep, albeit often-fleeting, sensibilities of the good and the divine, we must use Scripture, reason, theology, and concrete action to magnify as well as to interrogate these sensibilities. Through these means we can further an understanding of vulnerability and ambiguity, nurture repulsion of injustice and evil, and seek the glory of God made manifest in creaturely flourishing.

A CALL TO CRITIQUE THEOLOGY'S OWN IDOLATRIES

The French Reformed pastors found that to receive the call "Résister" required that their own theologies change. They had to uproot anti-Judaism and anti-Semitism from their own faith and culture and had to turn their heritage of protest back on their own theology. To take up "Résister" today likewise requires internal critique and continual reformation of theologies, institutions, and practices. As Calvin reminds us, idolatry is both commonplace and extremely dangerous. Contemporary idols may be intermingled in the way we speak and think, with where we live and work and worship, in what we buy and eat. We uphold and advance these idols in everyday language and the most prosaic of activities. Our inmost desires become corrupted: I may become preoccupied with possessing and consuming and fail to attend to neighbors or strangers. I may not consciously choose to affirm white privilege or to perpetuate poverty, to give other examples, but I nevertheless participate, advertently and inadvertently, in patterns of engaging the world that effectively uphold such choices. By being so "honored," these idols accumulate the power to describe and organize "reality," and thus they are, in a manner of speaking, more able to compel us to bow down. Christians and their communities must therefore extend their resistance to themselves and their theologies, to the assumptions, falsehoods, and injustices in which they are implicated, even as they are resisting other idolatries and tyrannies.

Resistance to idolatry—without and within Christian theology, institutions, and practice—has been foremost among the concerns of feminist and womanist theologies. For example, social ethicist Beverly Wildung Harrison sounded the classic Protestant theme of divine sovereignty, but in a way that questioned problematic construals of divine authority. God is "beyond our manipulation and control," she wrote, but "does not aspire to control us or require our obeisance."[28] Harrison has exposed theological complicity with cultural, racial, and gender dominance, with consumerism and economic exploitation, with imperialism and colonialism, and with misogyny and homophobia. Theologian Delores Williams has thematized resistance as integral to Christian faith by exploring Hagar's narrative in relation to those of contemporary African American women as narratives of survival and resistance.[29] Katie Geneva Cannon has examined how enslaved African Americans and their descendants have survived the dehumanizing "blight" in the dominant culture and religion by creating a counterculture through folklore, spirituals, and prayer.[30] Mary McClintock Fulkerson has read the places and practices of one congregation for signs of grace and redemption that appear in the ambiguities of everyday life.[31] In effect, they are charting new ethnographies of idolatry and right worship.

Mary Daly's classic 1973 book, *Beyond God the Father*, put the matter of idolatry simply: "If God is male, then the male is God." Her pithy statement implies all three aspects of idolatry. First, defining God as male is idolatrous in the narrow sense: the divine is falsely and reductively pictured as male. Second, elevating the male and thereby subordinating women is tyrannous and presents a false picture of humanity.

And third, any theology that endorses this definition perpetuates and promotes a false picture of "reality."[32] Daly focused on how theologies have fixed and objectified "God" in static symbols, especially but not only male ones, and how these theologies in turn have legitimated oppression and subordination. She saw the women's movement as an ontological rupture that broke through static symbols.

Iconoclasm has also featured prominently in Sallie McFague's work. Seeming to take a page from Calvin himself, she notes that persons forget that the metaphors they use for God are metaphors. They forget as well that metaphors inevitably limit understanding and thereby effectively limit God. Language about "God" is necessarily metaphorical and is therefore always finally inadequate.[33] Metaphors and models that may have been relevant in one context can become irrelevant, idolatrous, and even dangerous in another. Ways of speaking about God are always having to be re-formed. In McFague's work, the rejection of patriarchal, triumphalist, and imperialist models of God informs an expansive notion of human well-being as inseparable from the well-being of all life. At the same time, resistance to the idolatrous degradation of life, and a correlative reverence and care for life as a gift of God, inform capacious models of and for God.

Implicit in McFague's approach is a point worth making explicitly. While any metaphors or discourse may become idolatrous, use of metaphors itself is not. Metaphors and other discourse provide necessary means for conveying and responding to the grace of God.[34] Economies and polities, language, knowledge, and relations can be means for both losing and gaining a sense of God's glory, for both denying and being granted some comprehension of truth, and for both tearing down and striving toward "the good repair" of Christ's kingdom.

The call to safeguard the glory of God, to seek the truth, and to align thought and lives to what is worthy of honor and reverence, is a never-ceasing though always proximate task. Theology is more likely to become idolatrous when it pretends to somehow possess final truths apart from historical and cultural influences. Theology's work ought to be construed more modestly, as neither the achievement of a closed system nor with a final point of closure, but as requiring ongoing reformation and resistance.[35] At their best, theologies emerge from and fund a continuous this-worldly revolution.

If Marie Durand did not indicate how "Résister" must also be directed to her own Reformed theology and faith, this reflexive aspect of the call to resist was already implicit in the slogan *Ecclesia reformata sed semper reformanda*, "the church reformed but always being reformed." Beverly Harrison observes that this "continuously reforming theological stance . . . was, at best, our tradition's rhetorical ideal, even when honored more in the breach than in the practice."[36] Feminist and womanist theologians have tried to honor this stance, not only in the breach, but also in the practice of resistance, as did Marie Durand and mid-twentieth-century resisters. Moreover, they did so by making explicit, in their theologies and in their lived confession, the connection between the call to resist and the calling to be reformed. If we exegete these old slogans well for our day, "Résister" and "semper reformanda" can continue to spark and guide a venturesome faith and theology that never cease their attempt to bear truth amid the ravages and glories of life.

STRUGGLE AND A *VIA NEGATIVA*

Marie Durand's day-to-day resistance was waged at the most basic of levels in her struggle to eat, keep warm, be clothed, maintain community and communication, and worship without constraint. She took nothing for granted but the constancy of God and the responsibility to do what she could. She fashioned a way to survive that engaged her intellect and faith, strengthened her sense of self, widened her community through correspondence, and eventually allowed her actions to reach through history. The rest of this chapter considers how the practice of resisting shaped Marie Durand and, by extension, can shape other persons and communities. A way of always reforming and resisting can be compared to the ancient way of knowing God, the *via negativa*. In relation to it, I note the harsher and most often deadlier struggles faced in the Nazi death camps and as depicted by Primo Levi. His remembrances of Auschwitz portray resistance at its limits and also issue a severe caution against romanticizing "struggle."

To be always reforming and always resisting is a stance necessary for shared life before God and essential in the face of global threats and risks. It suggests a dialogical, ever-converting, ever-being-converted stance—an ongoing struggle—rather than a static state. We began this book with the persecution of early Christians, Irenaeus's depiction of the struggle "to receive and bear God," Augustine's "ache of discord," and Luther's wrestle with affliction and God. Calvin concludes that "in this life we are to seek and hope for nothing but struggle."[37] The language of "struggle" recurs throughout feminist, womanist, Black, and liberation theological accounts.[38] It typically connotes both an element of hardship or suffering and also activity to survive or change that situation over against passive acceptance of it. To picture human existence as struggle coheres with the call to resist and also with the underlying experience and theological judgment that creaturely life is vulnerable to damage and to healing, and that it is ambiguous, always being corrupted and yet being made glorious. In addition, to speak of struggle accents how moral and theological understanding are rooted in historical, material activity rather than in biological gender or identity. Persons and communities are thereby located in their engagement with others in the world rather than being identified by attributes or characteristics. In effect, "struggle" offers a metaphor for being situated and for situating one's self historically, politically, and personally.

At its best, struggle as metaphor and depiction preserves the particularities among many concrete efforts while also indicating shared goals among them. Used in this way, the shared language of struggle can relate specific efforts to other perspectives and involvements, and also relate intellectual work to real hardships and grassroots activism.[39] In this chapter, the language of struggle suggests analogies—of lived confession, of vulnerability to idolatry and tyranny, and of survival and transformation—among the experiences and efforts of Marie Durand, mid-twentieth-century resisters, womanists and feminists, and the readers. When "struggle" is used to refer to an always reforming and resisting stance, to connect intellectual work to political activism, and to indicate analogies among situations of vulnerability and agency, then it remains a crucial metaphor for interpreting life before God.

Yet struggle is not merely a metaphor (if good metaphors are ever "mere"). It points to deadly threats, real vulnerability, and tenacious hope for survival and transformation. Marie Durand confronted life-altering threats and profound loss. By the time she was twenty-one, her mother had disappeared, her brother had been executed, her father and her new husband were imprisoned, and she had been removed from the small hamlet of her birth and youth to a stone fortress tower in another region of France where, because she refused to abjure her faith, she would spend virtually her entire adulthood. Is love of God and of neighbors and strangers possible in the face of such loss? Can trust and loyalty continue to take root? Can hope persist? Very few letters survive from the first twenty years of her imprisonment. Perhaps she was able to write to her father while he was in prison and then after his release and before his death in 1749. Perhaps after her brother's execution she corresponded with her exiled sister-in-law until her death in 1747. Even supposing she was able to sustain communications through those years, she had been cut off from the nexus of persons and place that held her past and thus, to a significant extent, was cut off from her past existence itself. She also lost any future she might have hoped for and possibly even the hope of having any future to anticipate. Authorities did not expect persons or words to survive such repression, let alone that a call would rise, "Résister."

The interdependence of resistance, rich relations with others, and integrity become evident when their possibilities are imperiled. "Imagine a man who is deprived of everyone he loves," Primo Levi wrote in *Survival in Auschwitz*, "and at the same time of his house, his habits, his clothes, in short, of everything that he possesses: he will be a hollow man, reduced to suffering and needs, forgetful of dignity and restraint, for he who loses all often easily loses himself."[40] To enter Auschwitz, Levi explained, was to enter a system that "had as its primary purpose shattering the adversaries' capacity to resist." (The adversaries in this case were new arrivals to the camp.) It was to enter a world of "indecipherable" uncertainties where it was extraordinarily difficult to stand in relation with any other person or cause:

> The enemy was all around but also inside, the "we" lost its limits, the contenders were not two, one could not discern a single frontier but rather many confused, perhaps innumerable frontiers, which stretched between each of us. . . . There were instead a thousand sealed off monads, and between them a desperate covert and continuous struggle.[41]

In this terrible world of a thousand fronts of striving, there was no "we" to draw a common line of resistance, and there was no common resistance to create a "we."

In the death camps, persons became utterly encompassed by and abject to Nazi power; they were reduced to the choice of existing at all costs versus not existing. To use the language of fourth-century theologian Gregory of Nyssa, "All footholds have been left behind. There is nothing to 'take hold of,' neither place, nor time, nor dimension, nor anything else, nothing on which thought can take its stand."[42] In the death camps, there was virtually "nothing on which to stand"—no allies, no certainty, no memory, no agency reliably provided a foothold. However, the void that opened in the camps was not the Deity's surpassing mystery, as it was for Gregory and other theologians whose search for knowledge of God led them along the *via negativa*. It was Nazi power that appeared as abysmal: able to swallow up past, present, future, self, world, and God.

In the ancient *via negativa* (apophatic theology), knowledge of God begins with negations that draw attention to divine incomprehensibility.[43] Gregory of Nyssa said that at most we can be aware of God's presence; we can never know the divine essence. "The true knowledge and the true vision of what we see consist precisely in this—in not seeing: for what we see transcends all knowledge, and is everywhere cut off from us by the darkness of incomprehensibility."[44] The path of surrender of conscious effort before the depths of divinity contrasts sharply with the negations effected by mass technologies of degradation, torture, and extermination. In the latter, resistance is defeated, not surrendered. Moreover, a different darkness of incomprehensibility threatens: the overwhelming immanence of evil.[45] Yet in both, understanding must somehow begin by knowing the incomprehensibility in which one stands.

The ancient *via negativa* was, as its name implies, a *way* of knowing, that is, a way of knowing limits, not knowledge received once and for all. The twentieth-century Orthodox theologian Vladimir Lossky explained that apophaticism is a religious attitude toward divine incomprehensibility that does not start with or stop at the attainment of doctrine. It involves the dissolution of dogma into a plenitude that dogma cannot grasp and the constant and life-encompassing transformation of the creature before God. At best, "the mind feels the ungraspable escape its grasp." The problem of knowing is twofold: first, we cannot sense the full mystery of the divine and, second, our appropriation of what we do sense is even more difficult. As Basil the Great put it, "Our intellect is weak, and our tongue is weaker still."[46]

Centuries ago Symeon the New Theologian counseled, "Do not try to describe ineffable matters by words alone, for this is an impossibility. . . . But let us contemplate such matters by activity, labor, and fatigue. . . . In this way we shall be taught the meaning of such things as the sacred mysteries."[47] Virtuosity and mastery will not reach the ineffable. Rather, he taught, understanding will come by proceeding to work and live without presuming to comprehend the Divine, who encompasses all living and working. When stripped of ready formulas, the rhythm of work and life redounds to realities that surpass human understanding. By contrast, brutal tyranny strips humanity as well as doctrine. Intellect, tongue, *and agency* are weakened; the capacity to resist as well as capacities of knowing and naming are undermined. What, then, might we make of Symeon's counsel?

No monastic rhythm of "activity, labor, and fatigue" afforded ready contemplation of the unthinkable, unspeakable, immobilizing reality of Auschwitz. To be sure, there was labor: it led to hunger, which by calculation was never to be satisfied and served as a means for humiliation, dehumanization, and extermination. "When one works, one suffers, and there is no time to think," Primo Levi recalled. Work did not *macht Frei*, give freedom, as the entrance to the camp mocked. Free men think and talk about the purpose of life, he observed, recounting one day in Auschwitz. "But for us the question is simpler. Today in this place our only purpose is to reach the spring. At the moment we care about nothing else. Behind this aim there is not at the moment any other aim."[48]

With many canny, persistent acts, some good comrades, and a few turns of "good fortune"—he was sent to the camp late in the war and did not have to survive its reign as long as to reach the spring—Levi fashioned a way to survive from one week to the next. Survival required not only assuaging hunger and avoiding selection for death, but also refusing to be defined by hunger and by death. In contrast to the hovering threat of annihilation, his resistance took on a certain rhythm of purpose: "I almost never had time to devote to [the contemplation of] death. I had many other things to keep me busy—finding a bit of bread, avoiding exhausting work, patching my shoes, stealing a broom, or interpreting the signs and faces around me. The aims of life are the best defense against death: and not only in the Lager [camp]."[49] No activity, including avoiding exhaustion or attempting interpretation, could be taken for granted. Claiming his agency by using whatever measure of it he could, Levi also sustained his intellect, his tongue, and his life.

Whereas the ancient *via negativa* offered a way of knowing the limits to comprehension of God, we are considering a way of resistance at the limits of human dignity and survival. In chapter 1, we referred to Elaine Scarry's argument that acts of torture circumscribe the tortured person's world in a way that transfers power to the torturer; I am depicting resistance as the obverse. Acts of resistance push back against destruction and constraint in a way that rejects the sovereignty of "alien powers" and that expands the possibilities for personal and communal life before God. At such limits of thinking, speaking, and acting, resistance is more than negation and revolt. It is a *way* of surviving. Or better, it is a way *of living*, of pursuing the aims of life, to use Primo Levi's formulation. By pushing back against harm and destruction, resistance creates a sheltering space—at least a modicum of shelter—for vulnerable life. A modicum, because it may be a matter of survival at best, not of flourishing:

systematic programs of dehumanization and genocide defeat capacities for resistance, community, personhood, and dignity. To defeat a massive system of defeat requires that struggle under the system be joined by organized resistance from without.

ALWAYS REFORMING, ALWAYS RESISTING

Marie Durand pushed back against constricting powers by worshiping God as the source of all life and by naming other powers as idolatrous. She pushed back against destruction by reaching out to others in letters and by carving "Résister" into the stone of the ages. She pushed back by becoming more than a faithful daughter and a sister to a martyr: she became a witness in her own right.[50]

Clearly her life was better—safer, healthier, more autonomous, more richly related, more choice-filled—before she sustained imprisonment and immense losses. However, she refused to be defined by constraint and loss. Marie Durand lived by faith: she proceeded to live and work and worship without presuming full comprehension of God or of her constrained life. Perhaps she struggled to retain an "awareness of divinity" and the testimony of conscience against the obliteration of her family and her church, her past and her future. Perhaps the language of Scripture, the pattern of Christ, and the practices of worship, service, and writing served to magnify and strengthen what might otherwise have been fleeting experiences of goodness, justice, and God. We might imagine, good Calvinist that she was, that increased knowledge of God through the lens of Scripture and the mediation of Christ correlated with increased knowledge of herself and others. Yet, it was not knowledge of God or of self, attained once and for all; it was a matter of always seeking the reign and justice of God and of always resisting.

Repression and suffering in themselves do not generate better selves or stronger faith. However, we can and must be tutored by those who have faced profound threats and loss, who have looked into the abyss of evil and of loss and tried to name and mourn its depth, who have continued to push back against harm so as to allow space for the dignity and care of vulnerable human lives, and who thereby have found themselves at the heart of humanity and before God. Such examples crystallize a way of resistance. In them there is steadfast repulsion against harm and evil; protest to idolatry and tyranny cultivated in thought, word, and deed; and the consistent creation and preservation of a space of freedom where dignity, justice, and love may survive. Sometimes this space of freedom is created by the reciprocal and repeated extension of love among self, God, and others: that was how the villagers in Le Chambon understood resistance and the reception of vulnerable strangers to grow from the love of God and of neighbors and strangers.

Martin Luther argued that all vocations ought to serve the neighbor. Each individual stands accountable before God, *coram Deo*, and with other Christians in mutual accountability for support, assistance, and intercession. The two parts of this chapter have moved between a *call* to resist and a *calling*, a vocation of resistance. A vocation to be "always reforming, always resisting" suggests an ever-converting, ever-being-converted way of living before God that is ever seeking to be responsive in love and responsible in resistance. Such a way of resistance is not accomplished once and for all, but prayed as we can, lived as we are able, and worked as a vocation.

How might such a way of resistance translate to the different threats of our time? Struggles for survival are waged throughout the world's villages and cities. The deadly effects of contemporary idolatries are seen in places where the basic goods of life cannot be taken for granted, where constant vigilance is required to keep a child safe from violence and well-enough fed, where decent housing can be neither afforded nor found, where access to minimal health care or education cannot be assumed, where the lack of hope numbs minds and spirits. The effects of our day's idolatries also cut across relative privileges. They are seen in interpersonal abuse and violence, substance abuse, ragged relationships, lack of viable common life, contaminated food and water and air, and relative inability to access or affect political processes. To resist is to gain a foothold against the seemingly insurmountable accumulation of such ravages. In such contexts, "struggle" may mean marches and international coalitions, but it more likely involves an accumulation of daily practices that are equivalent to the Durand family's persistence in faith, to Marie's being taught to read by her father and in turn teaching an imprisoned child, and to writing her testimony in letters and in stone.

Here we have returned to the language of struggle, and a caution should be reiterated. I have noted that such struggles, some more fierce and brutal than others, are related by analogy and often by common cause; interrelations have to be built rather than assumed. Struggle at the limits of endurance and comprehension, such as we have been discussing, relativizes the quiet devastations of more comfortable lives. Relatively privileged persons can take many things for granted, even if we ought not. Although the diminishments and damage we face may differ qualitatively from the starkest struggles, it is imperative that we use whatever we face to deepen our comprehension of systemic and not-so-systemic threats, to connect our own with others' vulnerabilities, and to take up the call to resist as our own. Keeping a proportionate sense of one's own situation does not mean denying the real hardships and damage that one sustains; as I argued in the last chapter, all persons must "go through" suffering.

Perhaps the more instructive analogy for such a situation is with the Reformed resisters of the mid-twentieth century. If anyone could have survived the Vichy regime with minimal consequence, removed themselves from small and large collaborations with the Nazis, and maintained their lives with little change, it would have been them. They lived in remote areas where they were sustained by local produce and animals, where there were no manufacturing or transportation hubs relevant to the war, and where there were virtually no persons of Jewish descent. Rather than choosing a sectarian option of isolating themselves from the threats that others faced, they opened themselves to others and understood that, whether they became engaged or not, other persons' survival and human dignity in general were already threatened. For them, it was not enough to sustain the life they had, and particularly not as "given" by tyrannous powers that presumed at the same time to take life from others. Instead, they fashioned a middle way by resisting idolatry and tyranny while opening their doors to strangers. They extended the reach of their love of neighbors and strangers far beyond the high plateaus where they lived. They threaded a way between sectarianism and triumphalism; it was a way that made them more vulnerable to both devastation and transformation.

In the twenty-first century, it is not enough to rest in the relatively safe and relatively prosperous high plateaus of global capitalism and to secure one's life from the ravages that others suffer. And a sectarian option is not a real option: persons are already intricately and globally interconnected. For example, cell phones allow communication with persons around the world; they also connect their users to the Congo, from whence comes 80 percent of the mineral that allows the phones to hold an electrical charge, but where rural Congolese themselves cannot afford the technology and where exploitation and rape accompany international looting of mineral resources.[52] Neither a sectarian nor a triumphalist option acknowledges the threats and possibilities that are intrinsic to daily existence. We assimilate and promulgate idolatries by megabytes and gigabytes; we consume tyrannies with how we eat, work, and live; we transact them in the global marketplace and suffer them in globalized risks and damage. At the same time, as even these capacities for corruption and harm attest, within these interconnections and interdependencies persons and communities can pursue ways of thinking, speaking, and acting that may make real differences for others, self, and world.

Twenty-first-century North Americans are as apt to encounter ineffable selves and relations as to encounter the ineffability of the divine or the abyss of evil. We may feel giddy, lacking anything to take hold of or any place to stand, before even reaching the depths plumbed by the *via negativa* or rent asunder in the Holocaust. To confront the confounding ambiguities of our lives and world requires as well a way of resistance: pushing back ambiguity to make distinctions between what denies mercy and justice and what affirms it, resisting what degrades humanity, and opening a space of freedom where love for God and strangers can grow. Persons must begin where they are, at the thresholds of their lives. As Magda Trocmé at Le Chambon observed, "A person either opens the door or closes it in the face of a victim." There are no "Protestant saints," she noted. "There are only people who accept responsibility, and those who do not."[53] It wasn't then and isn't now a matter of first securing a surer place for one's self, but of learning when to welcome and when to resist.

CHAPTER 8

An Itinerary of Delight and Gratitude

Many August nights Avey had stood beside her great-aunt and watched the figures through the open doors of the Carolina Tidewater church. A handful of elderly women and men slowly circled the room, gliding on their toes and stamping their heels. Decades later, Avey Johnson, the main character in Paule Marshall's novel, *Praisesong for the Widow*, recalled: "Only their heels rose and then fell with each step, striking the worn pineboard with a beat that was as precise and intricate as a drum's. . . . They sang: *Who's that riding the chariot? / Well well well* . . . ; used their hands as racing tambourines, slapped their knees and thighs and chest in dazzling syncopated rhythm."[1] The Ring Shout became more animated as the night wore on. The steady trudge of feet affirmed the vulnerability of existence, as song and movement circled into dazzling glory.

The glory of God is alive in the cosmos and in creaturely life. Praising God, the psalmist declares, "You give them drink from the river of your delights. For with you is the fountain of life; in your light we see light" (Ps. 36:8–9). At the edge of a glacier lake on a brilliant day, with the strains of "Hallelujah!" on Easter, in the remembrance of a wise teacher or friend—the affirmation of glory nearly voices itself. However, the glory of God may be far from evident in the aftermath of a disaster or in the experience of betrayal and loss; there may be no sense of "aliveness" in dreary routines and mundane demands. Does an emphasis on "glory" detract from the pressing demands of everyday existence, neglect the cries of hungry and suffering people, and disregard the plight of the planet? Is delight in God and in life compensatory at best? To put it differently, in a world marked by suffering, should there be anything more to say about living before God beyond the call and testimony of resistance?

Immense suffering, tragedy, and harm are a manifest, not-to-be-denied part of living before God. Yet they do not complete or conclude what can be said. This book has linked vulnerability and glory—but not to minimize the risk and hazards that threaten persons, communities, cultures, and the earth itself, nor to deny the ambiguity and unimaginable harm and brutality that creatures suffer. Rather, the pairing of vulnerability and glory emphasizes the interrelation of vulnerability to devastation and vulnerability to transformation, and the interrelation of a living creation and a living God. Vulnerability and glory are not opposites. As the apostle Paul affirmed long ago, God's grace and glory are breathed into creatures and borne in earthen existence. How human creatures move toward and are turned toward the glory of God *in their vulnerability*—not by escaping or denying their vulnerability or by neglecting relations with and needs of others—is the subject of this chapter. The glory of God may not always be immediately evident to creatures, but through means of grace, creaturely attention and existence can be strengthened, step-by-step, to receive and bear the majesty of God. To use Paule Marshall's Ring Shout as a metaphor, when shared and trained, the steady trudge of mundane existence can come simultaneously to acknowledge the vulnerability of creatures and to circle into dazzling glory.[2]

This chapter explores an itinerary of delight and gratitude. The itinerary attends to the vulnerability of creatures and cosmos while fostering delight in and gratitude to God. This itinerary is the counterpart—the polar tension, not the opposite—of the testimony and calling of resistance. The way of resistance pushes back against what denies God and the dignity of earthly existence; in so doing it creates a sheltering space where love of neighbors and strangers may grow. The itinerary of delight and gratitude depicts persons and communities moving to receive creaturely life as a gift of God and to meet other persons and things with reverence and appreciation because God creates, redeems, and sustains all being.[3]

Paule Marshall's *Praisesong for the Widow*, which is a story of transformation and calling framed by ritual, can help us to explore such an itinerary. A movement similar to classic conversion narratives structures Marshall's novel. In this chapter, a theologically inflected reading of her protagonist's journey introduces the itinerary of delight and gratitude. Beginning with (1) dissatisfaction, this chapter and the itinerary (2) move through faith to (3) a reorienting acknowledgment of ambiguity and vulnerability. Conversion, which is ongoing, also involves (4) attunement to God, cosmos, and creatures through delight and gratitude; this attunement is (5) shaped by and expressed in corporate affirmations of God's beckoning and restoring grace.

Although much of this exploration is organized by a narrative of conversion, it should be emphasized that the "itinerary of delight and gratitude" is a metaphor or a metaphoric field more than it is a sequence of events.[4] The phrase itself already signals the play of tropes: it juxtaposes a metaphor of movement, "an itinerary," with "delight" and its roots in sensory perception and pleasure, and with "gratitude," which signals response to God and others. Historical resources from previous chapters are condensed together with interpretations of contemporary situations into tropes such as an itinerary to God, the *via affirmativa*, and the sweet taste of God.[5] Through relations within and among these condensed metaphors, multiple perspectives articulate with each other.[6] The aim, however, is not to resolve comparisons and contrasts into a final synthesis. Rather, what results is a field of multiple, interacting depictions—mutually contrasting, testing, and transforming tropes— that together evoke and pattern "an itinerary of delight and gratitude."

DISSATISFACTION

The widow in the title of Marshall's book is Avey Johnson, a sixty-four-year-old, middle-class African American from suburban New Jersey. As the novel opens, we find her stumbling in the dark of a cruise liner cabin, trying not to bump into furniture or decades-old memories that have resurged with unexpected force. Waking in the middle of the night, she made up her mind to leave the cruise and return home. As she stuffs her suitcases with clothing, it is as much her self that she is trying to force back into familiar contours. Yet the name of the ship, the *Bianca Pride*, and of her suburban home, North White Plains, New Jersey, signal that she may have been dislocated for a long time.

Marshall's novel connects her character's middle-class striving with the historical struggles of African Americans. The title of the first part, "Runagate," comes from Robert Hayden's similarly named poem. In the poem, a person "runs falls rises stumbles on" while fleeing slavery.[7] Unbeknownst to Avey Johnson, lying before her as before the figure in Hayden's poem, is "the night long and the river/to cross."[8] After decades of striving for middle-class attainments, Avey no longer finds those pleasures satisfying; her acceptable life is foundering. The journey ahead will require, in part, discerning what is "too much" to endure and what is "enough" for survival and flourishing.[9]

Two nights before Avey's decision to leave the cruise, she had entered the mirror-lined Versailles dining hall, where she glimpsed a tastefully coiffed and attired woman. "For a long confused moment" she failed to recognize the woman as herself.[10] Beneath the failure of self-recognition lurked the tacit question: how much had been compromised for her careful composure? The tacit answer is given in the onset of a mysterious clogged sensation: too much. The sensation rises when she is unable to swallow the fancy dessert that she has so anticipated. Her body registers what is not yet brought fully to consciousness: she has had too much.

Too much of the pretensions of middle-class life. Too much compromise required to gain access to their consumption.

The strange malaise haunts her the next day, causing her perceptions of reality to shift. In the surreality she enters, violence and decay are revealed beneath the polite recreations of a cruise holiday. Aging sunbathers turn to skeletons before her eyes. Sounds from a game being played on the deck below call up suppressed memories of the thud of a nightstick upon a Black citizen. Multiple tropes convey Avey's condition: she is disheveled and destabilized; she feels ill at ease and strangely bloated; her surroundings seem to lurch; she feels pursued; she fails to recognize herself and her world. Constriction is revealed beneath composure and violence beneath civility. What Avey had taken to be the good life is shown to be of profoundly "mixed nature."

If her body is afflicted with a clogged sensation and her mind by hallucinations, her soul is afflicted by her great-aunt Cuney. Her aunt erupts into a dream, summoning Avey to follow her down along the familiar route they had traversed together during many childhood summers. In the dream, Avey, no longer a girl, is on her way to an important luncheon and is not about to follow the old woman. As dusk falls, Cuney's summons turns to pleading. She strains toward Avey like "a preacher in a Holiness church imploring sinners and backsliders to come forward to the mercy seat." The woods behind become the church choir, beseeching, *"Come / Won't you come . . . ?"*[11] But Avey Johnson will not be moved.

For her part, Aunt Cuney will not let go. Like Jacob wrestling the mysterious stranger at the ford of the Jabbock, Avey becomes locked in battle. A silent tug-of-war with her great-aunt turns into a brawl, with her respectable neighbors looking on. Her stylish clothing is torn— threatening to leave her as naked as the soul in the bosom of Abraham. When Avey wakes from her dream, she remains embattled. By the end of the novel, like Jacob, she will receive a blessing from her adversary in the form of a name. Jacob receives the name Israel, "the one who strives with God," and the blessing of having met God face-to-face and yet being allowed to live.[12] Avey's blessing also comes in the form of a name. After refusing it for decades, she eventually embraces the full name that her great-aunt insisted be given to her, Avatara, "avatar, messenger," and the vocation that is its legacy. But here I am jumping ahead to the end of the story.

To contemporary ears, Avey's condition does not sound as dire as John Calvin's assessment of the human condition, but Marshall depicts something nearly as thoroughgoing. Calvin described humans as wounded by sin and in need of complete restoration. Harm, not only lack of capacity, was involved: sin's deadly wound caused a corruption that affects all humanity. The fruits of life become the fruits of sin, rotten from their core. Every person suffers corruption, and "the whole man is overwhelmed—as if by a deluge—from head to foot, so that no part is immune from sin."[13] Both Marshall and Calvin depict creatures who are unable to cure or escape their condition themselves.[14]

By juxtaposing these two accounts, I do not mean to imply that Marshall is offering a nascent theory of sin or that her portrait of Avey's condition ought to be judged by Calvin's. I do mean to suggest that tropes other than Calvin's may be used to develop a revised etiology of corruption/conversion. This revised etiology assumes that human creatures remain vulnerable to change, change that may be harmful or healing, and that we creatures, individually and collectively, have already been harmed (and transformed); moreover, those changes themselves foster vectors of destruction and transformation. As Calvin argued, human creatures have been incapacitated—they were created by a good God as part of a glorious creation; they are not merely dull, lacking a divine spark. Moreover, they have been changed by human ingenuity and choices, and they remain vulnerable to threats that humans, including themselves, have fostered, advertently or inadvertently. Persons and communities become who they are—and continue to change and be changed—in particular situations and relations.[15] They remain vulnerable to corruption and transformation as situated selves and communities, in and through their interactions and interdependencies. To use Marshall's novel again as an example, both the way Avey situates herself and is situated in the world, and also the way she dwells in the present, from the past, and toward the future, are distorted.

One of Marshall's most pervasive motifs, "the relationship of one's feet to the earth,"[16] begins to suggest the difference of attending to situated selves rather than enfleshed souls.[17] Chattel slavery and other degradations of human devising constrain movement. Even if persons are able to flee toward freedom, literally or figuratively, that journey takes place under the threat of new captivity and involves rising, falling, stumbling toward a not-yet-known destination. Marshall's contrasting image is of persons singing and circling together steadily, step-by-step, until their movement becomes a dazzling dance that rises in praise. Metaphors of gaining footing and steady movement can also be found in Calvin. Calvin's pilgrims could be plunged in darkness, sometimes "wavering and limping and even creeping along the ground," sometimes walking slippery slopes, but they were also capable of some progress and of forging "a straighter path."[18]

Marshall's trope suggests a realignment in relation with others and the earth as well as within individual bodies and, by analogy, within social and ecclesial bodies. There are hints of a balance etiology here as well as of an etiology of corruption/conversion. (Aspects of an invasion etiology are also suggested, with hallucinations and dreams representing alien impingements on conscious and unconscious processes.) What is amiss according to Marshall's telling—and also Calvin's—is something more thoroughgoing than being out of kilter and ill at ease. Her character, Avey, is ostensibly free, at least by consumer capitalism's account, but has become captive to illusions of glory—a fancy dessert served in a mirrored hall on a sleek ship, shared with persons who are as captivated as she—and has hindered her own movement, literally weighing herself down with excess luggage. She cannot free herself, but neither can others free her for herself. In Marshall's novel, the possibilities of glory signaled in the Ring Shout are eventually mediated through religiocultural resources and the unexpected ministrations of others and affirmed when Avey accepts her own calling alongside these mediators.

WALKING IN FAITH

At the core of Avey's transformation is her remembrance of a regular walk with her great-aunt Cuney during Avey's childhood summers in Tatem, South Carolina. Twice a week they set out for Ibo Landing. They passed the church and "Doctor" Benitha Grant's house, with her healing herbs. They saw the piles of broken, rusted implements in Pharo and Celia Harris's yard, a "gothic" memorial to former days of sharecropping and taking in washing. They crossed over what was once a huge plantation of sea island cotton and through the juniper tree forest to the river landing that led to the ocean. There her aunt would recount an incredible tale. Going and returning, they always greeted the ancient Mr. Golla Mack.[19]

Marshall's fictive geography reviews a cultural history of threats, such as chattel slavery, war's pillaging, sharecropping—and of means of survival, such as the church, arts of healing, preservation of memories, wisdom conveyed through folktale and myth.[20] Her characters traverse this history as they walk to the Landing. Their walks also link Avey and the generation she represents with older generations and more distant forebears.

The story of Ibo Landing was the center of the summer ritual. Aunt Cuney told the tale to Avey as she had heard it from her own grandmother Avatara.

Years before, a ship had arrived, and the Ibos, bound in chains and irons, had been brought to shore. Those tall proud Africans had looked around. Their long, hard looks encompassed all that there was to see— on that day and into the future. They saw slavery, the emancipation, . . . everything including the two of them standing there at that moment. With the same long looks the Ibos sized up the white folks who had brought them there. They studied, knew what was to come, and then turned and began to walk away. "They had seen what they had seen and those Ibos was stepping! . . . They just kept on walking like the water was solid ground." Leg irons didn't stop them. They kept on walking right past the ship, kept on walking over the water toward home. They were singing by then.[21]

What does it take to resist dehumanization and to survive with integrity and dignity? This question is at the heart of the novel. Marshall's rendering of the story of Ibo Landing answers: "Awareness." The Ibos, tall and proud, retain an awareness of the worth they possess. "Vigilance." They look both directions, into the past and into the future, to safeguard their worth and dignity from any who would destroy or appropriate it. "Strength." Despite iron collars and chains, the Ibos are able to turn away and keep on walking. "And distance." Not tempted by the nearby shore, they keep their eyes trained to the real prize: home, Africa, Zion, as it were. Enslavement did not constrain them, and neither does death.[22]

Once Avey asked whether the Ibos drowned. Her great-aunt replied, "Did it say Jesus drowned when he went walking on the water in that Sunday School book your momma always sends with you?"[23] Human worth and freedom were denied under the brutal conditions of enslavement; for Cuney, the story of the Ibos' dignity and ultimate freedom was to be believed as wholeheartedly as the story of Jesus' triumph over the water. Arguably, it's not belief in the literal ability of the Ibos and Jesus to walk on water that is crucial for Marshall's characters; of greater significance is that Aunt Cuney tells the story of the Landing to be believed and that Avey trusts her and believes the story that Cuney tells. What was to be believed was that even the harshest conditions could not deny human worth, dignity, and ultimate freedom; finally it is this vision, mediated by Cuney and the tale, that requires trust and loyalty.

My interpretation here bears the strong imprint of H. Richard Niebuhr's work. Regardless of how one interprets Marshall's novel, faith itself should not be construed as assent to the nonrational, but rather as a matter of trust in the source of value and loyalty to that which gives value.[24] Niebuhr found this basic structure of faith throughout human relations. A radically monotheist faith follows the faith of Jesus Christ in trusting God as the source and center of all value and in loyalty to God and God's creatures.[25] Trust in and loyalty to one God involves the self in a "continuous revolution" of mind and heart; such faith requires that "all beings, not only our friends, but also our enemies, not only men but also animals and the inanimate, be met with reverence, for all are friends in the friendship of the one to whom we are reconciled in faith."[26]

The polite constraints of a cruise ship do not compare with the shackles of a slave ship. Furthermore, worries about swallowing a fancy dessert and being smartly attired for its consumption are hardly pressing concerns in a hungry, needy world. But the plight of Avey Johnson points to what many others undergo. We postmoderns tend to assume that we are self-composed. In fact, we are often composed by and for consumption. Global cultural and economic forces mediate desire, beauty, choice, freedom. As consumer options multiply, choices of how to make one's way in the world are often reduced to the common denominator of monetary worth and to a single essentially passive option: to consume or not to consume. Our lives become clogged and devoid of delight; we consume but are not satisfied. "Why do you spend your money for that which is not bread, and your labor for that which does not satisfy?" Isaiah 55:2 asks. The prophet's ancient question has deep contemporary resonance. The realization to which Marshall's character finally comes is that she must choose not to choose: she must decide to disembark the sleek ship that carries her only toward more consumption and, in effect, to set out in faith.

REORIENTATION

As Avey's dissatisfaction grows, she begins to sense a different way of inhabiting and engaging the world. She sees it with peripheral vision, feels it with peripheral sensation, remembers it with peripheral memory. She is like Calvin's traveler, "passing through a field at night who in a momentary lightning flash sees far and wide, but the sight vanishes so swiftly that he is plunged again into the darkness of the night before he can even take a step—let alone be directed on his way by its help."[27] When she disembarks the cruise, she becomes more, not less, disoriented. She plans to catch the next flight north, but her stumbling journey leads her in the opposite direction.

Classic conversion narratives tell of being both turned toward a new way and turned from the past. Conversion circles one back through personal and shared history, often to repent of past actions, but also to give a thorough accounting of how the past prepared for something new and how a new horizon changes the significance of the past. At issue in such an accounting is the integrity of the self. Integrity comes from the consistent direction of a life, not from replacement of the past. Conversion involves realigning the past with an emerging future and reconstructing a basis for that future in the past, thereby shaping a new trajectory into the future; integrity must constantly be shaped in relation to the past and future as well as with others and God. Thus the past, whether as borne in memory or evidenced in a history of effects, cannot simply be "disembarked" upon arrival at some newly redeemed state. Conversion does not mean substitution or transfiguration but rather reorientation, turning around, of personal and shared life, life that remains vulnerable to damage and to further transformation.

Conversion requires acknowledgment of the ambiguity of one's life, including one's relations and community, and of ongoing vulnerability to damage and to transformation. Such acknowledgment necessitates tracing sources of harm so that damage can be assessed and redressed through the reconstruction of self and community.[28] These sources and the extent of harm are often suppressed—personally, and also culturally. In his 1951 essay "Many Thousands Gone," James Baldwin explored the cultural repression of racially inflected harm. Fear and contempt seep into black psyches and white psyches and have been masked and mythologized in American culture. "The man does not remember the hand that struck him, the darkness that frightened him, as a child; nevertheless, the hand and the darkness remain with him, indivisible from himself forever, part of the passion that drives him wherever he thinks to take flight."[29] While the seepage from a brutal history of human ownership of other humans and from race-based valuation, fear, and enmity may differ somewhat today from Baldwin's day, "the hand and the darkness remain."

When repressed pain is recognized and "believed," then it can be integrated into selves and communities and become the basis for response and action.[30] Like many accounts of actual trauma,[31] Marshall's story of Avey suggests the extent to which one's own pain may resist expression. In their early married years, Avey and her husband, Jay, do what they perceive has to be done in order to survive—and yet in the process they lose what sustains meaning and, effectively, they lose their selves. Only much later in life does Avey cry out for those losses: "How much had they foolishly handed over in exchange for the things they had gained? . . . *Too much!*"[32] The litany of lament pours out for several pages. Later in the novel, Avey's recognition of failure and loss is acknowledged by mediator figures; it is also connected to and relativized by historical devastation far beyond her own.

Like pain, profound joy evades language. But its force is dispersive, not destructive. Joy carries one out of place, out of language, and as Marshall suggests, it can connect persons to the broadest horizons of meaning and purpose. Conversely, to lose passion and delight is to lose connection and, to a large degree, the selves that are situated in those connections. Marshall portrays the difficulty of sustaining such connections in the face of pressures to survive and get ahead and also the challenge of attending to genuine delight among competing visions of satisfaction.

As Marshall's character recognizes the fuller ambiguity of her life— harm and joy, loss and love—she asks whether there might have been another way to meet the threats and possibilities she faced. What would it have taken? She comes to this realization: "Awareness. It would have called for an awareness of the worth they had possessed. Vigilance. . . . And strength. . . . and the will and even cunning necessary to withstand the glitter and the excess. . . . Above all, a certain distance of the mind and heart. . . ."[33] Marshall frames Avey's answer in relation to the story of Ibo Landing, but the answer also parallels the counsel of prophets and wisdom writers: Pay attention, stay alert. "Incline your ear, and come to me; listen, so that you may live" (Isa. 55:3).

DELIGHT IN GOD AND IN LIFE

We have been following one fictional narrative of conversion while also exploring an itinerary of delight and gratitude. I now turn more directly to that itinerary. The first part of this itinerary involves ongoing conversion—departing from inattentive consumption, walking in faith, and acknowledging the reaches of harm, joy, loss, and love in personal and shared life; the second part involves attunement to God, to life as a good gift of God, and to the glory of God alive in creatures and the cosmos.[34] In chapter 6, we noted aspects of a pedagogy of enjoyment and gratitude in Calvin's thought. Those aspects can be reengaged and compared with the traditional *via affirmativa*. I will look especially at delight in relation to the satisfaction of need and in relation to God, and at how the Psalms train perceptions, affections, and valuations.

The language of "delight" is the language of the Psalms and Wisdom literature. "Take delight in the Lord," Psalm 37 counsels. The sweet taste of God's law leads to understanding (Ps. 119:103); in Proverbs 24, wisdom's lessons are delightful, as good and sweet as honey.[35] In Scripture and in life, "delight" is often associated with senses that are fully engaged and needs that are fully satisfied. Delight can attest that perceived needs or senses are true. Moreover, deep satisfaction of needs and senses may serve as a symbol and means of transformation. In Isaiah 55:1–5, to "delight in rich food" parallels being fully alive, and both indicate the glory of God. The prophet calls his sluggish listeners to heed their own thirst and hunger and the God who can satisfy their true needs abundantly and "without price."[36] In this passage, delight signals the satisfaction of creaturely needs in relation to the fullness of God's purposes, of shared human life, and of the earth. In verses 10–13, the earth's abundant growth and harvest attest that God has also satisfied the thirst of the earth with rain and snow. Being satisfied, the earth and its vegetation are transformed into co-celebrants of joy: "The mountains and the hills before you shall burst into song, and all the trees of the field shall clap their hands" (55:12).

Delight that comes with the satisfaction of deep—perhaps previously unrecognized—thirst and hunger offers a key for hearing God's call and for imagining the flourishing of earthly existence. How can persons attend rightly to hungers, physical and other, and their reorienting satisfaction in God? Not by negating or sublimating delight, not by substituting spiritual delights for physical pleasures, but by learning to heed hunger's call and to pay attention to delight's reorientation. To attend well to delight involves being responsive to the basic needs of self and others and responsible for their satisfaction, being attentive to how that satisfaction signals the integrity of creatures and cosmos, aligning the felt pleasure of satisfaction with a sense of the fullness of God's glory, and reshaping personal and shared life in response to the sense of God's glory conveyed in delight.

To attend to delight is more than a matter of perception; it is a reflexive art that requires awareness, imagination, and action. The Psalms, with their vivid sensory language and their depiction of wide-ranging human affections, emotions, and interactions, have had extraordinary importance for shaping corporate worship and for shaping persons as worshiping creatures—creatures who are oriented in response and gratitude before God and others. In the Psalms, matters of creaturely capacity, perception, and response (or lack thereof) are taken up in relation to matters of divine initiative, knowability, mercy, and judgment.

Consider Psalm 34. It exults, "O taste and see that the LORD is good." It doesn't stop at tasting and seeing God; the psalm engages nearly a full sensorium to delight in and praise God. The congregation looks to God, radiantly and without shame (v. 5), while "the eyes of the LORD are on the righteous" (v. 15). The psalmist, poor souls, and the righteous cry to God (vv. 1, 6, 17), whose "ears are open to their cry" (v. 15). God's touch is almost palpable: God is "near to the brokenhearted," shielding spirits from being "crushed" and "keeping" the bones of the afflicted so that they will not be broken (vv. 18–20). Creatures and God are portrayed as "sensing" each other's value and need (or completeness). There is interrelation and response: vulnerable creatures cry out and delight in God, recognizing God's glory, justice, and goodness toward creatures. At the same time, God perceives and reaches toward creatures in a qualitatively different way than human creatures sense and reach to God.

In his *Confessions*, Augustine finds himself drawn by the sweetness of God and gathered together in the fire of God's love.[37] The Psalms teach him to call upon God and to rest in God's love. He exclaims, "How they set me on fire with love of you!" The Scriptures, "which are sweet with the honey of heaven and radiant with your light," also teach him that God's sweetness and radiance dwell within his own soul.[38] His scrutiny of sensory experience and of memory leads to the edges of God. "I shall go beyond this force that is in me, this force which we call memory, so that I may come to you, my Sweetness and my Light."[39] Finally, it is God who finds him:

> You called me; you cried aloud to me; you broke my barrier of deafness. You shone upon me; your radiance enveloped me; you put my blindness to flight. You shed your fragrance about me; I drew breath and now I gasp for your sweet odour. I tasted you, and now I hunger and thirst for you. You touched me, and I am inflamed with love of your peace.[40]

The opening chapter of Augustine's *Confessions* affirms, "[God's] gifts are good and the sum of them all is my own self. Therefore the

God who made me must be good and all the good within me is his."[41] The overarching movement of Augustine's journey toward God as the source of all good can be compared with later formulations of a *via affirmativa*. Affirmative, or cataphatic, theology "is a way which comes down towards us: a ladder of 'theophanies' or manifestations of God in creation," according to Orthodox theologian Vladimir Lossky. As God can be said to condescend toward humanity, Lossky explained, so can humans be said to ascend toward God. "The ladder of cataphatic theology which discloses the divine names drawn above all from Holy Scripture, is a series of steps up which the soul can mount to contemplation." In the *via affirmativa*, "speculation gives way to contemplation, knowledge to experience."[42] Augustine drew on the physical sensations of pleasure to provide analogies for his journey toward God. Ultimately, sensory pleasures do not reach to God but instead provide analogies for the way God calls Augustine and surrounds him with delight. Augustine's journey began with knowledge of God as the source of good and moved to the experience of being encompassed in the sound, radiance, fragrance, taste, and touch of God.

Augustine's affirmation of sensible delight was chastened and negated by his recognition of the lures of sensible temptation.[43] Historical theologian Margaret Miles argues that Augustine reconstructed pleasure through the practice and paradigm of continence. Through it, he offered a model of spiritual discipline as active withdrawal from attraction.[44] (This model also partakes of a balance etiology: swelling pride is constrained, scattered parts collected, and improper desires reordered.) His reconstruction indicated the limits, and more, the dangers, of any equation of the experience of sensible delight with the experience of God's goodness. Augustine incorporated important negations in the reconstruction of the self and in approaching God as ultimately unfathomable, as "sweetness beyond understanding."[45]

For reasons both similar to and different from Augustine's concerns, Protestants have often been averse to a *via affirmativa*. Martin Luther rejected the affirmative way of knowing God as presumptuous speculation about the majesty of God.[46] As we have seen, he dismissed such speculation as a theology of glory and instead favored a theology of the cross. In effect, he rejected a lived *via affirmativa*, moral or spiritual advance toward God, in addition to a speculative *via affirmativa*. At the same time, Luther viewed faith as being caught up with love and joy. "From faith thus flow forth love and joy in the Lord," he explained, "and from love a joyful willing and free mind that serves one's neighbor willingly."[47] The flow of love and joy is one-directional, from Christ and through the self as if a channel to the neighbor. Luther typically denounced any hint of self-propelled advance toward God (and, it seemed at times, to others) as works righteousness; Christians are to rely on God's gracious initiative in Christ alone.

It is possible to affirm such a flow of love and joy in faith while portraying a wider circulation of enjoyment among a living God and a living creation—a depiction suggested in the Psalms and elsewhere in Jewish and Christian thought. Indeed, neither synthesis (as in Augustine) nor paradox (as in Luther) is ultimately adequate to the connections of harm and joy, loss and love, that situate the self with others in the world before God and through which a living God moves and dwells among creatures and cosmos. Life before God involves ever-shifting tensions and multiple conversions, ongoing resistance and ongoing affirmation. Situated selves and communities are altered by vectors of devastation and transformation, and they remain vulnerable to further devastation and transformation. Living before God requires "going through" suffering and "moving against" idolatry, tyranny, and indignity. It also "moves toward" glory, coming to affirm and respond to a sense of God's grace and glory alive in creatures and cosmos. These interrelated movements require attunement of sensibilities and responsive engagement, not merely perception. Calvin's use of the Psalms can aid an interpretation of delight and gratitude as integral to the transformation of vulnerable creatures toward the glory of God.

Although Calvin followed Luther's suspicion of speculation and also held that perception was prone to distortion, he did not view knowledge of God that was gained from contemplation of the sensible world or the self as false. "Let us not be ashamed to take pious delight in the works of God open and manifest in this most beautiful theater [i.e., the universe]," he counseled.[48] God's works should not be viewed "cursorily"; rather, "we should ponder them at length, turn them over in our minds seriously and faithfully, and recollect them repeatedly."[49] Note that contemplation is directed to "God's works"; it cannot fathom the abyss of God. That said, everything from the macrocosm of the universe to the microcosm of selves can serve as "mirrors" in which to contemplate "God's inestimable wisdom, power, justice, and goodness." Calvin indicated that such contemplation could profit from the latest science and that it was potentially infinite: "For there are as many miracles of divine power, as many tokens of goodness, and as many proofs of wisdom, as there are kinds of things in the universe, indeed, as there are things

either great or small."[50] Moreover, this contemplation ought to lead creatures to thankfulness and trust in God.[51]

Calvin viewed the Psalms as providing a mirror for contemplating
the self[52] and a model for training sensibilities.[53] The Psalms advance
self-knowledge, diagnose human plights, and teach how life can be
ordered before God; Calvin called them "An Anatomy of All the Parts
of the Soul." They teach persons to plumb the depths of emotions and
affections, to offer them to God in prayer, and to reorient self and relations in response to them.[54] In the *Institutes*, Calvin wrote of "descending into one's self,"[55] as well as departing from one's self, and the Psalms
especially enable that descent. The Psalms "will principally teach and
train us to bear the cross."[56] David's psalms and example (whose mediation, for Calvin, foreshadowed Christ's) clarified Calvin's own sorrows,
eliciting from him "unnumbered groans and sighs."[57]

The Psalms also teach the goodness of God and foster delight and
gratitude. When it came to depicting perception of the goodness of
God, Calvin often turned to the metaphor of tasting God's sweetness,
found especially in the Psalms and in Wisdom literature. "We begin in
the present life, though various benefits, to taste the sweetness of the
divine generosity in order to whet our hope and desire to seek after the
full revelation of this. When we are certain that the earthly life we live is
a gift of God's kindness, . . . we ought to remember it and be thankful."[58]
In his commentary on Psalm 23, Calvin observed that "God, by his
benefits, gently allures us to himself, as it were by a taste of his fatherly
sweetness."[59] It is the sweetness of God's generosity and care as tasted
in God's "benefits," not a direct perception of God, that lifts hearts and
minds to God.

Benefits are the good things that God provides to "live happily under
his care." In Psalm 23, a grassy meadow in which a shepherd and his sheep
can rest and a gently flowing stream from which they can drink epito-
mize benefits. Good things—and Calvin notes that King David enjoyed
"the greatest abundance of temporal good things"—are not rightly used
unless they are referred to their end as means of God's care.[60] Benefits
ought not be viewed as personal possessions or entitlements but first as
God's. As we saw earlier, the right use and enjoyment of God's benefits
includes receiving them as gifts of God for sustenance and delight, using
them in moderation and with right stewardship, and sharing them with
fellow creatures in genuine love and kindness.[61] Elsewhere Calvin connected moderate use with concern for the poor: nothing can be rightly
used and enjoyed if it is at the neglect of the hungry poor.[62] In today's

global economy, "temporal good things," or at least temporal things, are multiplied exponentially while contemporary equivalents to a grassy meadow and a flowing stream—a safe place to rest, a sustainable liveli-hood, and the quenching of thirst—are not ensured for all the world's people. Although there is much more to say and do to ensure the basic goods of life and their fair distribution, at a minimum we can say that their distribution, use, and enjoyment affects both thinking about and living before God. Right use and enjoyment of the goods of life can afford a taste of God's sweetness and demands attention to the needs of others; such use and enjoyment can help to kindle genuine love and kindness and to shape a proportionate sense of self and community in relation to the vulnerability of others and the earth.

Calvin depicted David's contemplation of God's benefits as an ascent toward God: David makes remembrance of God's benefits "ladders by which he [David] may ascend nearer to him [God]."[63] Like Jacob who dreams of ladders (Gen. 28:12), David's contemplation of the goodness of God provides David—and Calvin through him—a glimpse of the glory of God descending and ascending like angels on a ladder set on earth and reaching to heaven.[64] Like many Christian commentators before him,[65] Calvin interpreted Jacob's ladder through John 1:51 (and also with Eph. 4:8–10), which has heaven opening and "the angels of God ascending and descending upon the Son of Man."[66] Calvin thought that the ladder symbolized Christ well: "the Mediator" was one of Calvin's favored depictions.[67]

Calvin pictured Christ as ascending to the incomprehensible glory of God and thereby lifting human hearts and minds, and also as descending to the depths of human life and struggle. Human sensibilities—joy and terror, fear and gentleness, awe and friendly feeling, all in one passage—move with and in response to Christ;[68] they are called forth by the work of Christ and heightened before the reality of God. In attending to those sensibilities, Christians also ascend with Christ and descend into human vulnerability and ambiguity, moving with and in some sense recapitulating the descent and ascent of God in Christ. This union with Christ was vividly portrayed in Calvin's interpretation of the Lord's Supper as providing its participants with a taste of Christ.[69]

In his commentary on Genesis 28:12, Calvin noted how "some Jewish commentators" treated Jacob's ladder, effectively agreeing with them that the ladder's symbolism refers to how heaven and earth are related in God, while rejecting their focus on providence as "not satisfactory." He argued that God's covenant, founded on Christ, was already revealed to the patriarchs (i.e., to Jacob), and that, because of human separation from God by sin, "it is Christ *alone* who joins heaven and earth."[70] Calvin regularly excoriated "the blindness of the Jews" to what Calvin viewed as the eternal truth of Christ. However, at some points in Calvin's work, possibilities can be glimpsed of varied covenants and mediations, ones that do not have to be viewed as superseding others. (In the last chapter, we saw twentieth-century Reformed resisters who also glimpsed those possibilities.) For example, David's psalms often stand on their own in Calvin's work; sometimes they also interpret the work of Christ, rather than the other way around. The anatomy the Psalms provide is more often mirrored in, rather than replaced by, the work of Christ. I want to insist, whereas Calvin does not, that the testimony of David, the Psalms, and Jacob's ladder need not be encompassed by Christ the Mediator; moreover, in their own right they bear witness to the glory of God, dwelling among and lifting up vulnerable creatures.

A CORPORATE *VIA AFFIRMATIVA*

When early Protestants sang the Psalms, raising their voices in praise and lifting their hearts in joy, they understood themselves to be meditating on God's benefits and goodness. Especially for followers of Calvin, right worship became a central theme for the whole of Christian life and for every Christian. The first question of the Westminster Shorter Catechism asks, "What is humanity's chief end?" and responds, "To glorify God and enjoy God forever." Calvin recommended singing the Psalms as an expression of spiritual joy. "Singing has great force and vigor to move and inflame the hearts of men to invoke and praise God with a more vehement and ardent zeal." (Conversely, the wrong kind of singing also had great power: "dishonest and shameless songs" not only conveyed perverse messages; their melodies could "pierce the heart" and inject "corruption" like "venom.") Calvin commended singing the Psalms in church and "even in the homes and in the fields."[71] Generations of French Protestants would do exactly that, including psalm-singing prisoners like Marie Durand and those walking to their executions like her brother. Early Protestants took their glorifying seriously.

As one might expect, Calvin advised moderation in songs: they should be "neither light nor frivolous," but have "weight and majesty."[72] In other words, the right mode of singing could enable worshipers to bear the weight and majesty of God. In their sober zeal, these singing Protestants were engaged in something quite radical: before the sixteenth century, boy choirs and cantors performed the chants and songs that were heard in services of worship. By contrast, most Protestant Reformers encouraged congregational singing and welcomed women's voices. One visitor to Strasbourg during that period observed in astonishment and appreciation: "Here, everyone sings, all sing together, men as well as women, and everyone has a [hymn]book in hand."[73] Calvin explained that the pleasure of singing has the power to lift hearts and minds to God, and "to console us by meditating on [God's] virtue, wisdom, and justice."[74] These singing Protestants were engaged in a corporate *via affirmativa*, pursued not in cloisters or by clergy but in the midst of daily life and by lay women and men joined in corporate worship.[75]

"Believers have no greater help than public worship. For by it God raises his own folk upward step by step," wrote John Calvin.[76] At its best, worship through singing the Psalms and observing the Lord's Supper and baptism—or circling the Ring Shout—does not bifurcate a "more theological" spirit from a "less theological" flesh. Rather, corporate worship can attune sensibilities, needs, and satisfactions toward the well-being of others and the grace and glory of God. Calvin "strongly commends" corporate prayer and singing because "they exercise the mind in thinking of God and keep it attentive—unstable and variable as it is, and readily relaxed and diverted in different directions, unless it be supported by various helps." Moreover, he continues, "the glory of God ought, in a measure, to shine in the several parts of the body," and especially in the tongue in corporate prayer and confession.[77]

Despite the language of delight found in the Psalms and echoed in Calvin himself, Protestant moderation often muffled enjoyment and sometimes replaced it with fear.[78] In many Calvinist traditions, strong accents on divine sovereignty and human depravity effectively closed off a corporate *via affirmativa*. Everyday practices and practices of corporate worship that might move through delight to glory were discouraged or never developed. Unlike for Calvin's David, contemplation of the good gifts of life did not offer "ladders" to the sweetness of God; seldom, too, was the mediating work of Christ viewed as moving persons through the heights and depths of creaturely life and, in concert with each other, to the threshold of God's glory. The writer M. F. K. Fisher recalled "that almost joyful stern bowing to duty typical of religious women" found in her grandmother's late Victorian Protestantism. "'Eat what's before you and be thankful for it,' Grandmother said often; or in other words, 'Take what God has created and eat it humbly and without sinful pleasure.'"[79] Similarly stern grandfathers could be found presiding at communion tables. In some churches, an emphasis on the proclaimed Word not only displaced regular observance of the Lord's Supper but also discouraged vivid sight, sound, taste, or movement—of bodies and emotions—in worship. Moreover, it was an abstracted Word, sometimes far removed from the anatomy of creaturely existence and from the affections and afflictions of Jesus' own life.

When psalms and corporate worship raise hearts and minds to God, they ought neither to suppress nor to simply release emotions and affections; rather, they can train attention to needs and satisfactions as crucial connections to God and to the needs and satisfactions of other creatures. Such attunement ought not be confused with a certain kind of propriety and order, as it has all too often been within Anglo-American and European Protestantism, or with more severe pieties that negate sensibilities and agency *as* human. Neither ought such attunement be confused with gaining "more," whether that be more emotions and "experiences," or excess things that high consumer culture may offer. Responsive attunement to the glory of God alive in creatures and cosmos moves between these options. How so? To explore a moderating way, I return briefly to taste and delight and then to the related delights of tables—tables that are formally eucharistic and others that are not. That exploration will return us, finally, to right witness and welcome and to the question raised by the early disciples of what is "enough."

The metaphor of taste is an instructive and complex one for "moving toward" God. When Psalm 34 invites persons to "taste and see that the LORD is good," it connects a judgment about God's goodness with an experience of God's reality. The ability to taste God as good, moreover, implies a process of learning. There are no technologies to correct tastebuds in the way that spectacles correct vision. In fact, medieval scholars used images of chewing and ruminating on the sweetness of Scripture to indicate the extensive care and time needed for the arts of memory and meditation.[80] In addition, the trope of tasting the sweetness of God builds on a bodily sense that is generally shared while lending itself to acknowledgment of pedagogical and cultural aspects of taste, hunger, and their distortions.[81] Finally, taste cannot be separated from the satisfaction of hunger; moreover, the needs of hungry people (and direct action to meet those needs) ought not to be separated from a sense of the fullness of God. Training response to hunger, one's own and the world's, and learning the delights of taste are lifelong tasks.

How are taste and delight related to each other and to creaturely vulnerability? Jean Anthelme Brillat-Savarin argued that taste, among all the senses, is the one "which gives us the greatest joy." The joy of taste is great, it seems, because it can be widely shared and is accessible throughout life, and not first because of the rarified heights it may reach.[82] In his classic meditation, *The Physiology of Taste* (1825), Brillat-Savarin also related the joy of taste to a background awareness of human finitude and loss: "In eating we experience a certain special and indefinable well-being, which arises from our instinctive realization that by the very act we perform we are repairing our bodily losses and prolonging our lives."[83] In this way, acknowledgment of vulnerability is intrinsic to the experience of joy. Brillat-Savarin distinguished between the pleasures of eating, "the actual and direct sensation of satisfying a need," and the pleasures of the table that extend and modify the pleasures of eating culturally and historically.[84] The pleasures of the table are seldom as intense as other pleasures, but they may be more lasting and more sustained, and they may enhance other pleasures or console us for their loss.[85] According to Brillat-Savarin, the moderate delight of taste, contemplated and enhanced in meals that are savored and shared, rightly acknowledges vulnerability and undergirds sociability.

M. F. K. Fisher believed that "the art of eating" must be encouraged and that it could be nurtured in better and worse ways. Over against "impatience for the demands of our bodies," inattention "to the voices of our various hungers," or "shameful carelessness with the food we eat for life itself," she counseled training in attention and enjoyment.[86] (Not incidentally, it was Fisher who translated Brillat-Savarin's work into English, and at the end of World War II.) This was a counsel she gave especially in times of scarcity. In a postscript to her book on cooking and eating during the World War II years, she concluded: "To nourish ourselves with all possible skill, delicacy, and ever-increasing enjoyment" is one of the ways persons can "assert and then reassert our dignity in the face of poverty and war's fears and pains." Moreover, she noted, such arts of nourishment can aid knowledge of other things, including of ourselves and the powers that threaten human survival and dignity.[87] Fisher commended "a kind of culinary caution," learned through the experience of wartime food rationing, that was attentive to food (butter, meat, spices, in particular) as precious and not to be wasted.[88] We might venture to say that in instruction about the art of eating, Fisher joined delight with something of her grandmother's firm insistence on gratitude, on receiving food as a gift.

A café in Bruges, Belgium, has a saying printed on the wall (or it did a few years ago) that, roughly translated from the French, says, "The one who does not honor daily bread has no taste for everlasting bread." Or was it "cannot taste"? "Can never taste"? In Jesus' teaching and parables, one gains a taste of everlasting bread, perhaps even participation in an everlasting banquet, by honoring daily bread, by offering a cup of cool water, by ensuring that there is enough for all. By learning how to nourish ourselves well and to delight in and be grateful for food, persons may begin to imagine the welcome to be received, the hunger to be met, and the joy to be shared at table. If we take food for granted while others go hungry and lack the basic necessities of existence, can we taste what has been provided with delight and gratitude? If daily bread is not honored, can we even begin to imagine with Jesus and the Gospels a welcome table set by God?[89]

When delight, which signals need and its satisfaction and which emerges in relation to an acknowledgment of vulnerability, combines with gratitude, which orients all creatures and things to their source in God, then we are at the heart of a life open to the glory of God alive in the cosmos and in creatures. This way of living before God, this itinerary of delight and gratitude, can be expressed and must be trained in corporate practices that join creatures and cosmos to the transforming reality of God. As Irenaeus taught centuries ago, vulnerable creatures can be strengthened to receive and bear the grace and glory of God. At their best, this is what both daily bread and the great celebration of the Lord's Supper do. Here is Calvin, once again: "We see that this sacred bread is spiritual food, as sweet and delicate as it is healthful for pious worshipers of God, who in tasting it, feel that Christ is their life, whom it moves to thanksgiving, for whom it is an exhortation to mutual love among themselves."[90]

Calvin offered this picture of being delighted, strengthened, transformed, and reoriented by partaking of the Lord's Supper in contrast to his own "culinary caution" about unworthy participation. He saw much at stake in rightful administration and participation: proper honoring and discernment of God, of Christ's body, of other members of the body, and of one's self, as well as the ability to offer healing, solace, and aid to sick, distraught, and needy persons. Such attention and care for right administration and participation, especially when combined with tendencies to order and restraint, may degrade into rigorism and formalism—and did at times. At their worst, corporate practices of worship may serve to divide insiders from outsiders, to close off participation, and to suppress delight and gratitude. Then, shared meals and other means of shaping response to God and the needs of others may not only fail to foster delight and gratitude; they may also serve to suppress hunger and other needs. Their suppression, in turn, limits the possibility of their satisfaction and thereby hinders the ability to anticipate the full welcome of God's table.

Something of this attention and moderation is also evident in the Ring Shout. Historically and in Marshall's novel, the Ring Shout was meant to be worship and not to be confused with dancing—not to be "light and frivolous," as Calvin said. (In the novel, Aunt Cuney had been banned from the Ring Shout for one night for "crossing her feet" in a dance step; she took that lesson severely, and doing so kept her, literally, outside the church for the rest of her life.) One's feet were never to leave the floor, but within that framework, atonal singing and syncopated movement rose in glorification. The Ring Shout conveyed the possibility of a steady but lively existence in contrast to the instability and hindrance—literal and figurative—caused by enslavement and racism. The shouters were taught to engage and turn the world, not as persons who had been brought low by racism and poverty, but as persons whom God had raised up, who rode high in a chariot of divine glory.[91] The Ring Shout offered means for the transformation of persons in community, and also for encircling and reinterpreting a wider world as before God, and it thereby extended possibilities for other relations and transformations. In the novel, it takes a lifetime for Avey to absorb the lessons of the Ring Shout and of the story of the Landing. The final section of Marshall's novel and its culminating ritual, the "Beg Pardon," is the context in which the curious trudge of the Ring Shout connects Avey Johnson to a broader world and an acceptance of her own vocation in it. The Beg Pardon, danced and prayed on the Caribbean island of Carriacou, is a great supplication for the mending and renewal of the generations and the world.[92] I will not recount here how Marshall's heroine comes to partake in the Beg Pardon. Suffice it to say that the movement of the ritual circles wider and draws Avey in, and she finds that the steps she first mimicked as a child allow her to participate. As she takes up the rhythmic trudge as her own, the older generations meet her with gestures of recognition. When they ask her name, she tells them, "Avatara," and accepts the calling that is her name.

Although persons and communities have been hindered, harmed, and remain vulnerable, they can be strengthened to bear the glory of God. In the face of the indignities of poverty and hunger, the destructions of war, disaster, and systemic hatred, and the diminishments of daily existence—small rituals and the great rituals are essential for understanding and living. At their best, these rituals can train awareness to the deepest needs and hungers, and foster delight in their satisfaction and gratitude for what is received and shared. Modest meals—shared by Jesus with Mary and Martha, offered to strangers, fashioned in times of war and devastation, partaken at the communion table—can be "enough." Such modest dignities and the relations they express and nurture may become means by which the glory of God is known as alive in creatures and cosmos.

The purpose of life before God is not to surpass vulnerability, but, in the words of the Westminster Shorter Catechism, to glorify and enjoy God. That, in turn, requires receiving and sharing life as a vulnerable yet glorious gift of God and bearing it toward the full glory of God. Life before God is a field of multiple transformations, a moving space of tensions and conversions, that involves both ongoing resistance and ongoing affirmation. Testimonies to and collective participation in the grace and glory of God are received, shaped, and shared as vulnerable creatures live with and for others and before God. This account of vulnerability and glory contrasts with both sectarian and triumphalist options: the call and testimony of resistance and the itinerary of delight and gratitude are not lived solely within Christian communities and traditions—although they ought to be shaped and exemplified there—but also in everyday ways and in the whole of life.

Vulnerability is part of being creatures who are interdependent with other persons, living things, and the cosmos. The complexity of vulnerability is indicated in the story of Jacob at the ford of the river Jabbock, wrestling through the night with a mysterious stranger, who leaves Jacob both limping and transformed. It is found at the very heart of the Christian gospel in the story of Jesus' life, death, and resurrection. Persons and communities remain susceptible to harm and therefore are almost inevitably marked by suffering and wrong, sometimes by unfathomable tragedy or brutality. And yet, even at the depths of suffering and devastation, human creatures and communities are always also vulnerable to transformation. Vulnerability is the situation in which earthly existence may be harmed and degraded; it is also the situation in which persons and communities may receive and bear the glory of God.

Notes

INTRODUCTION

1. Tracy Wilkinson, "Searching among a Haitian Cathedral's Ruins," *Los Angeles Times*, January 16, 2010, http://articles.latimes.com/2010/jan/16/world/la-fg-haiti-church16-2010jan16. See also Marc Lacey and Damien Cave, "Haitians Seek Solace amid the Ruins," *New York Times*, January 17, 2010, http://www.nytimes.com/2010/01/18/world/americas/18haiti.html.

2. Damon Winter and James Estrin, "On Assignment: Prayers in the Dark," Lens Blog, *New York Times*, January 15, 2010, 12:34 pm, http://lens.blogs.nytimes.com/2010/01/15/assignment-19.

3. The phrase "menace in the air" comes from James Baldwin's novel, *Go Tell It on the Mountain* (1952; repr., New York: Modern Library, 1995), 12. See also John Calvin, *Institutes of the Christian Religion* [1559], ed. John T. McNeill, trans. Ford Lewis Battles, 2 vols. (Philadelphia: Westminster Press, 1960), 1.17.10.

4. Thomas Aquinas, *Summa theologica*, I–II.85.3.

5. For a recent philosophical investigation of vulnerability to cultural devastation, see Jonathan Lear, *Radical Hope: Ethics in the Face of Cultural Devastation* (Cambridge, MA: Harvard University Press, 2006); for a meditation on vulnerability to mourning and violence in post-9/11 America, see Judith Butler, *Precarious Life: The Powers of Mourning and Loss* (London: Verso, 2004); idem, *Frames of War: When Is Life Grievable?* (London: Verso, 2009). See also Susan Sontag, *Regarding the Pain of Others* (New York: Picador, 2003); idem, "Regarding the Torture of Others," in *At the Same Time: Essays and Speeches* (New York: Farrar Strauss Giroux, 2007), 128–42. Also of interest are idem, *Illness as Metaphor; and, AIDS and Its Metaphors* (New York: Picador, 1990); Mary Douglas, *Purity and Danger: An Analysis of Pollution and Taboo*, with a new preface by the author (1966; London: Routledge, 2002); and Mary Douglas and Aaron

Wildavsky, *Risk and Culture: An Essay on the Selection of Technological and Environmental Dangers* (Berkeley: University of California Press, 1982).

6. Four kinds of contemporary theological responses can be compared with my focus on vulnerability to transformation and devastation in life before God. First, theologians have focused on particular threats such as ecological destruction, genocide and the suffering of innocents, sexual violence and the international sex trade, torture, and terrorism. Note also decades of important reflection on race, poverty, and oppression by African American and Latin American liberation theologians. Second, a number of recent theological and philosophical monographs have addressed suffering and evil, such as Douglas John Hall, *The Cross in Our Context: Jesus and the Suffering World* (Minneapolis: Fortress Press, 2003); and Emilie Townes, *Womanist Ethics and the Cultural Production of Evil* (New York: Palgrave Macmillan, 2006). Third, other works have taken up vulnerability and/or suffering in relation to the doctrine of God, soteriology, and Christology, perhaps most famously Jürgen Moltmann's *The Crucified God* (New York: HarperCollins, 1974). More recently see William Placher, *Narratives of a Vulnerable God* (Louisville, KY: Westminster John Knox Press, 1994); and a contrasting view in Rita Nakashima Brock and Rebecca Ann Parker, *Proverbs of Ashes: Violence, Redemptive Suffering, and the Search for What Saves Us* (Boston: Beacon Press, 2002).

Finally, "vulnerability" has a history in women's movements as well, especially as theorized in relation to sexual violence. In contrast to sexual victimization, activists and theorists accented women's agency and bodily integrity. Pioneering work by feminist and womanist theologians theorized bodies, passions, sexuality, and relations as intrinsic to human wholeness, as part of a good creation, and as possible means of grace over against views of these as lesser or deleterious aspects of human existence. For four more recent and diverse feminist theological treatments of risk and vulnerability, see Sharon Welch, *A Feminist Ethic of Risk* (Minneapolis: Fortress Press, 1990); Stephanie Paulsell, *Honoring the Body: Meditations on a Christian Practice* (San Francisco: Jossey-Bass, 2002); Wendy Farley, *The Wounding and Healing of Desire* (Louisville, KY: Westminster John Knox Press, 2006); and Sarah Coakley, *Powers and Submissions: Spirituality, Philosophy and Gender* (Oxford: Blackwell Publishers, 2002), esp. chap. 1, "*Kenōsis* and Subversion: On the Repression of 'Vulnerability' in Christian Feminist Writing."

7. See H. Richard Niebuhr on the error of self-defense in thinking, and on the need for a nonapologetic and nondogmatic approach to thinking theologically, in *The Meaning of Revelation*, (New York: MacMillan, 1941; repr., Louisville, KY: Westminster John Knox Press, 2006), xxxiv and passim; and "Toward New Symbols," in *Theology, History, and Culture: Major Unpublished Writings*, ed. William Stacy Johnson (New Haven, CT: Yale University Press, 1996), 19–33.

8. Sontag, *Regarding the Pain of Others*, 99. Sontag's essay about how photographic representation of others' pain in faraway places turns persons into

spectators includes many other observations relevant to viewing images of Haiti's devastation.

CHAPTER 1: FROM PAUL'S EARTHEN VESSEL
TO AUGUSTINE'S MIXED BODY

1. See Dale B. Martin, *The Corinthian Body* (New Haven, CT: Yale University Press, 1995). I have been informed by his reading of *sōma* (body) and *pneuma*; see esp. 123–32.

2. Victor Paul Furnish, *II Corinthians*, Anchor Bible 32A (Garden City, NY: Doubleday, 1994), 253, 280. See also idem, "2 Corinthians," in *HarperCollins Bible Commentary*, ed. James L. Mays (San Francisco: HarperSanFrancisco, 2000), 1097.

3. Martin, *The Corinthian Body*, 160–61, and chap. 6 passim. Martin's etiologies build upon Margaret M. Lock, *East Asian Medicine in Japan* (Berkeley: University of California Press, 1980); René Dubos, *Man Adapting*, enlarged ed. (New Haven, CT: Yale University Press, 1980); idem, *Mirage of Health: Utopias, Progress, and Biological Change* (New York: Harper & Brothers, 1959). Martin's tacit assumption is that, in Paul, the invasion etiology accounts for the threat of dangerous external agents and not the work of Christ. That is, Paul does not portray Christ as an external agent who somehow invades the Corinthian body; the Corinthians are already incorporated into Christ.

4. Martin, *The Corinthian Body*, 135.

5. See ibid., 131, and chap. 9 for Martin's exegesis of 1 Cor. 11. He concludes that Paul's assumed physiology of women's more porous and thus more susceptible bodies leaves the male-female hierarchy unquestioned. We can add that Paul seems also to have assumed that only dangerous spirits and not the spirit of Christ would "invade" the prophesying women.

6. At other times substitution rather than transformation seems to be portrayed; see, e.g., the "earthly tent" that is destroyed and replaced with a "heavenly dwelling" (2 Cor. 5:1–2).

7. Irenaeus, *Adversus haereses* 3.24.1, in Henry Bettenson, ed. and trans., *The Early Christian Fathers: A Selection from the Writings of the Fathers from St. Clement of Rome to St. Athanasius* (Oxford: Oxford University Press, 1956), 83 (cited below as Bettenson).

8. Peter Brown, *The Body and Society: Men, Women, and Sexual Renunciation in Early Christianity* (New York: Columbia University Press, 1988), 141.

9. Brown, *The Body and Society*, 68. See also Margaret Miles, *Fullness of Life: Historical Foundations for a New Asceticism* (Philadelphia: Westminster Press, 1981), 19–36.

10. See, e.g., Irenaeus, *Adversus haereses* 2.22.4; 3.16.6; 3.21.10; 3.22.3; 5.20.2–5.21.1; in Bettenson, 80–83. See also Miles, *Fullness of Life*, 28.

11. Irenaeus, *Adversus haereses* 5.8.1, in Bettenson, 84. Brown offers a more vivid translation in *The Body and Society*, 73: "accustomed, little by little, to receive and to bear the mighty weight of God." "Bearing the mighty weight of God" alludes to 2 Cor. 4:17: "For this slight momentary affliction is preparing us for an eternal weight of glory beyond all measure."

12. Eusebius of Caesarea, *Ecclesiastical History* 5.1.50, as quoted in Elizabeth A. Castelli, *Martyrdom and Memory: Early Christian Culture Making* (New York: Columbia University Press, 2004), 45–46.

13. "The Martyrs of Lyon," in *The Acts of the Christian Martyrs*, ed. and trans. Herbert Musurillo (Oxford: Clarendon Press, 1972), 9, 56.

14. Elaine Scarry, *The Body in Pain: The Making and Unmaking of the World* (New York: Oxford University Press, 1985), 4.

15. Ibid., 9.

16. Ibid., 36–38; see chap. 1 for her analysis of the structure of torture's "unmaking."

17. Ibid., 38–45.

18. Ignatius of Antioch, *Letter to the Romans* 4.1–2, in *Apostolic Fathers*, 2 vols., trans. Kirsopp Lake, Loeb Classical Library (Cambridge, MA: Harvard University Press, 1927), as adapted and quoted in Castelli, *Martyrdom and Memory*, 79. Also in Cyril Richardson, ed. and trans., *Early Christian Fathers* (New York: Macmillan, 1970), 104 (cited below as Richardson). See also the remembrance of the execution by burning of Polycarp, bishop of Smyrna, around 156–157, at the age of eighty-six. As he stood in the fire, a "sweet aroma" rose, "not as burning flesh, but rather as bread baking or as gold and silver refined in a furnace" (*Martyrdom of Polycarp* 15.2, in Richardson, 155). See also Brown, *Body and Society*, 71–72; Castelli, *Martyrdom and Memory*, 52–55; and Caroline Walker Bynum, *The Resurrection of the Body in Western Christianity, 200–1330* (New York: Columbia University Press, 1995), 43–51.

19. Castelli observes: "Read through Christian lenses, the story of Christian encounters with their Roman others is a cosmic battle narrative in which the opposition embodied by the Roman authorities takes on demonic auras and resonances. Read through Roman lenses, this same story is often an incidental account of a minor set of skirmishes with unruly subjects—or indeed, a story that does not even merit being recorded" (*Martyrdom and Memory*, 36).

20. Eusebius, *Ecclesiastical History* 5.1.56, as quoted in Castelli, *Martyrdom and Memory*, 54.

21. Castelli, *Martyrdom and Memory*, 54.

22. Ibid., 25.

23. Ibid., 48. In her epilogue, Castelli writes that an alternative interpretation of "martyr" might focus less on "the willful, the willing, the will-sublimating sacrifice of self (a sacrifice that can too easily, in its logic, enable a sacrifice of the other)" and more on witness and testimony. "The overprivileging of the self-

sacrificial dimensions of the 'martyr' results in a flattening out, the dangerous eclipsing of the possibility of recognizing the suffering of others" (ibid., 203).

24. Irenaeus, *Adversus haereses* 1.10.1–2, in Richardson, 360.

25. In *Adversus haereses* 5.13.2, Irenaeus refutes Gnostic "proof-texting" of 1 Cor. 15:50, "flesh and blood cannot possess the kingdom of God," as simplistic and mistaken. Instead, Irenaeus teaches that the whole economy of salvation involves the binding of the Spirit with the substance of flesh and blood. On Irenaeus's opponents, see Robert M. Grant, *Irenaeus of Lyons* (London: Routledge, 1997).

26. Irenaeus, *Adversus haereses* 4.18.5, in Bettenson, 96.

27. Irenaeus, *Adversus haereses* 3.4.1, in Richardson, 374.

28. This conclusion follows Irenaeus's statement that "where the Spirit of God is, there is the Church." *Adversus haereses* 3.24.1, in Bettenson, 83.

29. See B. C. Butler, *The Idea of the Church* (Baltimore: Helicon, 1962), 56–59.

30. Tertullian, *De resurrectione carnis* 7, as quoted in Miles, *Fullness of Life*, 19. In the preceding section, Tertullian describes God as lovingly absorbed in the task of molding the human form from clay, anticipating its ennobled condition in Christ (*De resurrectione carnis* 6, in Bettenson, 113).

31. Tertullian, *De resurrectione carnis* 8.2, as quoted in Bynum, *The Resurrection of the Body*, 43.

32. See Elaine Pagels: "The orthodox tradition implicitly affirms bodily experience as the central fact of human life. What one does physically—one eats and drinks, engages in sexual life or avoids it, saves one's life or gives it up—all are vital elements in one's *religious* development." *The Gnostic Gospels* (New York: Vintage Books, 1981), 122.

33. J. N. D. Kelly, *Early Christian Doctrines* (London: Adam & Charles Black, 1958), 191. See also Eric G. Jay, *The Church: Its Changing Image through Twenty Centuries* (Atlanta: John Knox Press, 1980), 63; and Jaroslav Pelikan, *The Christian Tradition: A History of the Development of Doctrine*, vol. 1, *The Emergence of the Catholic Tradition (100–600)* (Chicago: University of Chicago Press, 1971), 160.

34. Origen, *Homiliae in Jeremiam* 4.3, as cited in Henry Chadwick, "Introduction to *Exhortation to Martyrdom*," in *Alexandrian Christianity*, ed. and trans. Henry Chadwick and John Ernest Leonard Oulton (Philadelphia: Westminster Press, 1954), 391.

35. See H. J. Vogt, "Ecclesiology" in *Encyclopedia of the Early Church*, ed. Angelo Di Berardino, trans. Arian Walford, vol. 1, produced by Institutum Patristicum Augustinianum (New York: Oxford University Press, 1992), 260.

36. Origen, *Homiliae in Jeremiam* 4.3.

37. This chapter neglects an intricate set of theological negotiations about one particular body, the body of Christ, and how the church is related to that body. I will return to some of these themes in later chapters.

38. In tracing changing approaches to vulnerability and transformation in

relation to this figure, I am not seeking to establish a definitive "original meaning" of the figure or to trace distortions from such a fixed meaning. Neither am
I arguing that "treasure in earthen vessels" is *the* master trope for picturing the
relation of vulnerable and transformed life, only that its use is pervasive enough
to be instructive. That said, this figure (and later, Augustine's antithesis of the
visible and invisible church) is connected with other paired relations—mor-
tality/humility/weakness and glory, human and divine, the bodily or material
and the verbal, the structural and the organic, hidden and revealed, outer and
inner—and this constellation of relations is decisive.

39. H. Richard Niebuhr's *Christ and Culture* (New York: Harper & Row,
1951; repr., HarperSanFrancisco, 2001) is the background here. I take up his
argument in chapter 5.

40. Cyprian, *Letters* 54.3, as quoted in John Calvin, *Institutes of the Christian
Religion* [1559], ed. John T. McNeill, trans. Ford Lewis Battles, 2 vols. (Philadelphia: Westminster Press, 1960), 4.1.19 (cited below as *Inst.*). Calvin also refers
to the image of breaking vessels in the "Prefatory Address to King Francis I of
France," *Inst.*, 12.

41. *Martyrdom of Polycarp* 15.2, in Richardson, 155.

42. See S. L. Greenslade, "Introduction" to Cyprian, *On the Unity of the
Catholic Church*, in *Early Latin Theology*, trans. and ed. S. L. Greenslade (Philadelphia: Westminster Press, 1956), 120.

43. Cyprian, *Unity* 5.

44. See Kelly, *Early Christian Doctrines*, 209.

45. Cyprian, *Unity* 6.

46. Ibid., 23.

47. Ibid., 9.

48. Greenslade, "Introduction," 121.

49. Vogt, "Ecclesiology," 261, paraphrasing Augustine (*Enarrationes in Psal-
mos* 25.5). Augustine also uses the threshing-floor image in *On Baptism* 1.17–
26, in *Nicene and Post-Nicene Fathers* [cited below as *NPNF*], ed. Philip Schaff,
vol. 4 (1887; repr., Grand Rapids: Wm. B. Eerdmans Publishing Co., 1987).

50. Augustine, *De catechizandis rudibus* 25.48, as quoted in Peter Brown,
Augustine of Hippo: A Biography (Berkeley: University of California Press,
1967), 213. See also Augustine, *First Catechetical Instruction*, ed. Johannes
Quasten and Joseph Plumpe (1946; Mahwah, NJ: Paulist Press, 1996), 80.

51. Brown, *Augustine of Hippo*, 213.

52. Ibid., 215–20.

53. Augustine, *On Baptism* 1.16.25. For a striking twentieth-century reprise
of this image, see James Baldwin, *Go Tell It on the Mountain*, part 3, "The
Threshing Floor" (New York: Modern Library, 1995), 267–68.

54. Brown, *Augustine of Hippo*, 224.

55. Augustine, *On Baptism* 5.27.38. See Brown, *Augustine of Hippo*, 223; and
Pelikan, vol. 1, *The Emergence of the Catholic Tradition*, 302–4.

56. Augustine, *On Baptism* 1.6.8.

57. Pelikan, vol. 1, *The Emergence of the Catholic Tradition*, 302.

58. Augustine, *Retractionum*, 2.18, as quoted by Vogt, "Ecclesiology," 261.

59. Brown, *Augustine of Hippo*, 221–22. Brown cites Augustine, *Confessions* 12.11–13, as an example. On "only an imperfect shadow," Brown cites Alois Wachtel, *Beiträge zur Geschichtstheologie des Aurelius Augustinus* (Bonn: Röhrscheid, 1960), 118–19. The citation for "according to a certain shadow of the reality" is Augustine, *Contra epistolam Parmeniani* 2.4.8.

60. Brown, *Augustine of Hippo*, 222.

61. Martin, *The Corinthian Body*, 143.

62. Augustine, *Sermon 272*, in *NPNF*, vol. 7. See also *Sermon 268.2*, in *NPNF*, vol. 7.

63. Pelikan, vol. 1, *The Emergence of the Catholic Tradition*, 303; Kelly, *Early Christian Doctrines*, 417; Jay, *The Church*, 87; Brown, *Augustine of Hippo*, 223.

64. Brown, *Augustine of Hippo*, 225.

65. Augustine, *De moribus catholicae et de moribus Manichaeorum* I.30.63, as quoted in Brown, *Augustine of Hippo*, 225.

66. Calvin himself stopped short, just short, of making right order one of the marks of the church, arguing: "If churches are well-ordered, they will not bear the wicked in their bosom" (*Inst.* 4.1.15).

67. See Jay, *The Church*, 91.

68. Jaroslav Pelikan, *The Christian Tradition: A History of the Development of Doctrine*, vol. 4, *Reformation of Church and Dogma (1300–1700)* (Chicago: University of Chicago Press, 1984), 174. Whereas theologians before him and John Calvin after him explained that the church gives birth to, nourishes, protects, and strengthens Christians, Luther attributes this "mothering" agency to the Word of God. For relevant passages in Luther's works, see Brian Gerrish, *The Old Protestantism and the New: Essays on the Reformation Heritage* (Chicago: University of Chicago Press, 1982), 95 n. 23.

69. Martin Luther, *Table-Talk*, No. 453, as quoted in *A Compend of Luther's Theology*, ed. Hugh Thompson Kerr Jr. (Philadelphia: Westminster Press, 1943), 137. See Luther, No. 2962b, in Martin Luther, *Luther's Works*, ed. Helmut T. Lehmann, vol. 54, *Table Talk*, ed. and trans. Theodore G. Tappert (Philadelphia: Fortress Press, 1967), 185–86.

70. See Luther's extended invective against the "whore-church of the devil" in *Against Hanswurst* (1541), in Martin Luther, *Luther's Works*, ed. Lehmann, vol. 41, *Church and Ministry III*, ed. Eric W. Gritsch (Philadelphia: Fortress Press, 1966), esp. 205–28.

71. Brown, *Body and Society*, 425.

72. On "frailty," see ibid., 405; "twisted will," 422; "ache of discord," 427. Brown cites Augustine, *Enarratio in Psalmum* 147, 20, for "peace in its fullness," 427 n. 157.

CHAPTER 2: ASSEMBLED UNDER THE CROSS

1. Martin Luther, *Against Hanswurst* (1541), trans. W. P. Stephens, in Martin Luther, *Luther's Works*, ed. Helmut T. Lehmann, vol. 41, *Church and Ministry III*, ed. Eric W. Gritsch (Philadelphia: Fortress Press, 1966), 211 (*Luther's Works* cited below as *LW*).

2. See the end of chapter 1. The phrase is from Peter Brown, *The Body and Society: Men, Women, and Sexual Renunciation in Early Christianity* (New York: Columbia University Press, 1988), 427.

3. Scholars estimate that half to two-thirds of the population lived near or below subsistence levels, with natural disasters and market fluctuations constantly threatening to worsen their conditions. See Samuel Torvend, *Luther and the Hungry Poor: Gathered Fragments* (Minneapolis: Fortress Press, 2008), 17. He cites Catharina Lis and Hugo Soly, *Poverty and Capitalism in Pre-Industrial Europe* (Atlantic Highlands: Humanities, 1979), 53–96.

4. David C. Steinmetz, "Luther against Luther," in *Luther in Context*, 2nd ed. (Grand Rapids: Baker Academic, 2002), 1. On *Anfectung* and the social trauma of his age, see also Richard Marius, *Martin Luther: The Christian between God and Death* (Cambridge, MA: Belknap, Harvard University Press, 1999), esp. chaps. 1–4; Martin Marty, *Martin Luther*, A Penguin Life (New York: Lipper/Viking, 2004).

5. Steinmetz, "Luther and Calvin on the Banks of the Jabbock," in *Luther in Context*, 156–68; and Marty, *Martin Luther*, 25–27.

6. Martin Luther, *Predigten* 25.vii (1522), in *D. Martin Luthers Werke: Kritische Gresamtausgabe* (Weimar, 1883–) [cited as *WA*] 10.3:239 as translated and cited in Jaroslav Pelikan, *The Christian Tradition: A History of the Development of Doctrine*, vol. 4, *Reformation of Church and Dogma (1300–1700)* (Chicago: University of Chicago Press, 1984), 165. See Pelikan's discussion of Luther's theology of the cross, 155–67.

7. Martin Luther, *Heidelberg Disputation* (1530), in *Martin Luther's Basic Theological Writings*, ed. Timothy F. Lull (Minneapolis: Fortress Press, 1989), 43–44 (cited below as Lull).

8. Heiko A. Oberman, *Luther: Man between God and the Devil*, trans. Eileen Walliser-Schwartzbart (New Haven, CT: Yale University Press, 1989; New York: Doubleday, Image Books, 1992), 253–54.

9. Oberman, *Luther*, 270; also 263–64.

10. Martin Luther, *On the Councils and the Church* (1539), trans. Charles M. Jacobs, rev. Eric W. Gritsch, *LW* 41:164–65, with original brackets.

11. Ibid.,165. See also Oberman, *Luther*, 255.

12. Luther, *Against Hanswurst*, *LW* 41:197.

13. Ibid., 198–99, with original brackets.

14. Martin Luther, *The Freedom of a Christian* (1520), in Lull, 606.

15. Luther, *Heidelberg Disputation*, in Lull, 41, with original brackets. Note also his next point: "He knows that it is sufficient if he suffers and is brought low by the cross in order to be annihilated all the more."

16. Martin Luther, *The Pagan Servitude of the Church* [1520], in *Martin Luther: Selections from His Writings,* ed. John Dillenberger (Garden City, N.Y.: Doubleday, Anchor Books, 1961), 261, 271, 250. Scholars have challenged Luther's sweeping characterizations of the church's decay and corruption, including the "Babylonian Captivity" (i.e., the Avignonese papacy), the moral laxity of the popes, and the "stupid priest." See Susan E. Schreiner, "Church," *The Oxford Encyclopedia of the Reformation,* vol. 1, ed. Hans J. Hillerbrand (New York: Oxford University Press, 1996), 323–27.

17. Heiko Oberman argues that Luther understood the church and indeed, the whole of human life and history, as a battleground between God and the devil. According to Oberman, "the discovery that the wealthy, powerful Church was in fact a Church in captivity ignited the Reformation" (*Luther,* 270). Scholars have argued that the sixteenth-century Reformation debates were at least as much about the nature of the church as they were about justification or grace. See Schreiner, "Church"; Paul D. L. Avis, *The Church in the Theology of the Reformers* (Atlanta: John Knox Press, 1981), 1; Geddes MacGregor, *Corpus Christi: The Nature of the Church according to the Reformed Tradition* (Philadelphia: Westminster Press, 1958), 5; and Peter Hodgson, *Revisioning the Church: Ecclesial Freedom in the New Paradigm* (Philadelphia: Fortress Press, 1988), 44.

18. See, e.g., the concluding paragraphs of Luther's pivotal treatise, *The Freedom of a Christian,* in Lull, 625. There he contrasts his proposed "middle course" to the "unyielding, stubborn ceremonialists" of his day "who like deaf adders are not willing to hear the truth of liberty [Ps. 58:4] but, having no faith, boast of, prescribe, and insist upon their ceremonies as means of justification." To these already pungent polemics, Luther adds an entirely gratuitous comment: "Such were the Jews of old, who were unwilling to learn how to do good." He does not write, "Such were Paul's *opponents* of old," but rather "such were [all] the Jews of old"—and that is not the last disparagement of the paragraph. For brief overviews of Luther's often but not always hostile stance toward the Jews of his day and Judaism, see Marius, *Martin Luther,* 372–80; Marty, *Martin Luther,* 169–75; and Oberman, *Luther,* 292–97.

19. Luther, *The Ninety-five Theses,* in Dillenberger, *Martin Luther,* 496.

20. Luther, *Apology of the Augsburg Confession* 4.67, as quoted in Pelikan, vol. 4, *Reformation of Church and Dogma,* 166.

21. Luther, *Resolution concerning the Lutheran Thesis XIII on the Power of the Pope* (1519), WA 2:208, as cited in Eric W. Gritsch, "Introduction to *Church and Ministry,*" in *LW,* vol. 39, *Church and Ministry I,* ed. Eric W. Gritsch (1970), xii.

22. Luther, *On the Councils and the Church,* in LW 41:149–51.

23. Martin Luther, No. 4360, February 1539, in Luther, *LW,* vol. 54, *Table Talk,* ed. and trans. Theodore G. Tappert (1967), 333. Jaroslav Pelikan observes that the language of Luther's 1517 proposition about the true treasure of the gospel of the glory and the grace of God was not new in itself. "Yet, all the decisive terms in this axiom—such words as 'church,' 'gospel,' and 'grace'—come

to mean something in the sixteenth century that many of these [earlier] theologians would not quite have been able to recognize or acknowledge" (vol. 4, *Reformation of Church and Dogma*, 128). Regarding language, note also the "sexual politics" of Luther's images of vessels and treasure, the "whore-church of the devil," a potent word of God, and the true church as a "bride" with whom God "sleeps" (see below).

24. Luther construed doctrine or teaching as the chief expression of the gospel. The renewal of moral, religious, and sacramental life were secondary to the recovery of sound doctrine. Sound doctrine is the Word of God rightly heard, and centrally, justification by faith. Scripture alone (thus interpreted), not theological or philosophical speculation, can provide the basis for Christian life and thought. See Oberman, *Luther*, 55–57; also 117–19.

25. MacGregor notes that Luther's reformulation may have been informed by medieval conciliarist theories that favored the authority of the church as *congregatio fidelium* over the papacy and the curia (*Corpus Christi*, 28).

26. Martin Luther, *Concerning the Ministry* (1523), trans. Conrad Bergendoff, in *LW*, vol. 40, *Church and Ministry II*, ed. Conrad Bergendoff (Philadelphia: Muhlenberg Press, 1958), 19.

27. Martin Luther, *The Freedom of a Christian*, in Lull, 623.

28. Luther's revolutionary insight is expressed by the contemporary Catholic theologian Hans Küng: "The fundamental error of ecclesiologies which turned out, in fact, to be no more than hierarchologies . . . was that they failed to realize that all who hold [priestly] office are primarily (both temporally and practically speaking) not dignitaries but believers, members of the fellowship of believers." *The Church* (Garden City, NY: Doubleday, Image Books, 1976), 465.

29. Wilhelm Pauck observed that the priesthood of believers has served more as a critical principle against Roman Catholic clericalism than as a constructive ideal for Lutheran congregational life. "Luther's Conception of the Church," in Wilhelm Pauck, *The Heritage of the Reformation*, rev. ed., (Glencoe, IL: The Free Press, 1961), 51. Luther mitigated the import of a functionally defined vocation of the ministry—versus an ontologically distinguished ministry—with his assumption that women and others are excluded categorically from the ministry. Women, children, and "incompetent people," he wrote, have been "excepted" from the function of ministry by the Holy Spirit "even though they are able to hear God's word, to receive baptism, the sacrament, absolution, and are also true, holy Christians" (*On the Councils and the Church*, in *LW* 41:154–55).

30. Paul Tillich, "The Protestant Principle and the Proletarian Situation [1931]," in Tillich, *The Protestant Era*, trans. James Luther Adams (Chicago: University of Chicago Press, 1948; abridged ed., Phoenix Books, 1957), 175.

31. Ibid., 174–75. Compare H. Richard Niebuhr's argument that radical monotheism effects both "consistent secularization" *and* "the sanctification of all things," in *Radical Monotheism and Western Culture: With Supplementary*

Essays (New York: Harper, 1960; repr., Louisville, KY: Westminster/John Knox Press, 1993), 52; and as discussed below in chapter 5.

32. Luther excluded penance, marriage, priesthood, and unction from this list; he retained only baptism and the Lord's Supper among traditional sacraments (Luther, *Confession concerning Christ's Supper*, in Lull, 60). Article 7 of *The Augsburg Confession*, prepared in 1530 by Philip Melanchthon in consultation with Luther, offers what is now the best-known formulation: "That the Gospel be preached in conformity with a pure understanding of it and that the sacraments be administered in accordance with the divine Word." Augsburg elaborates baptism, the Lord's Supper, and modified forms of confession and repentance as sacraments.

33. On relics in medieval piety, see, e.g., Patrick J. Geary, *Living with the Dead in the Middle Ages* (Ithaca, NY: Cornell University Press, 1994); and Jonathan Sumption, *Pilgrimage: The Medieval Journey to God* (1975; repr., Mahwah, NJ: Hidden Spring, 2003).

34. Luther, *On the Councils and the Church*, LW 41:166.

35. Ibid., 167.

36. On the contrast between the explanatory and the apologetic use of the attributes of the church, see Küng, *The Church*, 344–45.

37. Luther, *On the Councils and the Church*, LW 41:199.

38. Ibid., 167.

39. Luther, *Against Hanswurst*, LW 41:211.

40. Luther, *On the Papacy in Rome, Against the Most Celebrated Romanist in Leipzig* (1520), trans. Eric W. and Ruth C. Gritsch, LW 39:65.

41. "A Christian lives not in himself, but in Christ and in his neighbor. Otherwise he is not a Christian. He lives in Christ through faith, in his neighbor through love. By faith he is caught up beyond himself into God. By love he descends beneath himself into his neighbor. Yet he always remains in God and in his love" (Luther, *The Freedom of a Christian*, in Lull, 623).

42. Ibid., 619.

43. Luther, *On the Papacy in Rome*, LW 39:65.

44. As H. Richard Niebuhr put it in his interpretation of Luther, faith does not depend upon the mediation of the church to interact with culture; rather, it "find[s] its way in culture through culture's methods." Niebuhr, *Christ and Culture* (New York: Harper & Row, 1951; HarperSanFrancisco, 2001), 216.

45. "The holy church is not bound to Rome; rather, it extends to the end of the earth, assembled in one faith" (Luther, *On the Papacy in Rome*, LW 39:75).

46. Similarly, in *On the Councils and the Church* (1539), Luther rejected the visible accouterments of medieval holiness—"the prescription of chasubles, tonsures, cowls, garb, food, festivals, monkery, nunning, masses, saint-worship"— because they are "items of an external, bodily, transitory nature" (LW 41:147). More exactly, Luther viewed them as "purely external," that is, *merely* external, and as neither essential to salvation nor instituted by God.

47. In *On the Papacy in Rome*, Luther quotes Col. 3:3 to make a similar point: "Our life is not on earth, but hidden with Christ in God" (*LW* 39:69).

48. Luther, *Table Talk*, No. 624, *LW* 54:110.

49. Luther, *The Freedom of a Christian*, in Lull, 607, with original brackets.

50. Luther, *On the Papacy in Rome*, *LW* 39:65–66.

51. Ibid., 67.

52. Ibid., 66. Compare Augustine: "In that unspeakable foreknowledge of God, many who seem to be without are in reality within, and many who seem to be within yet really are without." Augustine, *On Baptism* 5.27.38, in *Nicene and Post-Nicene Fathers*, ed. Philip Schaff, vol. 4 (New York, 1887; repr., Grand Rapids: Wm. B. Eerdmans Publishing Co., 1987).

53. Luther editor Eric Gritsch notes that Luther consistently maintained a "paradoxical dialectic" between the visible fellowship and the hidden church. According to Gritsch, in Luther's view "the church is neither an invisible Platonic reality nor an unchanging institution. Rather, like the individual Christian, the church is continually struggling and constantly re-created and sustained by the word of God" ("Introduction to *Church and Ministry*," *LW* 39:xvi).

54. Luther, *On the Papacy in Rome*, *LW* 39:70.

55. Luther, in a sermon on Luke 19:1–10, preached in 1527. Cf. *WA* 17.2:501, as cited by Gritsch, "Introduction to *Church and Ministry*," *LW* 39:xiii.

56. Hodgson, *Revisioning the Church*, 45, with original emphasis.

57. Oberman, *Luther*, 250.

CHAPTER 3: CALVIN ON CORRUPTION AND TRANSFORMATION

1. John Calvin, *Institutes of the Christian Religion*, ed. John T. McNeill and trans. Ford Lewis Battles, 2 vols. (Philadelphia: Westminster Press, 1960), 4.1.1. Citations in this chapter are from this translation of the 1559 Latin edition, and location will be given in the text; cited in the notes as *Inst.*

2. While the *Institutes* constitute only a small portion of Calvin's teaching and writing, he offered it as the central statement of Christian teaching and revised it throughout his career. I also take its structure to be representative of the structure of his thought.

3. John Calvin, "Prefatory Address to King Francis I of France," in *Inst.*, 9–31. Citations are given as page numbers in the 1960 translation. Calvin's address responded to the king's brutal retaliation against French Protestants after the affair of the placards in late 1534. See chapter 7 below and also Carlos N. M. Eire, *War Against the Idols: The Reformation of Worship from Erasmus to Calvin* (Cambridge: Cambridge University Press, 1986), 189–93.

4. Echoing in Calvin's "Prefatory Address to King Francis I of France," as in much of his thought, were Paul's words from Rom. 1:21: "Though they knew God, they did not honor him as God or give thanks to him, but they became futile in their thinking, and their senseless minds were darkened."

5. Hilary of Poitiers, *Against the Arians or Auxentius of Milan* xii (Migne, PL 10.616), as cited in Calvin, *Inst.*, 25 n. 43.

6. Some of this discussion of idolatry appeared previously in my chapter "Always Reforming, Always Resisting," in *Feminist and Womanist Essays in Reformed Dogmatics,* ed. Amy Plantinga Pauw and Serene Jones (Louisville, KY: Westminster John Knox Press, 2006), 152–68.

7. Let me be clear: I do not mean to suggest that an "idolatry critique" à la Calvin is fully adequate to the complexity of current situations and thereby to eschew the use of other critical theories. A theological diagnosis of any situation also necessitates the use of a range of political, cultural, and social theories, using both theology and theory to inform transformative engagement with and for others and before God.

8. Eire, *War Against the Idols*, 232.

9. William J. Bouwsma suggests that Calvin's construal of the thoroughgoingness of original sin had an equalizing effect on his interpretation of history and that it effected a "Copernican revolution" in the moral and social universe—a point similar to the one I make here. See Bouwsma, *John Calvin: A Sixteenth-Century Portrait* (New York: Oxford University Press, 1988), 144.

10. See Stephen D. Benin, *The Footprints of God: Divine Accommodation in Jewish and Christian Thought* (Albany: State University of New York Press, 1993). I am indebted to Margaret Mitchell for this reference. Calvin's first published book, his commentary on Seneca's *De clementia*, discusses Seneca's use of accommodation to advance his philosophical position. See Bruce Gordon, *Calvin* (New Haven, CT: Yale University Press, 2009), 24–25.

11. See the full passage in *Inst.* 2.11.13 and also the discussion of it in Benin, *The Footprints of God*, 190. See also Calvin's discussion of the Word of God in its various manifestations—the Law, the Prophets, and the apostles—relative to the authority of the church, in 4.8.

12. See Ford Lewis Battles, "God was Accommodating Himself to Human Capacity," *Interpretation* 31 (January 1977): 19–38. See also Edward Dowey, *The Knowledge of God in Calvin's Theology*, expanded ed. (Grand Rapids: Wm. B. Eerdmans Publishing Co., 1994), esp. chap. 1; and Serene Jones, *Calvin and the Rhetoric of Piety* (Louisville, KY: Westminster John Knox Press, 1995).

13. Bouwsma accents Calvin's innovative approach to theology itself as a nonspeculative, nonsystematic, useful, and empirically informed knowledge that addresses the intellect and affections, even while acknowledging the limits of human comprehension (*John Calvin*, 160). I am characterizing Calvin's approach as entailing the recognition of the genuine ambiguity of life and as undergirded by his notion of divine accommodation, by contrast, Bouwsma characterizes Calvin as accepting Luther's paradoxical view but being "less enthusiastic" and "ambivalent" about it (161).

14. Calvin, *Sermon No. 30 on Deuteronomy*, 238, as quoted in Bouwsma, *John Calvin*, 192.

15. Bouwsma, *John Calvin*, 277. Bouwsma cites passages in several of Calvin's works for these images: *Comm. Ps.* 119:35 for "God's school"; *Comm. Jer.* 32:40 for God looking over the shoulder of his pupils; *Inst.* 1.6.4 for Scripture as textbook; *Serm. No. 34 on Job 9:7–8*, 419, for the repeating schoolmaster; and *Supplex exhortatio*, CO [Calvini Opera] 6:490–91, for the Protestant emphasis on preaching as teaching.

16. Susan E. Schreiner observes that "Calvin was equally (if not more) concerned with the visible church" than Luther. In Schreiner, "Church," *The Oxford Encyclopedia of the Reformation*, ed. Hans J. Hillerbrand, vol. 1 (New York: Oxford University Press, 1996), 325. For comparisons among sixteenth-century Reformed theologians and with Luther, see also John T. McNeill, "The Church in Sixteenth-Century Reformed Theology," *Journal of Religion* 22 (July 1942): 251–69.

17. Calvin did not understand worship as a private affair between an individual and God, as something that could take place apart from actual communities of faith. He prized the benefits of proper corporate worship and called French Protestants to leave everything behind—home, trade, nation—to go into exile for its benefits. See Eire, *War Against the Idols*, 262; and Bouwsma, *John Calvin*, 216. Both Eire and Bouwsma relate Calvin's insistence on the benefits of actual worshiping communities to Calvin's "anti-Nicodemism." See Eire, *War Against the Idols*, chap. 7, "Calvin against the Nicodemites," 234–75.

18. By contrast, Geddes MacGregor argued that Calvin was the first theologian to develop a "definite theory" about the invisible church. *Corpus Christi: The Nature of the Church according to the Reformed Tradition* (Philadelphia: Westminster Press, 1958), 43.

19. "The church is founded upon the teaching of the apostles and prophets, with Christ himself as the chief cornerstone" (*Inst.* 4.2.1). Calvin cites the phrase "the teaching of the apostles and prophets," based on Eph. 2:20 and 4:11, perhaps more often than any other biblical text in his sections on the church. See, e.g., *Inst.* 4.1.1; 4.2.1; 4.2.4.

20. "Nonessentials" include matters such as "that souls upon leaving bodies fly to heaven." Essential doctrines pertaining to the sum of religion are "God is one; Christ is God and the Son of God; our salvation rests in God's mercy; and the like" (*Inst.* 4.1.12).

21. Bouwsma, *John Calvin*, 100.

22. See also *Inst.* 1.2.2 and 3.2.8 and the discussion in Bouwsma, *John Calvin*, 158–59. On the civil and ecclesiastical order in Geneva, see William Naphy, *Calvin and the Consolidation of the Genevan Reformation* (Louisville, KY: Westminster John Knox Press, 2004); and idem, "Calvin's Geneva," in *The Cambridge Companion to John Calvin*, ed. Donald K. McKim (Cambridge: Cambridge University Press, 2004), 25–37.

23. Luther, *On the Papacy in Rome* (1520), in *Luther's Works*, ed. Helmut T. Lehmann, vol. 39, *Church and Ministry I*, ed. Eric W. Gritsch (Philadelphia: Fortress Press, 1970), 65.

24. It would be incorrect to blame Calvin for the ills of all modern bureau-cracies, including bureaucratic religion; yet later Calvinists engaged readily in capitalism's rationalized economic order and the modern bureaucratic state. For the most part, bureaucratic churches did not presume to align modern societies in proper offices and relations as did older ecclesiastical hierarchies; instead, they brokered power with economic and political forces.

25. Philip Benedict, *Christ's Churches Purely Reformed: A Social History of Calvinism* (New Haven, CT: Yale University Press, 2002), 117. See also Gordon, *Calvin*, 276.

26. Carlos Eire notes that "though Calvin accepts the possibility of martyr-dom, he never advises this sacrifice as the norm for those who stay behind," that is, for French Calvinists who do not flee into exile. "Instead of calling for an aggressive struggle against 'idolatry,' Calvin calls for an assertive but quiet withdrawal which is to be coupled with exemplary adherence to the Gospel" (*War Against the Idols*, 265).

27. Ibid., 266.

28. Heiko A. Oberman, *Luther: Man between God and the Devil*, trans., Eileen Walliser-Schwarzbart (New Haven, CT: Yale University Press, 1989; New York: Anchor Doubleday, Image Books, 1992), 250.

CHAPTER 4: MODERN TREASURE?

1. James M. Gustafson, *Treasure in Earthen Vessels: The Church as a Human Community* (New York: Harper & Brothers, 1961; Louisville, KY: Westminster John Knox Press, 2009), 110.

2. Jaroslav Pelikan, *The Christian Tradition: A History of the Development of Doctrine*, vol. 5, *Christian Doctrine and Modern Culture (since 1770)* (Chicago: University of Chicago Press, 1989), 302. Peter Hodgson. *Revisioning the Church: Ecclesial Freedom in the New Paradigm* (Philadelphia: Fortress Press, 1988), 53.

3. Note, by way of contrast, Karl Rahner's judgment that the emergence of the "world-church" after the Second Vatican Council (1962–65), that is, the emergence of indigenous forms of Christianity around the world, was perhaps the Council's most significant achievement. See his *Theological Investigations*, vol. 20, *Concern for the Church*, trans. Edward Quinn (New York: Crossroad Publishing, 1981).

4. See Joseph Haroutunian, *God with Us: A Theology of Transpersonal Life* (Philadelphia: Westminster Press, 1965).

5. See also the works of Daniel Day Williams, James Luther Adams, and Claude Welch. Related themes of sociality and community can be found in the work of Josiah Royce, Howard Thurman, Martin Luther King Jr., Bev-erly Wildung Harrison, Sallie McFague, Margaret Farley, and Katie Cannon, among others. When generalizing about an "American strand," I am referring to such social interpreters of Christian life in the United States. For additional

observations, see Kristine A. Culp, "Introduction" to *"The Responsibility of the Church for Society" and Other Essays by H. Richard Niebuhr*, ed. Kristine A. Culp (Louisville, KY: Westminster John Knox Press, 2008).

6. In its day, Brunner's treatment was arguably more influential among Protestant theologians and ecumenical church leaders than that of his now more widely read contemporaries Karl Barth, Karl Rahner, and Paul Tillich.

7. Emil Brunner, *The Christian Doctrine of the Church, Faith, and the Consummation*, vol. 3 of *Dogmatics*, trans. David Cairns with T. H. L. Parker (1960; Philadelphia: Westminster Press, 1962), 74. Brunner's critique turned on Calvin's treatment of the church as an external means of grace. However, his reading of Calvin conflated several senses of "external" in ways that Calvin arguably did not: extrinsic as opposed to intrinsic to faith, externally or instrumentally related as opposed to internally related, exterior or historical-social-political as opposed to interior or spiritual. See Emil Brunner, *The Misunderstanding of the Church*, trans. Harold Knight (Philadelphia: Westminster Press, 1953), 9–10. By contrast, I have accented the sociability and historicality of Calvin's approach.In *God with Us*, Haroutunian read Calvin differently while nevertheless identifying the same problems of individualism and institutionalism in Protestant theology. Haroutunian viewed flawed treatments of Christian love in Brunner and in Anders Nygren's work as being related problems.

8. Brunner rejects faith as consent to doctrine, found in Karl Barth's theology, as "objectivism"; he rejects faith as an event, found in Rudolf Bultmann's theology, as "subjectivism."

9. Brunner, *Dogmatics*, 3:339–43.

10. Ibid., 42.

11. Ibid., 37. Compare Haroutunian, *God with Us*, 25: For him, an interpretation of faith rightly changes when attention is given to the sociality of Christian life; however, unlike Brunner, his argument did not appeal to the authority of an "authentic" Pauline *Ekklesia*.

12. Brunner, *Dogmatics*, 3:5.

13. Ibid., 53.

14. Ibid., 46–47.

15. Ibid., 33.

16. Ibid., 43.

17. Brunner, *Misunderstanding*, 107. Note that *Misunderstanding* uses *Ecclesia* whereas *Dogmatics* uses *Ekklesia* with no apparent distinction in use.

18. Emil Brunner, *The Church in the New Social Order* (London: SCM Press, 1952), 11.

19. Brunner, *Dogmatics*, 3:75. Here Brunner quotes Luther, *On the German Mass* (1526). See also Brian Gerrish, *The Old Protestantism and the New: Essays in the Reformation Heritage* (Chicago: University of Chicago Press, 1982), 98 n. 36.

20. Emil Brunner, "The *Mukyokai* ('Non-Church') Movement in Japan," in *Religion and Culture: Essays in Honor of Paul Tillich*, ed. Walter Leibrecht (New

York: Harper, 1959), 289. See also Brunner, *Dogmatics*, 3:113–14. Founded by Uchimura Kanzō (1861–1930), it was a highly literate movement of Christians who met primarily in Bible study.

21. Brunner, *Misunderstanding*, 5. He treats Calvin's doctrine of the church as the root of these "false solutions."

22. It may be more accurate to say that the problem of the relation of church as fellowship to existing institutions that faced Brunner and other mid-twentieth-century ecumenists was a legacy of sixteenth-century debates about the true church. Brunner's reframing of the problem may have disregarded the felt concerns about life, death, and salvation that fueled sixteenth-century debates.

23. Gustafson, *Treasure in Earthen Vessels*, xviii, with original emphasis.

24. Ibid., 14–28.

25. Ibid., 8. See subsequent work by feminist theologians. For example, Nelle Morton asked, "Should not all that one eats be valued both physically and spiritually? Is it not time to rescue the powerful symbolism surrounding the sacrament from a preoccupation with things, and restore it to eating and drinking out of the people's common humanness at the deepest source of their existence?" Morton, "Preaching the Word (1973)," in *The Journey Is Home* (Boston: Beacon Press, 1985), 50.

26. Gustafson engaged the work of social theorists and philosophers such as Durkheim, Weber, Malinowski, Mead, Royce, and Dilthey. Subsequent theoretical perspectives would nuance, expand, and critique his work—e.g., Mary Douglas on condensed symbols, feminist theorists on the body and on language, and interpretation and discourse theories. See also Gustafson's own later attention to the biological sciences and to critiques of anthropocentrism. Still as notably absent today as it was then is a treatment of economic theory.

27. Gustafson, *Treasure in Earthen Vessels*, 109.

28. Ibid., 105; also 6–7. See Claude Welch, *The Reality of the Church* (New York: Charles Scribners' Sons, 1958), 66–67, for a related critique of Karl Barth's contrast between the "apparent church" and the "real church." See also H. Richard Niebuhr's critique of the neo-orthodox revival of the Augustinian visible/invisible distinction in "The Hidden Church and the Churches in Sight," in Culp, "*Responsibility*," 52–61; and also the concluding paragraphs of H. Richard Niebuhr, *Faith on Earth: An Inquiry into the Structure of Human Faith*, ed. Richard R. Niebuhr (New Haven, CT: Yale University Press, 1989), 116–17.

29. Gustafson, *Treasure in Earthen Vessels*, xviii.

30. Ibid., 105.

31. Ibid., 110.

32. Ibid., 109.

33. Ibid., 111.

34. Ibid., 13. For example, Gustafson explains that "loyalties and deeds are common to all communities; the specific object of loyalty and its consequent

effect upon actions marks the differentiation between the church and other communities" (13).

35. Ibid., 110.

36. H. Richard Niebuhr, "The Church Defines Itself in the World," in *Theology, History, and Culture: Major Unpublished Writings,* ed. William Stacy Johnson (New Haven, CT: Yale University Press, 1996), 69–70.

37. H. Richard Niebuhr, "The Responsibility of the Church for Society," in Culp, *"Responsibility,"* 67.

38. For example, see Mary McClintock Fulkerson, *Places of Redemption: Theology for a Worldly Church* (New York: Oxford University Press, 2007); and Rebecca Chopp's depiction of the "community of transformation" gathered around the Word as "perfectly open sign," in *The Power to Speak: Feminism, Language, God* (New York: Crossroad Publishing, 1989). Compare Serene Jones's discussion of the "bounded openness of church," in *Feminist Theory and Christian Theology: Cartographies of Grace* (Minneapolis: Fortress Press, 2000), 152. See also Mary E. Hines, "Community for Liberation," in *Freeing Theology: The Essentials of Theology in Feminist Perspective,* ed. Catherine Mowry LaCugna (San Francisco: HarperSanFrancisco, 1993), 161–84; Amy Plantinga Pauw, "The Graced Infirmity of the Church," in *Feminist and Womanist Essays in Reformed Dogmatics,* ed. Amy P. Pauw and Serene Jones (Louisville, KY: Westminster John Knox Press, 2005), 189–203; Rosemary Radford Ruether, *Sexism and God-Talk: Toward a Feminist Theology* (Boston: Beacon Press, 1983); idem, *Women-Church: Theology and Practice of Feminist Liturgical Communities* (San Francisco: Harper & Row, 1985); Letty M. Russell, *Church in the Round: Feminist Interpretation of the Church* (Louisville, KY: Westminister/John Knox Press, 1993); Natalie K. Watson, *Introducing Feminist Ecclesiology* (Cleveland: Pilgrim Press, 2002).

39. Mercy Amba Oduyoye, *Daughters of Anowa: African Women and Patriarchy* (Maryknoll, NY: Orbis Books, 1995), 185.

40. While Ruether directed her criticisms primarily to the Roman Catholic Church, Protestant churches were not exempt from her critique, even if those churches are often more bureaucratic than classically hierarchical. Nevertheless, her discussion neglected, e.g., how language bears and hides power, and how even the relatively powerless may consent to and manipulate power. By contrast, see Mary McClintock Fulkerson's exploration of how traditional Presbyterian laywomen fashioned usable theologies despite exclusion, in *Changing the Subject: Women's Discourse and Feminist Theology* (Minneapolis: Fortress Press, 1994); and Cheryl Townsend Gilkes's study of laywomen's subversion of language and power, in "'Some Mother's Son and Some Father's Daughter': Gender and Biblical Language in Afro-Christian Worship Tradition," in *Shaping New Vision: Gender and Values in American Culture,* ed. Clarissa W. Atkinson, Constance H. Buchanan, and Margaret R. Miles (Ann Arbor, MI: UMI Research Press, 1987), 73–99.

41. Rosemary Radford Ruether, *Women and Redemption: A Theological History* (Minneapolis: Fortress Press, 1998), 274. In that passage, she defines patriarchy "as a multilayered system of domination, centered in male control of women but including race and class hierarchy, generational hierarchy, and clericalism, and expressed also in war and in domination of nature."

42. Ruether, *Women-Church*, 5.

43. Ibid., 32.

44. Ibid., 72–73; cf. Mary Daly's treatment of women's journey from sexism as "exodus community," in *Beyond God the Father: Toward a Philosophy of Women's Liberation* (Boston: Beacon Press, 1973), 157–60.

45. Ruether, *Women and Redemption*, 279; *Women-Church*, 37.

46. Ruether identified four marks by which a community of liberation can be known: "The Church is where the good news of liberation from sexism is preached, where the Spirit is present to empower us to renounce patriarchy, where a community committed to the new life of mutuality is gathered together and nurtured, and where the community is spreading this vision and struggle to others" (*Sexism and God-Talk*, 213).

47. Ibid., 206. These spirit-filled movements also offer traditions of women's leadership.

48. Ruether, *Women-Church*, 35.

49. Ruether looks for "a dynamic dialectical synthesis of the Catholic understanding of ongoing inspired development and the Protestant model of return to origins that dismantles distorted developments, seeing this not as a literal 'return' to some first-century world view, but as an insightful encounter with root stories that releases space for radically new envisionings." "Glimmers of truth" emerge and are submerged in various traditions through history. The critical retrieval of symbols and experiences can allow new points of convergence and thereby new possibilities for "situat[ing] oneself meaningfully in history." Ruether, *Women and Redemption*, 280. See also Ruether, *Liberation Theology: Human Hope Confronts Christian History and American Power* (New York: Paulist Press, 1972), 4–5; idem, *Sexism and God-Talk*, 18.

50. Ruether's *Women-Church* book in particular relies on a dichotomy between the institutional church, which is ambiguous at best for women, and autonomous feminist bases. To be sure, her quasi-typological interpretation of spirit-filled community and historical institution places her work more in continuity with the modern social-historical approaches of Max Weber, Ernst Troeltsch, and H. R. Niebuhr than with the modern philosophical-theological logic that we have been considering in this chapter. Like others who use these social-historical approaches, she neither distinguished between the more theological and the less theological in common life nor denigrated the significance of political, socioeconomic, and cultural processes.

51. Ruether, *Sexism and God-Talk*, 215–16.

52. Ruether, *Women-Church*, 3.

53. For theoretically thicker accounts of oppression/sin and liberation/ salvation, see, e.g., María Pilar Aquino, *Our Cry for Life: Feminist Theology from Latin America* (Maryknoll, NY: Orbis Books, 1993); Chopp, *The Power to Speak*; Jones, *Feminist Theory and Christian Theology*; Kwok Pui-Lan, *Postcolonial Imagination and Feminist Theology* (Louisville, KY: Westminster John Knox Press, 2005); McClintock Fulkerson, *Changing the Subject*; idem, *Places of Redemption*; and Mary M. Solberg, *Compelling Knowledge: A Feminist Proposal for an Epistemology of the Cross* (Albany: State University of New York Press, 1997).

54. See Simone de Beauvoir's rejection of a "Hegelian act of surpassing" in favor of an existentialist account of "conversion." *The Ethics of Ambiguity*, trans. Bernard Frechtman (New York: Philosophical Library, 1948; repr. New York: Citadel Press, 1991), 13.

55. "We were blind in our distrust of being, now we begin to see; we were aliens and alienated in a strange, empty world, now we begin sometimes to feel at home; we were in love with ourselves and all our little cities, now we are falling in love, we think, with being itself, with the city of God, the universal community of which God is the source and governor." H. Richard Niebuhr, "Responsibility and Christ," in *The Responsible Self: An Essay in Christian Moral Philosophy*, intro. James M. Gustafson (New York: Harper & Row, 1963; repr., Louisville, KY: Westminster John Knox Press, 1999), 177–78. See also H. Richard Niebuhr, "Faith in Gods and in God," in *Radical Monotheism and Western Culture: With Supplementary Essays* (New York: Harper & Row, 1960; repr., Louisville, KY: Westminster/John Knox Press, 1993), 126.

56. Niebuhr, *Theology, History, and Culture*, 72–73.

57. See H. Richard Niebuhr, "Christianity as a Movement: Preface to *The Kingdom of God in America*," in Culp, "*Responsibility*," 50. See also Haroutunian, *God with Us*, 41–61.

CHAPTER 5: A FIELD OF TENSIONS AND CONVERSIONS

1. H. Richard Niebuhr, "Faith in Gods and in God," in *Radical Monotheism and Western Culture: With Supplementary Essays* (New York: Harper & Row, 1960; repr., Louisville, KY: Westminster/John Knox Press, 1993), 126.

2. "Hyogo Declaration," from the final report of the World Conference on Disaster Reduction, January 18–22, 2005, Kobe, Hyogo, Japan, http://www .unisdr.org/wcdr.

3. See, e.g., studies in public health: Constance Urciolo Battle, ed., *The Essentials of Public Health Biology: A Guide for the Study of Physiopathology* (Sudbury, MA: Jones & Bartlett Publishers, 2008); and conversation with the author, June 27, 2009.

4. "UNISDR Terminology on Disaster Risk Reduction (2009)," http://www .unisdr.org/eng/terminology/terminology-2009-eng.html.

5. Historian Peter Brown provides this helpful characterization of the changed world: "By the time that [Jesus'] sayings and the story of his death and resurrection were collected in what later became the Gospels, Jewish Palestine had changed profoundly. Jerusalem had been stormed by the Romans in 70 A.D. The Temple lay in ruins. Judea was devastated. The eccentric settlements by the Dead Sea lay deserted. In the Gospels we meet, not the world of Jesus, but the very different, more tense world of his disciples. The stories in them had been collected in that terrible period, to meet the needs and to validate the activities of a group of wandering preachers, who claimed to be his true followers." Brown, *The Body and Society: Men, Women, and Sexual Renunciation in Early Christianity* (New York: Columbia University Press, 1988), 41.

6. Mishnah *Berakot* 9.5, as cited in Joseph A. Fitzmyer, SJ, *The Gospel according to Luke (I–IX)*, Anchor Bible 28A (Garden City, NY: Doubleday, 1981), 754.

7. Flavius Josephus, *Jewish War* 2.125.

8. *Didache* 11.3–6, from "The Teaching of the Twelve Apostles, Commonly Called the *Didache*," in *Early Christian Fathers*, trans. and ed. Cyril C. Richardson (Philadelphia: Westminster Press, 1953), 176. "The gospel precept" referred to in *Didache* 11.3 is Matt. 10:40–41.

9. See the classic sermon of Martin Luther King Jr. on the Good Samaritan text, "On Being a Good Neighbor," in *Strength to Love* (Philadelphia: Fortress Press, 1963), 26–35; and the haunting reprise in his final speech, "I've Been to the Mountaintop," in *A Call to Conscience: The Landmark Speeches of Dr. Martin Luther King, Jr.,* ed. Clayborne Carson and Kris Shepherd (New York: Warner Books, 2001), 217–19.

10. This reading contrasts with a quasi-typological interpretation in which Mary and Martha represent different sets of values. For a typical example, see Elwyn E. Tilden's note on Luke 10:42: "With delicate ambiguity Jesus rebuked Martha's choice of values. . . . Jesus approved Mary's preference for listening to his teachings as contrasted with Martha's unneeded acts of hospitality"; in *The New Oxford Annotated Bible with the Apocrypha, Revised Standard Version,* ed. Herbert G. May and Bruce M. Metzger (New York: Oxford University Press, 1977), 1261.

11. See, e.g., Gustavo Gutierrez, *A Theology of Liberation: History, Politics, Salvation,* trans. and ed. Sister Caridad Inda and John Eagleson (Maryknoll, NY: Orbis Books, 1972; 15th anniversary ed., 1988), 112–16.

12. My depiction is indebted to Gloria Anzaldúa's exploration of contemporary borderlands, specifically the lower Rio Grande valley, which currently divides the United States and Mexico, but also metaphorically other places—perhaps the situation of persons living within the Roman Empire in the days of Jesus and the early Christian missionaries? Borderlands are places of change and contention. On either side of the borders, "normal" and "alien" are defined; within the borderlands, persons are constantly in transition, often literally of

mixed cultures and races, and subject to control, sometimes brutal subjugation, by those who define and enforce the borders. Anzaldúa narrates not simply the negotiation of intersecting cultures, communities, and ideologies, but more precisely the tensions and connections across these various intersections and borders. A multiplicity of tensions, threats, and possibilities arise from inhabiting and negotiating multiple cultural spaces at once. She is especially interested in how "*mestiza* consciousness"—a critical and resourceful way of existing, thinking, and acting—is formed reflexively within the borderlands. Such a critical consciousness/agency within the borderlands does not involve simply combining one culture with another, resisting one culture for another, or somehow stepping outside all cultures into something new. Rather, it involves continual evaluation, negotiation, and re-creation through multiple strategies of "toleration," resistance, and affirmation. See Gloria Anzaldúa, *Borderlands/La Frontera: The New Mestiza*, 2nd ed., intro. Sonia Saldívar-Hull (San Francisco: Aunt Lute, 1987; 2nd ed., 1999); idem, "*La conciencia de la mestiza*: Towards a New Consciousness," in *Making Face, Making Soul: Haciendo Caras*, ed. Gloria Anzaldúa (San Francisco: Aunt Lute, 1990), 377–82.

13. Rebecca Chopp, e.g., contends that Christian proclamation itself must be loosed from its "ecclesial prison" if it is to "speak of freedom" to women and to the world. Chopp, *The Power to Speak: Feminism, Language, God* (New York: Crossroad Publishing, 1989), 4–5. Similarly, see Joan Martin, "A Sacred Hope and Social Goal: Womanist Eschatology," in *Liberating Eschatology: Essays in Honor of Letty M. Russell*, ed. Margaret A. Farley and Serene Jones (Louisville, KY: Westminster John Knox Press, 1999), 211.

14. Susan Suleiman, "(Re)Writing the Body: The Politics and Poetics of Female Eroticism," in *The Female Body in Western Culture*, ed. Susan Suleiman (Cambridge, MA: Harvard University Press, 1986), 24; as quoted in Susan Bordo, "Feminism, Postmodernism, and Gender-Scepticism," in *Feminism/ Postmodernism*, ed. Linda J. Nicholson (New York: Routledge, 1990), 143. Suleiman is specifically rejecting the use of "the grid of gender" as the organizing pattern for feminist theories. I do not disagree with her general critique, only with the implication that moving outside of this pervasive—and often dualistic—grid also entails rejecting all dialectics.

15. Hazel V. Carby, "The Multicultural Wars," in *Black Popular Culture*, "a project by Michelle Wallace," ed. Gina Dent (Seattle: Bay Press, 1992), 193.

16. H. Richard Niebuhr, "The Hidden Church and the Churches in Sight," in *"The Responsibility of the Church for Society" and Other Essays by H. Richard Niebuhr*, ed. Kristine A. Culp (Louisville: Westminster John Knox Press, 2008), 60–61. On conversion as a "permanent revolution" and as turning from defensiveness to gratitude toward God and love of the neighbor, see also H. Richard Niebuhr, *The Meaning of Revelation* (New York: Macmillan, 1941; repr., Louisville, KY: Westminster John Knox Press, 2006), esp. 58–72 and 86–100; and idem, "Faith in Gods and in God," in *Radical Monotheism*, 122–26.

17. H. Richard Niebuhr, *The Kingdom of God in America* (New York: Harper & Row, 1937; Harper Torchbooks, 1959), xiv, also xiii–xvi; repr. as "Christianity as a Movement," in Culp, *"Responsibility,"* 50–51. Niebuhr rejected a Hegelian understanding of dialectic (*Kingdom of God*, 14), and favored instead the approach of Henri Bergson in *The Two Sources of Morality and Religion* (1935; repr., Notre Dame, IN: University of Notre Dame Press, 1977).

18. H. Richard Niebuhr, *Christ and Culture* (New York: Harper & Row, 1951; repr., San Francisco: HarperSanFrancisco, 2001).

19. Ernst Troeltsch, *The Social Teaching of the Christian Churches*, intro. H. Richard Niebuhr, trans. Olive Wyon, 2 vols. (Chicago: University of Chicago Press, 1960).

20. H. Richard Niebuhr in collaboration with Daniel Day Williams and James M. Gustafson, *The Purpose of the Church and Its Ministry: Reflections on the Aims of Theological Education* (New York: Harper & Brothers, 1956), 19; repr. in Culp, *"Responsibility,"* 85. For discussions of the polar method, see Jon Diefenthaler, *H. Richard Niebuhr: A Lifetime of Reflections on the Church and the World* (Macon, GA: Mercer University Press, 1986), chap. 4; and James W. Fowler, *To See the Kingdom: The Theological Vision of H. Richard Niebuhr* (Nashville: Abingdon, 1974; repr., Lanham, MD: University Press of America, 1985), esp. 27–29.

21. H. Richard Niebuhr, "The Position of Theology Today," in *Theology, History, and Culture: Major Unpublished Writings*, ed. William Stacy Johnson (New Haven, CT: Yale University Press, 1996), 3–18.

22. Ibid., 10. Niebuhr seems to be rejecting metaphysical dualisms here as well as defining terms and also to be positioning himself in the history of Christian moral and philosophical debates, but he does not make those moves explicit.

23. H. Richard Niebuhr, "The Church and Its Purpose," in Culp, *"Responsibility,"* 85–90. Notably, Niebuhr does not include a polarity of visible and invisible. For his deconstruction of that distinction, see idem, "The Hidden Church," in Culp, *"Responsibility,"* 52–61.

24. For the principle of balance, see H. Richard Niebuhr, "The Position of Theology Today," in *Theology, History, and Culture*, esp. 8 and 18.

25. Niebuhr, *Radical Monotheism*, 126.

26. Ibid., 52–53.

27. On the relation of Niebuhr's polar method and use of the polarity of protestant principle and catholic vision to Paul Tillich's well-known—and roughly similar—contrast of protestant principle and catholic substance, see Kristine A. Culp, "Introduction," in Culp, *"Responsibility,"* xv.

28. Niebuhr, "The Church and Its Purpose," in Culp, *"Responsibility,"* 89.

29. See H. Richard Niebuhr, "The Gift of the Catholic Vision," in Culp, *"Responsibility,"* 113.

CHAPTER 6: VULNERABILITY IN A WORLD MARKED BY SUFFERING

1. James Baldwin, "The Fire Next Time," in *The Price of the Ticket: Collected Nonfiction, 1948–1985* (New York: St. Martin's Press, 1985), 349.

2. Venancia (pseudonym), a Salvadoran mother and catechist, as translated in Renny Golden, *The Hour of the Poor, The Hour of Women: Salvadoran Women Speak* (New York: Crossroad Publishing, 1991), 90–99.

3. Ibid., 193.

4. Jon Sobrino, *The True Church and the Poor*, trans. Matthew J. O'Connell (Maryknoll, NY: Orbis Books, 1984), 121. See also idem, *No Salvation outside the Poor: Prophetic-Utopian Essays* (Maryknoll, NY: Orbis Books, 2008); Gustavo Gutiérrez, *We Drink from Our Own Wells: The Spiritual Journey of a People*, trans. Matthew J. O'Connell (Maryknoll, NY: Orbis Books, 1984), esp. 114–21; idem, *On Job, God-Talk and the Suffering of the Innocent* (Maryknoll, NY: Orbis Books, 1987).

5. María Pilar Aquino, *Our Cry for Life: Feminist Theology from Latin America* (Maryknoll, NY: Orbis Books, 1993), 153. She refers to Luz Beatríz Arellano, "Women's Experience of God in Emerging Spirituality," in *With Passion and Compassion: Third World Women Doing Theology*, ed. Virginia Fabella and Mercy Amba Oduyoye (Maryknoll, NY: Orbis Books, 1988), 203.

6. This is Peter Brown's framing of a central concern of Irenaeus and Melito of Sardis in *The Body and Society: Men, Women, and Sexual Renunciation in Early Christianity* (New York: Columbia University Press, 1988), 68. See the discussion above in chapter 1.

7. Irenaeus, *Adversus haereses* 5.8.1, in *The Early Christian Fathers: A Selection from the Writings of the Fathers from St. Clement of Rome to St. Athanasius*, ed. and trans. Henry Bettenson (Oxford: Oxford University Press, 1956), 84. "To bear God" alludes to 2 Cor. 4:17.

8. Golden, *The Hour of the Poor*, 89.

9. Yann Arthus-Bertrand, *Earth from Above*, rev. ed. (New York: Harry N. Abrams, 2002). Working with the support of Unesco, Arthus-Bertrand took photographs over six continents during a five-year period.

10. On photography and the representation of atrocity, see Susan Sontag, *Regarding the Pain of Others* (New York: Picador, 2003).

11. Martin Luther, *Against Hanswurst* (1541), trans. W. P. Stephens, in Martin Luther, *Luther's Works*, ed. Helmut T. Lehmann, vol. 41, *Church and Ministry III*, ed. Eric W. Gritsch (Philadelphia: Fortress Press, 1966), 198–99.

12. Martin Luther, *Heidelberg Disputation*, #21, in *Martin Luther's Basic Theological Writings*, ed. Timothy Lull (Minneapolis: Fortress Press, 1989), 31, 44.

13. When Bernard Madoff was sentenced for his massive financial fraud, his changed appearance was covered prominently and taken as symbolic: "He was no longer the carefully tailored and coiffed financier. His hair was ragged," noted the *New York Times* headline story. Diana B. Henriques,

"Madoff, Apologizing, Is Given 150 Years," *New York Times,* vol. 158 (June 30, 2009), 1.

14. Luther, *Heidelberg Disputation*, #21, in Lull, *Luther's Writings*, 31, 44.

15. See Samuel Torvend, *Luther and the Hungry Poor: Gathered Fragments* (Minneapolis: Fortress Press, 2008).

16. Elaine Scarry, *The Body in Pain: The Making and Unmaking of the World* (New York: Oxford University Press, 1985), 4.

17. Ibid., 9. See also Mary McClintock Fulkerson, *Places of Redemption: Theology for a Worldly Church* (Oxford: Oxford University Press, 2007). Note her contrast between obliviousness and a place or frame for appearing.

18. See Isa. 58:9–14; also see Matt. 25:34–40.

19. This example comes from the work of Rev. Gregory Boyle, SJ, and Homeboy Industries in Los Angeles, as observed on March 21, 2005.

20. Tertullian, *De resurrectione carnis* 8,2, as quoted in Caroline Walker Bynum, *The Resurrection of the Body in Western Christianity, 200–1330* (New York: Columbia University Press, 1995), 43. See the discussion in chapter 1.

21. Ernst Troeltsch's later church- and sect-types correspond roughly to each of Calvin's rejected options. In Troeltsch's categories, this third way would retain the universal concern and embracing scope of the church-type without its triumphalism, and the emphasis on this-worldly transformation without sectarian exclusion.

22. Calvin effectively takes up Paul's argument in 2 Corinthians with the Stoics of his day. See Victor Paul Furnish, *II Corinthians*, 2nd ed., Anchor Bible 32A (Garden City, NY: Doubleday, 1994), 281–82.

23. John Calvin, *Institutes of the Christian Religion* [1559], ed. John T. McNeill, trans. Ford Lewis Battles, 2 vols. (Philadelphia: Westminster Press, 1960), 3.8.9 (cited below as *Inst.*).

24. Possibly he picked up the verb from Rom. 8, where it is associated with labor pains and also anticipates and contrasts with "the glory about to be revealed to us" (Rom. 8:18, 21); throughout his writings he described Christians as "groaning." See *Inst.* 3.8.9; also 2.1.3, 5; 3.3.16.

25. *Inst.* 3.8.10. Susan Schreiner explains that for Calvin, "Christ's suffering is the fundamental reality that lies at the heart of faithful and obedient existence." Yet, she clarifies, "it is not simply suffering for the sake of Christ or the gospel that is so important; suffering in itself is definitive of the spiritual life." Schreiner, *Where Shall Wisdom Be Found? Calvin's Exegesis of Job from Medieval and Modern Perspectives* (Chicago: University of Chicago Press, 1994), 95. She cites *Inst.* 3.8.7; and Ronald S. Wallace, *Calvin's Doctrine of the Christian Life* (Grand Rapids: Wm. B. Eerdmans Publishing Co., 1959), 67–68.

26. Calvin, *Inst.* 3.8.11.

27. Ibid., 3.8.1.

28. Ibid., 3.8.11.

29. Ibid., 3.4.3.

30. Ibid., 3.6.5.

31. Ibid., 3.7.1.

32. See McClintock Fulkerson, *Places of Redemption*, 254. See also M. Shawn Copeland, "'Wading through Many Sorrows': Toward a Theology of Suffering in Womanist Perspective," in *A Troubling in My Soul: Womanist Perspectives on Evil and Suffering*, ed. Emilie M. Townes (Maryknoll, NY: Orbis Books, 1993), 109–29; and Rosemary Radford Ruether, *Women and Redemption: A Theological History* (Minneapolis: Fortress Press, 1998), 279.

33. See the discussion of "overhumanization" and "hypertheism" in David E. Klemm and William Schweiker, *Religion and the Human Future: An Essay on Theological Humanism* (Oxford: Wiley-Blackwell, 2008); see also William Schweiker, *Theological Ethics and Global Dynamics: In a Time of Many Worlds* (Oxford: Blackwell, 2004).

34. Calvin, *Inst.* 1.17.1, 10–11.

35. Ibid., 3.4.3; 3.7.5.

36. Ibid., 3.7.6.

37. Ibid., 3.10.2–3. Note also Calvin's polemical caricature of gluttonous adversaries who are preoccupied with keeping "their belly full" and whose "kitchen [is] their religion," in his "Prefatory Address to King Francis I of France," *Inst.*, 14.

38. Beverly Wildung Harrison, *Making the Connections: Essays in Feminist Social Ethics*, ed. Carol S. Robb (Boston: Beacon Press, 1985), 20.

39. See several decades of feminist critiques of sin interpreted centrally or solely as pride, beginning with Valerie Saiving's landmark essay, "The Human Situation: A Feminine View," *Journal of Religion* (1960): 108; and as elaborated in Judith Plaskow, *Sex, Sin, and Grace: Women's Experience and the Theology of Reinhold Niebuhr and Paul Tillich* (Washington, DC: University Press of America, 1980). Anne E. Carr summarized the early critique and reformulation: Feminist thinkers have shown how dominant theological "understandings of sin as pride and rebellion against God . . . have failed to attend to the sin of those who are powerless, who lack agency, selfhood, and responsibility, who have suffered violence and abuse. . . . Sin is understood, in a feminist perspective, as the breaking of relationship with both God and human beings that can take the form of weakness as well as pride in its denial of the importance of human responsibility in both the personal and the political realms." Carr, *Transforming Grace: Christian Tradition and Women's Experience* (New York: Continuum, 1988; with new intro., 1996), 186.

40. Calvin, *Inst.* 3.7, esp. 3.7.1–2.

41. See Elizabeth V. Spelman, *Fruits of Sorrow: Framing Our Attention to Suffering* (Boston: Beacon Press, 1997).

CHAPTER 7: ALWAYS REFORMING, ALWAYS RESISTING

1. The French Musée virtuel du protestantisme cautions that attribution of the ascription to Marie Durand, symbolically powerful as it may be, is made "without true certainty." See http://www.museeprotestant.org/Pages/Notices .php?scatid=144&noticeid=543&lev=1&Lget=FR. However, most popular and scholarly sources assume the attribution, and there are good reasons to do so: few of the women imprisoned with her could write; on several occasions she was the one who wrote letters and signed them on behalf of the group; and finally, she grew up with testimonies of faith that her father had inscribed in the stone doorway and chimney of their home. I follow the conventional attribution.

2. Chamson explained that he was offering an exegesis of the old slogan "résister" for the present. His address, "La Résistance d'un Peuple (Après la Révocation de l'Édit de Nantes)," marked the 250th anniversary of the edict's revocation and the 150th anniversary of the Edict of Tolerance. See Philippe Joutard, Jacques Poujol, and Patrick Cabanel, eds., *Cévennes: Terre de Réfuge, 1940–1944*, 3rd ed. (Montpellier: Presses du Languedoc / Club Cévenol, 1994), esp. 53, 221, and 251.

3. See the third stanza of the "Complaint du maquis cévenol," by Jacques Poujol: "Sur les drapeaux de la France, / Pour garder leur liberté / Comme à la Tour de Constance / Ils ont écrit: « Résister» [On the flags of France, / To guard their liberty / As in the Tower of Constance / They wrote 'Résister']." As cited in Patrick Cabanel, Jacques Poujol, and Bernard Spiegel, "Quelques Juifs dans les Cévennes," in Joutard, Poujol, and Cabanel, *Cévennes*, 207.

4. See Beverly Wildung Harrison, "The Power of Anger in the Work of Love," in *Making the Connections: Essays in Feminist Social Ethics*, ed. Carol S. Robb (Boston: Beacon Press, 1985), 3–21.

5. On Marie Durand and her family, see Étienne Gamonnet, ed. and intro., *Lettres de Marie Durand (1711–1776): Prisonnière à la Tour de Constance de 1730 à 1768*, 2nd ed. (Montpellier: Les Presses du Languedoc, 1998). See also André Chamson's fictionalized portrayal in his novel *La Tour de Constance* (Paris: Éditions J'ai lu, 1970). In English, but dated, is Charles Tylor, *The Camisards* (London: Simpkin, Marshall, Hamilton, & Kent, 1893), esp. part 3, chaps. 13–15.

6. On the struggle of eighteenth-century French Protestants to secure political and civil rights, see Margaret Maxwell, "The Division in the Ranks of the Protestants in Eighteenth Century France," *Church History* 27 (June 1958): 107–23.

7. As quoted in Tylor, *The Camisards*, 293.

8. Citing Jean Crespin's 1564 *Actes des Martyrs*, Brad S. Gregory discusses how sixteenth-century French Huguenots often sang psalms on their way to their executions. See Gregory, *Salvation at Stake: Christian Martyrdom in Early Modern Europe* (Cambridge, MA: Harvard University Press, 1999), 136 and 408

n. 148. Pierre Durand and other eighteenth-century Huguenots would have known Crespin's book well. See also Barbara B. Diefenthaler, *Beneath the Cross: Catholics and Huguenots in Sixteenth-Century Paris* (New York: Oxford University Press, 1991), 136–44.

9. For example, see Marie Durand to Anne Durand, November 25, 1755, in Gamonnet, *Lettres*, 111.

10. Ibid., 52. He cites chap. 1 of John Calvin, *De la connaissance de Dieu*. See also Calvin, *Comm. Rom.* 1:20 in *Calvin's New Testament Commentaries*, ed. David W. and Thomas F. Torrance, 12 vols. (Grand Rapids: Wm. B. Eerdmans Publishing Co., 1959–72), 8:32.

11. "Anéantir l'être, c'est la loi de toute tyrannie; écraser toute personnalité intellectuelle et religieuse qui se dresse, briser les cœurs en même temps que les esprits et les volontés. C'est contre cette tentative des autorités, plus que pour la survie ou la sauvegarde du patrimoine, que Marie Durand eut à «résister»." Gamonnet, *Lettres*, 43.

12. John Calvin, *Corpus Reformatorum* 14:638, as quoted in Carlos N. M. Eire, *War Against the Idols: The Reformation of Worship from Erasmus to Calvin* (Cambridge: Cambridge University Press, 1986), 264.

13. John Calvin, *Institutes of the Christian Religion* [1559], ed. John T. McNeill, trans. Ford Lewis Battles, 2 vols. (Philadelphia: Westminster Press, 1960) (cited below as *Inst.*), "Prefatory Address to King Francis I of France," 11.

14. I have relied on Eire's account of the affair of the placards, *War Against the Idols*, 189–93, and more generally, on his argument about the central role of idolatry in sixteenth-century Calvinist thought.

15. Compare the explicit iconoclasm in *Inst.* 1.11, where Calvin charged "the papists" with putting "monstrosities" like statues of saints and elaborate rituals in place of God, denounced these seductive "pictures," and counseled Christians to rely on Scripture alone.

16. See Calvin, *Inst.* 4.1.17, and chapter 3 above.

17. Note that the accent on divine sovereignty has also served to promote fear of God and evasion of human responsibility. When the potentially creative tension between divine sovereignty and human responsibility has been removed, the result has been the creation of and submission to authoritarian religious and political regimes.

18. Philip Benedict, *Christ's Churches Purely Reformed: A Social History of Calvinism* (New Haven, CT: Yale University Press, 2001), 145–46. In an earlier version, I referred to ten thousand reported deaths in Paris alone. The most conservative estimate is two thousand in Paris and another two to three thousand in the provinces. On the massacre in historical, sociological, and religious context, see Diefenthaler, *Beneath the Cross*.

19. Eire, *War Against the Idols*, 310.

20. In 1933 a confederation of Lutheran, Reformed, and United Churches had joined together in opposition to Hitler's rising power and the pro-Nazi

stance of the Reich Church and convened themselves as the Confessional Synod of the German Evangelical Church, or more simply, the Confessing Church. They united behind "the inviolable foundation" of "the gospel of Jesus Christ as it is attested for us in Holy Scripture and brought to light again in the Confessions of the Reformation," a statement drafted substantially by Karl Barth.

21. For the text of the 1934 Theological Declaration of Barmen, see Arthur C. Cochrane, *The Church's Confession under Hitler* (Philadelphia: Westminster Press, 1962), 237–42.

22. Calvin railed against this third group, referring to them as "Nicodemites." On anti-Nicodemism, see Eire, *War Against the Idols,* chap. 7; and Gregory, *Salvation at Stake,* 150–62.

23. Eire, *War Against the Idols,* 266.

24. Philippe Joutard, "Postface," in Joutard, Poujol, and Cabanel, *Cévennes,* 333.

25. Georges Gillier as recorded in "Table ronde des pasteurs à Valleraugue (Août 1984)," in Joutard, Poujol, and Cabanel, *Cévennes,* 240. "Nous en avons pris conscience: la question juive n'était pas simplement une question biblique, mais une réalité."

26. Philip P. Hallie, *Lest Innocent Blood Be Shed* (New York: Harper & Row, 1979; HarperPerennial, 1994), 85. When I visited Le Chambon-sur-Lignon in 2001, the museum docent clarified that the effort was shared by seven villages in the Lignon plateau and ecumenically with various Protestant congregations and a Catholic parish.

27. Cabanel, Poujol, and Donadille, "Pasteurs en Cévennes," in Joutard, Poujol, and Cabanel, *Cévennes,* 216. They summarize an article by Avril W. Monod, "Deux métaphysiques (à propos de Karl Barth)," *Revue du Christianisme social* (April 1934): 258–61.

28. Beverly Wildung Harrison, "Restoring the Tapestry of Life: The Vocation of Feminist Theology," *The Drew Gateway* 54 (Fall 1984): 45. See also Harrison, *Making the Connections,* 221 and 228.

29. Delores S. Williams, *Sisters in the Wilderness: The Challenge of Womanist God-Talk* (Maryknoll, NY: Orbis Press, 1993), esp. chap. 5. See also her "Women's Oppression and Lifeline Politics in Black Women's Religious Narratives," *Journal of Feminist Studies in Religion* 2 (Fall 1985): 59–71.

30. Katie Geneva Cannon, "Surviving the Blight," in *Katie's Canon: Womanism and the Soul of the Black Community* (New York: Continuum, 1996), 28–37.

31. Mary McClintock Fulkerson, *Places of Redemption: Theology for a Worldly Church* (Oxford: Oxford University Press, 2007).

32. Mary Daly, *Beyond God the Father: A Philosophy of Women's Liberation* (Boston: Beacon Press, 1973), 19, 13.

33. Sallie McFague, *Models of God: Theology for an Ecological, Nuclear Age* (Philadelphia: Fortress Press, 1983), ix.

34. This was effectively James Gustafson's argument, although he made it in relation to processes of the church's life rather than in regard to theological metaphors and models. See the discussion in chap. 4.

35. Beverly Wildung Harrison, "Feminist Thea(o)logies at the Millennium: 'Messy' Continued Resistance or Surrender to Post-Modern Academic Culture?" in *Liberating Eschatology: Essays in Honor of Letty M. Russell,* ed. Margaret A. Farley and Serene Jones (Louisville, KY: Westminster John Knox Press, 1999), 159. See also Mary McClintock Fulkerson, *Changing the Subject: Women's Discourses and Feminist Theology* (Minneapolis: Fortress Press, 1994), 376–77, and chap. 7.

36. Harrison, "Feminist Thea(o)logies," 157.

37. Calvin, *Inst.* 3.9.1.

38. See, e.g., Ada María Isasi-Díaz, *En la Lucha / In the Struggle: Elaborating a Mujerista Theology* (Minneapolis: Fortress Press, 2004). Much modern use of the language of struggle can be traced to Charles Darwin's notion of "the struggle for existence," which he uses in a "large and metaphorical sense" to refer to individual life and to continuation of the species in *The Origin of Species.* See John Dewey, "The Influence of Darwinism on Philosophy," in *Essays on Pragmatism and Truth, 1907–1909: The Middle Works of John Dewey, 1899–1924,* vol. 4, ed. Jo Ann Boydston (Carbondale: Southern Illinois University Press, 1977), 3–14. I am indebted to Jennifer K. Thompson for this reference. Note also Simone de Beavoir's depiction of women's bodies as the site of struggle between species being and individual freedom in *The Second Sex.* Note too that the language of struggle enters human rights discourse. See, e.g., Eleanor Roosevelt's 1948 speech "The Struggle for Human Rights," in *American Rhetoric from Roosevelt to Reagan,* ed. Halford Ross Ryan (Prospect Heights, IL: Waveland Press, 1987), http://www.americanrhetoric.com/speeches/eleanorroosevelt.htm.

39. See Harrison, *Making the Connections,* 270 nn. 6–7; and idem, "The Power of Anger," passim; also see idem, "Feminist Thea(o)logies."

40. Primo Levi, *Survival in Auschwitz: The Nazi Assault on Humanity,* trans. Stuart Woolf (1958; New York: Touchstone, 1993), 27.

41. Primo Levi, *The Drowned and the Saved,* trans. Raymond Rosenthal (New York: Vintage International, 1988), 38.

42. As quoted by Margaret Miles, *Fullness of Life: Historical Foundations for a New Asceticism* (Philadelphia: Westminster Press, 1981), 97 n. 35.

43. See ibid., 96–97; and Jaroslav Pelikan, *The Christian Tradition: A History of the Development of Doctrine,* vol. 2, *The Spirit of Eastern Christendom (600–1700)* (Chicago: University of Chicago Press, 1974), 30–36.

44. Gregory of Nyssa, *On the Life of Moses,* from Migne, PG 44:337A, 87; as quoted in Kallistos Ware, "Christian Theology in the East (600–1453)," in *A History of Christian Doctrine,* ed. Hubert Cunliffe-Jones with Benjamin Drewery (Edinburgh: T&T Clark, 1978; Philadelphia: Fortress Press, 1980), 216.

45. According to Jewish theologian Arthur Cohen, the experience of the abyss opened by the death camps was neither of the terrible presence nor the terrible absence of God. Its monstrous immensity is an "ontological gathering of evil." He called the abyss the *tremendum* to compare and contrast it with Rudolph Otto's depiction of the terror-mystery of God's presence, the *mysterium tremendum*. In the death camps, "the sovereignty of evil has become more real and immediate and familiar than God." Evil can no longer be regarded as simply a privation of good, a defect, a void. Evil exists, has force; "its negativity and destructiveness are no less an aspect of the human structure than is that structure's potency for good." Cohen contends that persons must stop trying to protect God by denying the reality of evil. In the face of the *tremendum*, the relevant theological question "is not how God can abide evil, but how can God be affirmed meaningfully in a world where evil enjoys such dominion." Cohen, *The Tremendum: A Theological Interpretation of the Holocaust* (New York: Crossroad Publishing, 1981), 34, also 33; on the *tremendum*, see 29–30.

46. Basil the Great, *Letter 7,* in Migne, PG 32:345A, as quoted by Ware, 216.

47. Symeon the New Theologian, *Orations* 26, in Migne, PG 120:451, as translated and quoted in Pelikan, vol. 2, *The Spirit of Eastern Christendom*, 258. For a different sort of meditation on the inability of virtuosity, see Adrienne Rich, "Transcendental Etude," in *The Fact of a Doorframe: Poems Selected and New, 1950–1984* (New York: W. W. Norton, 1984), 264–69.

48. Levi, *Survival*, 55, 71; on hunger, see also 73–76.

49. Levi, *Drowned*, 148.

50. Gamonnet, *Lettres*, 67.

51. Martin Luther, *The Freedom of a Christian* (1520), in *Martin Luther's Basic Theological Writings,* ed. Timothy F. Lull (Minneapolis: Fortress Press, 1989), 623.

52. Eliki Bonanga, president of the Community of Disciples of Christ in the Congo (CDCC), speaking in Indianapolis, Indiana, on July 31, 2009. As reported at http://www.disciplesworld.com/newsArticle.html?wsnID=15640.

53. Hallie, *Lest Innocent Blood*, 154.

CHAPTER 8: AN ITINERARY OF DELIGHT AND GRATITUDE

1. Paule Marshall, *Praisesong for the Widow* (New York: E. P. Dutton, 1983), 34.

2. To portray the Ring Shout and the fictive coastal island of Tatem, South Carolina, where she places it, Marshall drew upon ethnographic studies of coastal Georgia and South Carolina from the 1940s. See Lydia Parrish, comp., *Slave Songs of the Georgia Sea Islands* (1942; repr., Athens: University of Georgia Press, 1992), on the Ring Shout: "The feet are not supposed to leave the floor or to cross each other, such an act being sinful. The shouting proceeds with a curious shuffling, but controlled step which taps out with the heel a resonant

syncopation fascinating in its intricacy and precision" (85). For a more recent study, see Art Rosenbaum, *Shout Because You're Free: The African American Ring Shout Tradition in Coastal Georgia* (Athens: University of Georgia Press, 1998). Note also the study of Tatemville, Georgia, in *Drums and Shadows: Survival Studies among the Georgia Coastal Negroes*, Savannah Unit, Georgia Writers' Project, Works Progress Administration (1940; repr., Athens: University of Georgia Press, 1986).

3. See the discussion of radical monotheism in H. Richard Niebuhr in chap. 5.

4. "Itinerary," like "movement" and "way," are metaphors that help to depict life before God as dynamic and ever converting (noting that "before God" is already itself metaphorical). "Itinerary of delight and gratitude" not only depicts the dynamism of persons and communities before God; as a metaphoric field it also provides a "place" to gather, relate, and reinterpret theological tropes, patterns, and practices that have situated and continue to resituate persons and communities in history and cultures.

5. See anthropologist Mary Douglas's discussion of the sacraments as "condensed symbols" and the Eucharist as among the most condensed symbols in *Natural Symbols: Explorations in Cosmology* (1970; with a new introduction, London: Routledge, 1996), 10; also see chap. 3. Other instructive comparisons and contrasts could be made with Douglas's mapping of social life and symbolic expression.

6. This method of "condensation" can be compared to Marshall's own approach. Her novel gains a multilayered, almost mythic texture because Marshall "condenses" historical and personal material into metaphors and lets these metaphors, together with a ritual structure, guide the reader's attention. These metaphors allow the reader to navigate the novel's layers of significance while also leaving contradictions and multiplicity in play. Literary critic Susan Willis discusses "condensation" and the use of metaphor in *Specifying: Black Women Writing the American Experience* (Madison: University of Wisconsin Press, 1987), 21–25. Compare Paul Ricoeur's discussion of the overdetermination of symbols in *Freud and Philosophy: An Essay on Interpretation* (New Haven, CT: Yale University Press, 1970); and David Tracy's treatment of intensification in *The Analogical Imagination: Christian Theology and the Culture of Pluralism* (New York: Crossroad Publishing, 1981), 125–26, 201–3. See also Peter Homans, *Theology after Freud: An Interpretive Inquiry* (Indianapolis: Bobbs-Merrill, 1970).

7. Robert Hayden, "Runagate Runagate," in *Angle of Ascent: New and Selected Poems* (New York: Liveright Publishing, 1975), 129. The poem praises Harriet Tubman.

8. Marshall uses this phrase from Hayden's poem as her first chapter's epigraph (*Praisesong*, 8).

9. The refrain "too much" patterns one of the novel's chapters; see below and Marshall, *Praisesong*, 134–45; "enough" refers to the discussion of discipleship and "enough" attention and welcome in chapter 5, above.

10. Ibid., 48.

11. Ibid., 42.

12. Gen. 32. Marshall does not refer to Jacob's wrestle or Abraham. She does use a quote from James Baldwin's 1951 essay, "Many Thousands Gone," to interpret the anxiety expressed in the dream (*Praisesong*, 45). See Baldwin, *The Price of the Ticket: Collected Nonfiction, 1948–1985* (New York: St. Martin's Press, 1985), 68.

13. John Calvin, *Institutes of the Christian Religion* [1559], ed. John T. McNeill, trans. Ford Lewis Battles, 2 vols. (Philadelphia: Westminster Press, 1960), 2.1.9 and 2.1.8–11 (cited below as *Inst.*).

14. See also Marilynne Robinson, "Facing Reality," in *The Death of Adam: Essays on Modern Thought* (New York: Picador, 2005), 76–86.

15. On situation and situatedness, see Simone de Beauvoir, *The Second Sex*, trans. H. M. Parshley (New York: Alfred A. Knopf, 1952); trans. of *Le deuxième sexe*, 2 vols. (Paris: Gallimard, 1949). My reading of Beauvoir and use of "situation" and "situatedness" is indebted to Toril Moi, *What Is a Woman? And Other Essays* (Oxford: Oxford University Press, 1999).

16. Barbara Christian, "Ritualistic Process and the Structure of Paule Marshall's *Praisesong for the Widow*," in *Black Feminist Criticism: Perspectives on Black Women Writers* (New York: Pergamon Press, 1995), 150.

17. The view of the flesh or body as the prison house of the soul is sometimes used by Calvin, esp. in *Inst.* 3.9.4–5, but also, e.g., in 3.6.5; 4.1.1.

18. Ibid., 2.2.18; 3.6.5; 3.10.1; 3.10.2.

19. Marshall, *Praisesong*, 32–37.

20. Here esp., but also elsewhere in the novel, Marshall provides "a subversive and critical fictional ethnography," to borrow sociologist of religion Cheryl Townsend Gilkes's characterization from Gilkes, "'A Conscious Connection to All That Is': *The Color Purple* as Subversive and Critical Ethnography," in *Embracing the Spirit: Womanist Perspectives on Hope, Salvation, and Transformation*, ed. Emilie M. Townes (Maryknoll, NY: Orbis Books, 1997), 279–80. See also Townes's discussion of *Praisesong* in her work *In a Blaze of Glory: Womanist Spirituality as Social Witness* (Nashville: Abingdon, 1995), chap. 5.

21. Marshall, *Praisesong*, 38–39. According to Gay Wilentz, Marshall drew upon material from the 1940 WPA project, *Drums and Shadows* (cited above) for the story of Ibo (Igbo) Landing. See Wilentz, *Binding Cultures: Black Women Writers in Africa and the Diaspora* (Bloomington: Indiana University Press, 1992), 102. The story of Ibo Landing is a variation of the flying African legend. See Julius Lester, *Black Folktales* (New York: Grove, 1969); and the 1991 film by Julie Dash, *Daughters of the Dust*. The legend has a historical basis: in 1803, Igbos who had been captured in Africa and sold as slaves in Savannah revolted en route to St. Simon's Island, Georgia; upon their arrival, they walked away from enslavement and into Dunbar Creek. See Timothy B. Powell, "Ebos Landing," in *New Georgia Encyclopedia* (Athens: Georgia Humanities Council

and the University of Georgia Press, 2004–2009), http://www.georgiaencyclo
pedia.org.

22. I am anticipating a later passage in summarizing the Ibo Landing story
this way. See Marshall, *Praisesong*, 139, and below.

23. Ibid., 40.

24. See H. Richard Niebuhr, *Radical Monotheism and Western Culture: With
Supplementary Essays* (New York: Harper & Row, 1960; repr., Louisville, KY:
Westminster/John Knox Press, 1993), 16.

25. H. Richard Niebuhr, *Faith on Earth: An Inquiry into the Structure of
Human Faith*, ed. Richard R. Niebuhr (New Haven, CT: Yale University Press,
1989), 94–95.

26. Niebuhr, *Radical Monotheism*, 125–26.

27. Calvin, *Inst.* 2.2.18.

28. See Mary McClintock Fulkerson on tracing the harm of (white) obliviousness as theological work, in *Places of Redemption: Theology for a Worldly
Church* (New York: Oxford University Press, 2007), 12–22.

29. Baldwin, *The Price of the Ticket*, 68.

30. In chaps. 1 and 5, I noted Elaine Scarry's argument that intense pain
"actively destroys" language and has to be "believed." Scarry, *The Body in Pain:
The Making and Unmaking of the World* (New York: Oxford University Press,
1985).

31. On the enduring effects of trauma, see, e.g., Eva Hoffman, *After Such
Knowledge: Memory, History, and the Legacy of the Holocaust* (New York: Public
Affairs, 2004). For a theological engagement, see Serene Jones, *Trauma + Grace:
Theology in a Ruptured World* (Louisville, KY: Westminster John Knox Press,
2009).

32. Marshall, *Praisesong*, 139–40.

33. Ibid., 139.

34. Compare Calvin, *Inst.* 3.6.5; 3.7.1.

35. In the Psalms and Wisdom literature, as well as in the history of Jewish
and Christian thought, language of delight and of desire are often intertwined,
with the Song of Songs epitomizing the combined use of these metaphors. This
chapter's focus on delight and consequent minimizing of metaphors of desire
should be taken only as a recognition of some differences between the registers
of delight and of desire, and not as an argument for their segregation. I am
indebted to Stephanie Paulsell, *Honoring the Body: Meditations on a Christian
Practice* (San Francisco: Jossey-Bass, 2002), and to her work in progress on the
Song of Songs.

36. See also John Calvin, "Isaiah 55:1–13," in Calvin, *Steward of God's Covenant: Selected Writings*, ed. John F. Thornton and Susan B. Varenne (New York:
Vintage Spiritual Classics, 2006), 243, 245.

37. Augustine, *Confessions*, trans. and intro. R. S. Pine-Coffin (Harmonds-
worth, UK: Penguin Books, 1961), 2.1 and 11.29.

38. Ibid., 9.4. Augustine is offering an extended meditation on Ps. 4.

39. Ibid., 10.17.

40. Ibid., 10.27.

41. Ibid., 1.20; also see 1.6.

42. Vladimir Lossky, *The Mystical Theology of the Eastern Church* (Crestwood, NY: St. Vladimir's Seminary Press, 1976), 39–40.

43. Augustine, *Confessions*, 10.30–35, reviews the temptations presented by each of the senses. For an exposition of the relationship of delight and desire in Augustine's construal of voluntary actions and sin, see Scott MacDonald, "Petit Larceny, the Beginning of All Sin: Augustine's Theft of Pears," in *Augustine's Confessions: Critical Essays,* ed. William E. Mann (Lanham, MD: Rowman & Littlefield, 2006), 45–69.

44. Margaret Miles, *Desire and Delight: A New Reading of Augustine's Confessions* (New York: Crossroad Publishing, 1992), esp. chap. 3.

45. Augustine, *The Confessions*, trans. Maria Boulding, OSB (New York: Vintage Spiritual Classics, 1997), 10.40, 65.

46. See chap. 3 and also Benjamin Drewery, "Martin Luther," in *A History of Christian Doctrine,* ed. Hubert Cunliffe-Jones with Benjamin Drewery (Edinburgh: T&T Clark, 1978; Philadelphia: Fortress Press, 1980), 319–20. Against Anders Nygren's influential interpretation of Luther, David C. Steinmetz suggests that some of Luther's exegesis included measures of both speculative ascent and practical approach to God. See Steinmetz, "Luther and the Ascent of Jacob's Ladder," in *Luther in Context,* 2nd ed. (Grand Rapids: Baker Academic, 2002), 142–55; Anders Nygren, *Agape and Eros* (Philadelphia: Westminster Press, 1953), 621–37.

47. Martin Luther, *The Freedom of a Christian* (1520), in *Martin Luther's Basic Theological Writings,* ed. Timothy F. Lull (Minneapolis: Fortress Press, 1989), 619, also 623.

48. Calvin, *Inst.* 1.14.20.

49. Ibid., 1.14.21. See also his discussion of the universe as a mirror that reflects God's glory, even if creatures' perception is dull, in 1.5.1, 3, 11.

50. Ibid., 1.14.21; see also 1.5.5 and 2.2.13–17.

51. Ibid., 1.14.22.

52. In the Psalms, "there is not an emotion of which anyone can be conscious that is not here represented as in a mirror." John Calvin, "The Author's Preface to the Commentary on the Psalms," in Calvin, *Steward of God's Covenant,* 164. Jason Byassee notes that in Augustine, the mirror of the Psalms "directs us, tells us how to feel anew, shows us what is the case, gathers up our affections and converts them. Augustine's mirror *gives* us our faces." Byassee, *Praise Seeking Understanding: Reading the Psalms with Augustine* (Grand Rapids: Wm. B. Eerdmans Publishing Co., 2007), 110.

53. I favor the language of "sensibilities" for conveying the lived, practical knowledge with which Calvin is concerned (e.g., *Inst.* 1.1.2; 1.2 passim;

1.5.9–10) and with which I also am. Sensibilities can be understood to have epistemic, moral, affectional, emotional, volitional, and aesthetic dimensions.

54. Calvin, "Preface to the Commentary on the Psalms," 164–65. In the preface Calvin offered a brief anatomy of his own soul (and thereby also attested to his qualifications as an interpreter of the Psalms). See also Serene Jones, "Soul Anatomy: The Healing Acts of Calvin's Psalms," in *Trauma + Grace*, 43–67; and idem, "Soul Anatomy: Calvin's Commentary on the Psalms," and Carlos Eire, "Calvin's Geneva and the Psalms," both in *Psalms in Community: Jewish and Christian Textual, Liturgical, and Artistic Traditions,* ed. Harold W. Attridge and Margot E. Fassler (Atlanta: Society of Biblical Literature, 2003), 265–92.

55. Calvin, *Inst.*, 1:54 n. 11; see 1.1.2; 1.5.3; 1.5.10; 2.16.1; 3.3.16; and elsewhere. These passages can be compared to Augustine's self-examination in the *Confessions.*

56. Calvin, "Preface to the Commentary on the Psalms," 166.

57. Ibid., 167. Calvin alludes to Rom. 8:22–23; see *Inst.* 2.1.3, 5; also 3.3.16 and 3.8.9. Augustine writes: "If the psalm is praying, pray yourselves; if it is groaning, groan too; if it is happy, rejoice; if it is crying out in hope, you hope as well; if it expresses fear, be afraid. Everything written here [in the Psalms] is like a mirror held up to us." Augustine, *Expositions of the Psalms 1–32*, trans. Maria Boulding, OSB, in *The Works of Saint Augustine: A Translation for the 21st Century*, part. 3, vol. 14., ed. John Rotelle, OSA (Hyde Park, NY: New City Press, 2000), 347. See also Michael C. McCarthy, SJ, "An Ecclesiology of Groaning: Augustine, the Psalms, and the Making of the Church," *Theological Studies* 66 (2005): 23–48.

58. Calvin, *Inst.* 3.9.3; see also, e.g., 1.14.22; 2.7.12; 3.2.7; 3.2.34; 3.2.41.

59. John Calvin, "Psalm 23," as excerpted from his *Commentary on the Psalms,* in Calvin, *Steward of God's Covenant*, 194; also *Inst.* 1.16.1. Elsewhere, however, Calvin depicted human "depravity" that "compels God to use severity in threatening us. *For it would be vain for him [God] gently to allure* those who are asleep" (*Inst.* 3.3.7, with emphasis added; note also the odd language about God being compelled). Here the most troubling aspects of Calvin's pedagogy of suffering recur—aspects that we rejected in chapter 5 as both dangerous and as inadequate to the best insights of Jewish and Christian thought. I am thinking with *and against* Calvin about a middle way of transformation, rather than attempting a wholesale retrieval.

60. Calvin, "Psalm 23," 195.

61. Calvin, *Inst.* 3.10.1. Randall A. Zachman considers charges that Calvin's instruction about creaturely use and enjoyment of God's benefits shares rightful blame for the ecological crisis. Zachman counters, arguing that for Calvin, "our use and enjoyment of the good things of creation is not intended by God to be an end in itself, but is rather the way God allures and invites us to seek him as the source of every good thing." "The Universe as the Living Image of God: Calvin's Doctrine of the Universe Reconsidered," *Concordia Theological Quarterly*

61 (October 1997): 303–4. It is another matter whether the framework of use and enjoyment alone is adequate to the complexity of ethical considerations involved in the contemporary mass production, marketing, acquisition, and consumption of things.

62. See Calvin's comments on the church's use of wealth, esp. *Inst.* 4.5.18.

63. Calvin, "Psalm 23," 194. See also the discussion of benefits as ladders in Calvin's commentary on Psalm 128, http://www.ccel.org/ccel/calvin/calcom12 .xii.i.html. I note with interest but have not yet seen the forthcoming volume by Julie Canlis, *Calvin's Ladders: A Spiritual Theology of Ascent and Ascension* (Grand Rapids: Wm. B. Eerdmans Publishing Co., 2010).

64. Note that Calvin understood "ascent to heaven" as metaphoric. Commenting on Eph. 4:8–10, he wrote: "When we say Christ is in heaven, we must not imagine that he is somewhere among the cosmic spheres. . . . When we speak of it [heaven] as another place outside the universe, we do so because we must speak of the Kingdom of God using the only language which we have." *Calvin: Commentaries*, ed. and trans. Joseph Haroutunian with Louise Pettibone Smith (1958; Louisville, KY: Westminster John Knox Press; 2006), 174.

65. See Steinmetz, "Luther and the Ascent of Jacob's Ladder," 142–55.

66. In addition to Calvin's commentary on Gen. 28:12 (*Calvin: Commentaries*, 147), see Calvin, *Inst.* 2.9.2; and his commentary on John 1:51, http://www .ccel.org/ccel/calvin/calcom34.vii.xi.html.

67. See, e.g., Calvin, *Inst.* 2.12.1–3; also 2.14; 2.15.5–6; 2.16.10–16.

68. *Calvin: Commentaries*, 147–48.

69. Calvin, *Inst.* 4.17.2–3.

70. *Calvin: Commentaries*, 146–47 with emphasis added.

71. John Calvin, "Preface to the Genevan Psalter (1543)." From the facsimile edition of "Les Psaumes mis en rime françoise par Clément Marot et Théodore de Béze. Mis en musique à quatre parties par Claude Goudimel. Par les héritiers de François Jacqui (1565)." Published under the auspices of La Société des Concerts de la Cathédrale de Lausanne; ed. in French, Pierre Pidoux; ed. in German, Konrad Ameln (Kassel: Baeroenreiter-Verlag, 1935), http://www.ccel .org/ccel/ccel/eee/files/calvinps.htm. In *Inst.* 3.20.32, Calvin follows Augustine's account of how psalm-singing was introduced from the Eastern church to Milan by Ambrose, and then to elsewhere in the West (see Augustine, *Confessions* 9.7, 15).

72. Calvin, "Preface to the Genevan Psalter." See also Calvin, *Inst.* 3.20.32.

73. From a letter written in Strasbourg by an Antwerp refugee, as quoted in Édith Weber, "13 Psalms from the Reformation" (39), notes to Chœur La Camerata Baroque, *Psaumes de la Réforme*, by Claude Goudimel, Jan Pieterszoon Sweelinck, and Samuel Mareschal (DDD, Hortus 064, ©2009, a compact disc).

74. Calvin, "Preface to the Genevan Psalter."

75. See also Gilbert I. Bond, "Psalms in a Contemporary African American Church," in Attridge and Fassler, *Psalms in Community*, 313–23. Compare

Howard Thurman's reflections on corporate singing of the spirituals in *Deep River* (1945; rev. ed. 1955) and *The Negro Spiritual Speaks of Life and Death* (1947), published as a single volume (Richmond, IN: Friends United Press, 1973), esp. "Jacob's Ladder," 77–86. On corporate formation and uplift through singing in contemporary African American and Anglo-American congregations, see Thomas Hoyt Jr., "Testimony," and Don E. Saliers, "Singing our Lives," both in *Practicing Our Faith: A Way of Life for a Searching People,* ed. Dorothy C. Bass (San Francisco: Jossey-Bass, 1997), 91–103 and 179–93. Compare also Gwen Kennedy Neville's treatment of open-air worship, camps, retreat centers, and reunions as Protestant corporate inversions of pilgrimage in *Kinship and Pilgrimage: Rituals of Reunion in American Protestant Culture* (New York: Oxford University Press, 1997).

76. Calvin, *Inst.* 4.1.5.

77. Ibid., 3.20.31.

78. See Lynn Japinga, "Fear in the Reformed Tradition," in *Feminist and Womanist Essays in Reformed Dogmatics,* ed. Amy Plantinga Pauw and Serene Jones (Louisville, KY: Westminster John Knox Press, 2006), 1–18.

79. M. F. K. Fisher, "The Gastronomical Me," in *The Art of Eating* (New York: Macmillan, 1990), 355, 361.

80. Relatedly, monastic rules associated eating and reading through practices of oral reading at meals. See Mary Carruthers, *The Book of Memory: A Study of Memory in Medieval Culture* (Cambridge: Cambridge University Press, 1990), 161–67.

81. It also opens up complicated matters of "good taste," which are beyond the scope of this chapter. See Frank Burch Brown, *Good Taste, Bad Taste, and Christian Taste: Aesthetics in Religious Life* (Oxford: Oxford University Press, 2000).

82. He was, after all, a French appellate judge writing on the other side of the tumult of the revolution, who had followed humanist, not monarchist, affirmations all along.

83. Jean Anthelme Brillat-Savarin, *The Physiology of Taste; Or, Meditations on Transcendental Gastronomy,* trans. and ed. M. F. K. Fisher (1949; New York: Everyman's Library, Alfred A. Knopf, 2009), 52–53.

84. Ibid., 188.

85. Ibid., 189–90.

86. Fisher, "How to Cook a Wolf," in *The Art of Eating,* 350, 188.

87. Ibid., 350.

88. Ibid., 188.

89. See Matt. 8:11; 22:1–10; Mark 14:15–24; also Isa. 25:6–8. See Alice Walker's short story, "The Welcome Table," in *In Love and Trouble: Stories of Black Women* (San Diego: Harcourt Brace, 1973), 81–87, which suggests a metaphorical power that transcends the harsh ambiguities of the actual community.

90. Calvin, *Inst.* 4.17.40.

91. Writing about the church and its ministry, Calvin notes that by "earthly means" God "bears us up as if in chariots to his heavenly glory" (*Inst.* 4.1.5).

92. The ritual's remembrance and lamentation, praise and celebration, reconnect the new world with Africa.

Index

Luther on, 36, 51, 60, 63, 72
patterns and processes necessary to,
79, 80, 105
resistance and, 122, 125, 130, 141,
149, 153, 172
shifting interpretations of, 23, 51, 52
as space of existence, 5–6
struggle as metaphor for, 149–50
and suffering, 111, 114–16, 121–22,
125, 129, 131
neither triumphalist nor sectarian,
83, 106, 111, 122, 180
vulnerability and, 5, 52, 87, 88, 94,
96, 102, 110–11, 114, 129–31, 153,
180
ways of living before God, 129–31,
155, 159, 172, 179
See also before God; Christian life,
the; itinerary of delight and gratitude; resistance, call and testimony
of
Lord's Supper, 43, 45, 64, 174, 176, 177,
179, 193n32
Lossky, Vladimir, 152, 171
Louis XV, King of France, 137
love, 2, 3, 6, 104, 106, 120, 150
Calvin on, 63, 64, 127–28, 173–74,
179
of God, Augustine on, 30, 46, 170
of God and neighbor, double command to, 139, 144
Le Chambon, France, and, 145, 155,
156
loss and, 2, 149, 168, 172
Luther on, 46, 171–72, 193n41
of neighbors, strangers, enemies,
144, 155, 156, 160
Niebuhr (H. R.) on, 89, 202n55,
204n16
resistance and, 136, 139, 145, 154–
55, 160
space of freedom and, 136, 154–55,
157
Luther, Martin, 6, 35–52, 64–65, 66–67,
71–72, 78–79, 116–19, 193nn32,
45–46; 196n16, 217n46
anti-Judaism in, 40, 48, 191n18

on authority, 32–33, 39–40, 43, 48,
51, 66, 192n25
captivity of the church, 39–41,
191n16
vs. church as mother, 32–33, 189n68
on the devil, 36, 37, 40, 41, 49, 51,
55, 191n17
on faith, 35, 36–37, 38, 40, 46–51,
118, 171–72, 192n24, 193nn41, 44
forms of ministry, 43, 45, 193n32
on grace, 35, 39, 41–42, 46–47, 48,
49, 51, 191n23
and paradox, 36, 48–49, 51, 60, 64,
66, 72, 117–18, 194n53, 195n13
on vocation, 43–44, 48, 51, 155,
192n29
See also under affliction(s); faith;
glory; gospel; joy/enjoyment; life
before God; love; marks of the
church; poor, the; poverty; Psalms,
use of; sacraments; salvation;
Scripture; unity; visible and invisible church; vulnerability; Word of
God

MacGregor, Geddes, 192n25, 196n18
Marius, Richard, 190n4, 191n18
marks of the church, 130, 201n46
Calvin on, 55, 63–67, 71–72,
189n66
Luther on, 37, 41, 42, 44–45, 51, 67,
71–72, 78, 116–17
Word and the sacraments, 55, 63–67,
193n32
See also cross, the: sign of; suffering:
as sign; suffering: world marked
by
Marshall, Paule, 130, 159–68, 180,
213n2, 214n6, 215nn20, 21
Martin, Dale, 15–16, 30, 185nn1, 3, 5
Marty, Martin, 190n4, 191n18
martyrs, 18–21, 22–23, 25–26, 76, 99,
104, 118–19, 125, 186–87n23,
197n26, 209–10n8
Mary and Martha, 101, 181, 203n10
McFague, Sallie, 148, 197n5
McNeill, John, 196n16

by Christian Mothers (El Salvador),
114
of conscience, 6, 144, 146, 154
by Durand (M.), 136, 138–40, 155
of faith, resistance as, 136, 137–40
of God's power, church as, 14, 18, 19,
82
in the Gospels, 95, 98, 135
See also resistance, call and testimony of; *Résister*
Theis, Éduard, 145
theodicy, 2, 121, 126, 129
Theological Declaration of Barmen
(1934). *See* Barmen Declaration
(1934)
theology, North American strand of,
75, 83, 89–90, 197n5
Thompson, Jennifer, 212n38
Thurman, Howard, 197n5, 219–20n75
Tillich, Paul, 44, 198n6, 205n27
torture, 16, 18–20, 37, 114, 115, 118,
119, 146, 152, 153, 184n6
Torvend, Samuel, 190n3
Tower of Constance (Aigues-Mortes,
France), 139, 209nn3, 5
Townes, Emilie, 184n6, 215n20
Tracy, David, 214n14
transformation. *See* God: transforming
reality of; vulnerability: to devastation and transformation
trauma, 16, 52, 116, 168, 216n31
triumphalism, 7, 13, 70, 83, 84, 86, 87,
106, 108, 111, 122, 148, 156, 181,
207n21
Trocmé, André, 145
Trocmé, Magda, 157
Troeltsch, Ernst, 108, 201n50, 207n21
tropes, 5, 8, 14, 15, 16, 160–61, 162–64,
187–88n38, 214n4
tyranny, 118, 135, 136, 139, 145–46,
152, 156, 172

Uchimura Kanzō, 198–99n20
United Nations International Strategy
for Disaster Reduction (UNISDR),
93

unity
of the church, 24, 25–26, 31, 46, 49,
64, 89
of the human race, Augustine on, 28,
33
spiritual, in faith and in Christ,
Luther on, 46–47, 49, 50, 76

Vatican Council, Second (1962–65),
197n3
via affirmativa, 129, 161, 169, 171–72,
175–76. *See also* ascent
via negativa, 129, 149, 151–53, 157
visible and invisible church, 22, 76, 79,
187–88n38
Augustine on, 13, 24, 28, 31, 49–50,
51, 194n52
Calvin on, 62–65, 71–72
and historical/ideal dialectic, 17, 71,
73–75
inadequacy of dialectic, 73–75, 89,
106–7
Luther on, 42, 47, 49–50, 51, 64–65,
71–72, 194n53
vocation, 43–44, 48, 51, 120, 142, 155,
162, 180, 192n29
vulnerability
account of distinguished from theodicy, 2, 129
and ambiguity, 5, 23, 41, 70–71, 74,
88, 102–3, 121, 146, 167
in the Bible, 3, 96, 181
and delight, 177–79, 181
to devastation and transformation, 2,
3, 94, 115, 120, 156, 163, 167, 172
and dignity, 144, 154
distinguished from suffering, 129,
131
earthen vessels and, 13–16, 87, 88,
94, 103, 160, 187–88n38
as enduring feature of earthly existence, 2, 94, 120, 122, 159
and glory, 4–5, 103–4, 122, 159–60,
181
as pivot of salvation, 120, 129, 160
and risk, 2–3, 4, 16, 93–94